JESUS CHRIST
THE TRUTH

J.JOHN & CHRIS WALLEY

CONTENTS

FOREWORD

What now seems a long time ago I had an idea. It was to produce a book about Jesus for anybody who wanted to know more about the man who is considered the most important figure in history. So in 2003 my friend Chris Walley and I wrote *The Life*, a book that has gone through many printings.

But things move on and it's time for a completely new version. What's changed? Well our world has changed: for instance in 2003 there were neither smartphones nor social media. It's not just technology that has changed: we are now more sensitive about matters of diversity, cultural awareness and gender. There have been other possibly more significant changes. We have increasingly drifted from a world in which facts were solid and immovable into one in which they are fluid and negotiable. In the past what you believed about something was determined by truth; now, increasingly, what you believe determines what you consider to be truth. In the past the head governed the heart; now it seems the opposite is true.

Christianity has always had opponents but in the last decade they seem to have become more aggressive and their arguments more wide-ranging. I find their criticisms no more convincing than they ever were but it means that to talk about Jesus now is difficult: less can be assumed, more must be defended and the arguments we use must be better supported.

This book focuses on two things: the truth about Jesus the man and the truth about his message. 'Who was this man?' and 'What did he teach?' are two of the most important questions anyone can ask about Jesus. After all, for nearly 2,000 years Jesus' followers have claimed that in this man, God became one of the human race. This is the most astonishing of claims, and whether it is true or false has profound implications. If it is not true then Jesus becomes a minor curiosity of history. If it is true then to follow Jesus and obey his teaching is quite simply the most important thing any of us can ever do. There is an awful lot at stake!

J.John

INTRODUCTION

THE QUESTIONS AND THE QUEST

We all know the really big questions of life. What am I here for? How am I to live? Does my life, with its hopes and fears, end with my death? In short, what's it all about? If we seek to answer these big questions we find we cannot avoid the greatest and most fundamental ones of all: is there 'someone' behind and beyond this world? And if there is, is this figure accessible to us? This issue of God is not just a big issue, but a difficult one: after all, any being worthy of the title 'God' is not going to sit in a test-tube to be analysed. In a quest for whether any god exists we need a guide, someone who will tell us clearly and truthfully what really is going on.

Now there is no shortage of individuals with claims to answer these fundamental questions. We live in a vast, noisy and crowded marketplace of beliefs: a world full of prophets and philosophers, mystics and materialists, atheists and astrologers. But who among these figures past or present do we listen to? Who are we to trust? Who tells the truth?

Amongst those figures who offer guidance, one individual stands out. He has the greatest claims attached to him: that he was God in the flesh; that he stood above all created beings; and that, one day, he will judge the whole world. As a guide to everything, he claimed to be not just the bearer of the truth, but somehow to *be* truth. Perhaps most remarkably of all, Jesus promised that he would not only give wisdom but, beyond all years and all distances, would be actually present with his followers as a companion. These are claims of an overwhelming enormity. They have been believed – even to the point of death – not by a mere handful of people but by billions over twenty centuries. Jesus is celebrated in art in every major language and culture. He has been loved and literally worshipped by billions who have found him to grant them strength in difficulty, comfort in sorrow and support in life.

If Jesus was all he claimed to be then our quest for someone to guide us to the truth is over: we have found who we are looking for. If he is not, then either we must look elsewhere or we must admit that any search for meaning is doomed. Everything hinges on Jesus and his claims.

THE IMPORTANCE OF JESUS

Let's begin. Jesus was a man from a low social background who was born over two thousand years ago into a despised race at the edge of a vast empire. He travelled no great distance, held no public office and left no writings. In the briefest of careers, barely three years, he trained twelve disciples from equally unpromising backgrounds, infuriating the religious leadership of his day and being publicly and shamefully executed. To say that he had an undistinguished life would be an understatement.

And yet . . .

- About a third of the world's population today consider themselves to be followers of Jesus.

- Although it may prefer to overlook the fact, Western culture is firmly rooted in the Christian faith centred on Jesus. The emphases on such things as truth, honesty, the value of every individual and a concern for the poor and weak, can all be traced back to the ethical teachings of Jesus.

- The followers of Jesus are not restricted to a single culture, social level or language but occur in their hundreds of millions in every inhabited continent.

- Jesus' teaching has proved to be extraordinarily durable. Throughout the last 2,000 years it has frequently found itself in opposition to great powers, brutal regimes and influential ideologies. Such bodies have often sought to erase the faith yet, when the dust has settled, the empire or the kingdom is gone and Jesus' teachings and his followers remain.

- English, the most commonly spoken language in the world, has been enormously influenced by Christianity. Three texts have moulded it: the Authorised Version or 'King James' Bible, the

Book of Common Prayer and the works of Shakespeare. The first two are, of course, Christian while the third frequently dwells on Christian themes and ideas. Whenever you utter such commonplace phrases as 'a prodigal son', 'turning the other cheek', 'not casting stones', 'love your neighbour' or 'judge not, lest you be judged', you repeat the words of Jesus.

• Millions of people from every culture, race and background can testify that believing in Jesus has transformed their lives.

• Jesus arouses astonishing devotion and commitment. Indeed he is quite literally worshipped; a phenomenon that would be idolatry unless, as mainstream Christianity has always believed, you hold to the astonishing idea that, in this Jesus, God became one of us.

And Christianity claims that on the third day after he was killed and buried, Jesus appeared alive in the flesh to his followers. From the very beginning, human beings have known three sad and unchallengeable things about death's grip on humanity: it is universal, inevitable and irreversible. Yet if Christians are correct, Jesus broke that rule. Astonishingly, utterly unique amongst the untold numbers of the dead, this Jesus is talked about in the present tense by billions. If we can indeed say not just that Jesus *lived* but that he *lives* then how we think about *everything* changes. It's not just that death is no longer final but, beyond our greatest hopes (or, possibly, worst fears) Jesus is alive and active in the world and one day will judge the human race. That's a claim whose truth definitely needs investigating.

TRUTH, FAITH AND THE SUPERNATURAL

We live in a world where terms such as 'alternative facts' and even 'post-truth' are thrown around and where some people think it's possible to ignore what you don't like simply by calling it 'fake news'. Faced with such ideas it's tempting to believe that either truth doesn't matter or that it is infinitely flexible. However attractive such views may seem they are, of course, nonsense. The truth of the matter is that truth matters and it can't be changed just because you don't like it. Every time you catch a plane, take medicine or drive over a bridge you rely on the fact that pilots, doctors and engineers operate on the basis of what they know to be true, not what they wish was true. The whole edifice of science and technology is based on things being either true or false and you won't hear the phrase 'post-truth' being used in any laboratory. Truth exists.

Yet if truth does exist it's undeniable that today people do seem to hold lightly to it. The result is an extraordinary paradox. On the one hand we see widespread scepticism about what is claimed to be truth by any authority, whether scientific or religious. On the other there is an astounding credulity when it comes to mysteries, theories and conspiracies. We are in an age when an 'alternative viewpoint', even if unsupported by facts, seems to compel more support than 'the traditional view', even if it is defended by an entire library of facts. The Internet must take some of the blame. There was a time when to promote an idea it was necessary to persuade someone to take the costly risk of publishing it in a book; a process that normally involved the checking of facts. Today anybody can publish anything and anybody does. The Internet has democratised knowledge in the worst possible way: now you don't need to know anything to be an expert!

Truth matters, and certainly so in the case of Jesus. The Bible claims that he is someone who controls our eternal destiny and demands our allegiance. How we live – and certainly how we die – hinges on the truthfulness of that claim.

Yet if modern culture is wrong to downplay truth it does have reasons for doing so. One source of the disfavour towards truth is a widespread certainty that there is more to the universe than can be described by cold scientific facts. 'There must be more than this!' was a powerful advertising catchphrase for the Alpha Course that echoed a near universal sentiment in twenty-first-century minds. The reality is that faith of all sorts, whether as religion, spirituality or simply superstition, is everywhere and seems to be becoming more widespread. There is a reason for this: human beings have hungry hearts and all the tricks and trinkets offered by the modern world leave us unsatisfied and malnourished. The result is that progress has produced a mind-set that is more open to the possibility of the supernatural – and hence the Bible's view of the way the world works – than many people expected.

Now of course the major reason that some people consider the Gospels to be fictional or fictionalised is because they do not believe in anything beyond what they normally see or feel. The idea that there might be the possibility of unusual events beyond the understanding of science – things that we might call *supernatural* – is ruled out. On the basis of this belief (something that is in fact an act of faith) any account that mentions such things as angels, miracles or resurrections must *automatically* be untrue. We devote a whole chapter to the miracles of Jesus and discuss and defend the idea of the supernatural there. Here let's just simply say that Jesus was an extraordinary and unique man and if what we label 'the Laws of Nature' *can* be broken by anyone then this was the man who could do it.

VIEWS OF JESUS: TRADITION AND ITS ALTERNATIVES

This book is all about Jesus and we need to acknowledge at the start that there are a vast number of different understandings of who Jesus was (or is) and what he means (or doesn't). Even if we do not always refer to them, these differing views form the backdrop to what we write in this book. At a very basic level we could divide these views into two: the traditional and the alternative.

The 'traditional' view

Let's start with the 'traditional' or 'mainstream' view of Jesus which is what we believe and defend in this book. This view, held by almost all Christians across all denominations through nearly twenty centuries, is that Jesus was in some special, unique way, God; that he died but a few days later rose bodily from the dead and is still alive today as the Lord and Saviour of the human race. And as believers in traditional Christianity we consider the Bible is a trustworthy record of who Jesus was, what he did and what he said. (There's a certain logic in linking these two views: after all, if God did go through the effort and agony of becoming human in Jesus then it would seem, well, *careless* not to have ensured a reliable record of what happened.)

Nevertheless, it's important to point out that our commitment to tradition extends only to our views of who Jesus really was and is.

We are not traditionalists in the sense that we automatically and unthinkingly endorse everything the church does simply because 'it's always been done that way'. Not all traditions are good – Jesus himself could be critical of tradition – and we think that there are areas where the church has done a poor job of reflecting its founder's teachings.

Incidentally, do be wary of thinking that any sort of 'traditional view of Jesus' must involve the sort of church practices that, for better or worse, you may be familiar with. It's worth remembering that, increasingly, Christianity is a global and diverse faith and, as a result, there is a vast range of ways of expressing faith in Jesus, many of which are likely to be very different to what's happening on Sunday in your nearest church. The traditional view can quite easily be expressed in a pretty non-traditional manner.

Now it's often assumed that the 'traditional view' of Jesus is quietly fading away. It isn't. It's alive, and thriving. Churches that hold to a traditional theology are growing and university theological departments that used to be full of individuals who thought about God only as some philosophical abstraction now contain thoughtful academics who have a living Christian faith.

The 'alternative' views

This traditional view finds itself opposed by broadly four 'alternative' views of Jesus which we could simplistically term as *myth, mystic, magician* or *militant*.

- Some people consider Jesus *mythical*. For them either Jesus is an entirely imaginary creation or, if he did exist, his reputation has been distorted beyond all recognition.

- Other people consider that the 'authentic Jesus' was primarily a *mystic*: someone claiming to be close to God and to receive messages from him. In one version of this, Jesus is just another in a long line of prophets. Perhaps increasingly more widespread is a version which sees Jesus as a universal guru or sage who dispensed words of wisdom.

- Others see Jesus as a *magician*: some sort of shaman who

those around him believed carried out healings and exorcisms. Depending on your belief in the supernatural these were either faked or psychosomatic events, or Jesus was indeed genuinely the master of spiritual powers.

- Still others would suggest that Christianity has hijacked a figure who was primarily a political *militant*. They imagine Jesus as an activist who stood up for his people against both the oppressive Roman occupation of his homeland and the injustices perpetuated by the corrupt religious leaders of his time.

In the course of this book we want to interact with these views. But let's make some general points here.

- None of these views do justice to what we know about Jesus. However respectfully presented ('Jesus was a wonderful teacher', 'the best man who ever lived', a 'great spiritual master', etc.) there is a vast gap between these alternative descriptions of Jesus and the unique and authoritative figure of traditional Christianity.

- Like fashions in clothes, these various views come, go, and then come back again. So some new sceptical bestseller will emerge and for the next year its explanation of who Jesus was will suddenly be in vogue. Then it will either be refuted or some other view will appear with another perspective on Jesus. And so on: repeat *ad infinitum.*

- Although some of these views of an alternative Jesus are held by individuals who have some awareness of theology and history, it is far more common to find that people hold such views on Jesus without any serious examination of the facts. A hundred years ago what you might call the 'unexamined default position' in the culture of most Western countries was some sort of traditional belief in Jesus. Now it is increasingly one of disbelief in that tradition. This shift probably has very little to do with, say, the discovery of new manuscripts or new ideas. The reality is that the Jesus of traditional Christianity fits very clearly into that category of 'things that are inconvenient because they have implications and make demands'. Here's an interesting quote from biblical scholar Craig Keener: 'I have talked with a number of sceptics about Christian faith who, after extended conversation, admitted that their objections to the basic Gospel portrait stemmed from their concern that acknowledging more about Jesus historically would entail greater moral demands on their lives.'[1] Sometimes it's not belief that needs to be challenged, it's unbelief. In a phrase, we may need to be more sceptical about scepticism.

- It's a curious fact that we all find something attractive about a challenge to an accepted opinion. There's an instance of this with two Bishops of Durham. When in 1984 one Bishop of Durham made a comment that was construed as denying the resurrection of Jesus, it made the headlines across the popular press; when in 2003 a successor (N. T. Wright) wrote an 800-page book of deep scholarship affirming the resurrection,[2] the popular press ignored it. When it comes to well-known events, a sober chronicling of the facts is likely to arouse much less interest than some sensational challenge. You don't get invited onto chat shows if you believe the earth is round.

- For all the noise and publicity that the alternative views of Jesus make, the fact is that their assertions have been answered and continue to be answered. There is the very strongest evidence that the Gospels are trustworthy in their depiction of Jesus.

In thinking about who Jesus was (and is) we need to be aware of a particular problem. It is precisely because Jesus is so important there is always a temptation for individuals to deal with the evidence about him in such a way that he can be moulded into a shape that pleases them. So quite frequently you hear people talk about Jesus with such words as '*I* like to think of him as . . .' The result is that, for some people, Jesus becomes the stern defender of the nation, the upholder of the family and the supporter of tradition. For others Jesus is the pioneering martyr of revolutionary socialism, proclaiming liberty and inclusion for all. Those fascinated by mysticism find Jesus mystical; those enthralled by politics find him political. Some want Jesus to be full of anger (particularly towards *their* enemies); while others want Jesus to be the gentle consoler (particularly towards *their* problems).

It's not just individuals who try to squeeze Jesus into their mould. Every age and culture seeks to do the same. In an astonishing triumph of wishes over facts, the Nazis tried to create a distinctly un-Jewish and Aryan Jesus.[3] At the end of the psychedelic, free-love 1960s there was a brief explosion of publicity around a view that suggested that the 'Jesus Cult' was – surprise, surprise – really all about hallucinogenic mushrooms and sex.[4]

We wish we could say that the temptation for individuals to create Jesus in their own image is confined to unbelievers. But it isn't. Even Jesus' most devoted followers have frequently dwelt almost exclusively on those passages of his teaching that fall comfortably on their ears while skipping over his more challenging words, even though they may be in the very next verse. There is a universal temptation to interpret Jesus in a way that renders him acceptable. After all, what better way of self-affirmation is there than to believe in a Jesus who shares your concerns and endorses your actions? Actually, it's probably true to say that if the Jesus you believe in doesn't challenge you and, at least periodically, make you feel uncomfortable, then he isn't authentic.

In thinking about someone who claimed to be the truth[5] made flesh it's important to force ourselves to think about what is not just convenient, but true.

THIS BOOK

The title *Jesus Christ – The Truth* was chosen because it expresses the twin aims of this book. The first is to express what we believe can be said with confidence about Jesus in terms of who he was and what he did. The second is to cover something of his teaching, which was frequently introduced by the phrase 'I tell you the truth . . .'

One audience for this book is simply anyone who wants to know more about Jesus the man and his message. So, for instance, you might be someone, entirely outside Christianity, who has an intellectual curiosity about the one who founded the faith that lies at the heart of Western culture. Alternatively, you might be an individual, equally outside the faith, who has a spiritual hunger and wants to explore, however cautiously, the possibility that Jesus might be the one who might satisfy that hunger. We hope this book will help both types of reader.

We believe that a book like this is no substitute for the Bible itself and the indispensable companion to this book is, of course, a copy of the New Testament, preferably in a version that is easy to read. The world is full of people who have picked up the Gospels and found, often to their consternation, that the Jesus they are reading about is no dead historical figure but a living person who demands a response. Yet the reality is that there are also those who, as they pick up the pages of the New Testament, want something of a guide to what they're reading.

Another audience for this book is those people who see themselves as Christians but who realise, perhaps in the face of challenges, that their knowledge about Jesus could be deepened. Our hope and prayer is that some of the truths that we write will not just illuminate heads but warm the hearts. We are also aware that, in a way unprecedented in the West for over a millennium, we live in times where Christians can find themselves asked to justify their faith and even to face opposition. Here, too, we have tried to help.

If you are an outsider to faith in Jesus can we just say one thing at the start? This book doesn't demand faith but instead presents evidence for a faith that we believe can be trusted. In thinking how you respond we simply ask that for the purposes of this book you consider for the moment the *possibility* that behind this vast and extraordinary edifice of atoms and stars, bacteria and black holes, goldfinches and galaxies that you inhabit, there might be an all-powerful, all-seeing, all-knowing, all-present God. You see, the Christian claim – believed over time by billions – is that this God doesn't just exist but has intervened in human history personally, physically and permanently in Jesus.

Now at this point we can hear someone say, 'Hang on, you two believe this stuff. Why should I read this? You are believers so you are obviously biased.' Let's make a few responses to that.

First, it's a weak argument for sceptics to say believers are biased because they 'have faith'. Precisely because we cannot put God under our scrutiny, all verdicts to do with his existence or nonexistence are based on faith.

Second, and related, is that the arguments for bias cut both ways. It's not simply the Christian community which only considers the data that suits its position and which excludes other data; it's also true of the sceptical community as well. There are many sceptics who tend to play fast and loose with language, presenting those of us who hold the traditional views as being biased because of our theological position and our supernatural worldview, while claiming for themselves the position of dispassionate and neutral historians or scholars. Unfortunately, there is no position of philosophical neutrality. To believe or disbelieve in God and the supernatural are both acts of faith. Yes, there are religious fundamentalists, but there are also 'atheistic fundamentalists' who would resolutely continue to deny the existence of the supernatural even if they were confronted by a dozen angels in celestial glory standing before them ('It must be a hologram!', 'What a remarkably convincing hallucination!' or even 'I guess I'm having a breakdown').

Third, can we play the numbers game? Christianity has been tried and tested for nearly 2,000 years by cultures across the globe and now has over two billion adherents. Despite some spectacular and shameful failures it has done a remarkable job of 'comforting the afflicted and afflicting the comfortable'. The mainstream view of Jesus behind it deserves serious concern.

What we can say is that, in keeping with the title of this book, we have done our best to be honest in presenting what we consider to be truth. We are well aware of books and websites by enthusiastic Christian believers where exaggerated and unsubstantiated claims have been made. Wishful thinking or bending the truth is not acceptable even if it is in the right cause. Jesus spoke an awful lot about truth and we value it.

ABOUT US

We come from very different backgrounds. J.John comes from a Greek Cypriot background and grew up speaking Greek. He has an MA in theology, is a speaker and teacher, and is a canon of Coventry Cathedral and Wroxall Abbey. He and his wife Killy have three adult sons and two grandchildren and live near London, England.

Chris Walley has a doctorate in geology and has had careers both as a lecturer and consultant in geology and as a writer. He is married to Alison and they have two adult sons and four grandchildren. He and his wife Alison live in France where he is involved in the Anglican Church in Cannes and the conservation work of A Rocha France.

SOME WORDS ON WORDS

We have deliberately chosen to use ordinary language. There is a good precedent for this: the Gospels and the letters that form the New Testament are written in the everyday, ordinary Greek of the marketplace rather than in the formal academic language of the scholars and philosophers.

Where we have quoted from the Bible we have used the New Living Translation. In order not to break the flow of the text, we have put the relevant Bible references with other notes at the end of the book.

A few specific notes:

- Jesus is a personal name (Hebrew *Yeshua*, Greek *Iesus*), and Christ ('Messiah') is a title. So Jesus Christ is a contraction of 'Jesus the Christ'. However, most Christians use the names 'Jesus' and 'Christ' interchangeably. We have used 'Jesus'.

- Almost all the activity of the Gospels takes place in a small strip of land, around 200 km long and 100 km wide, between the Mediterranean and the Jordan Valley. Following most authorities on the subject, we use the ancient geographic term 'Palestine'.[1] 'Israel' refers here, as it does in the New Testament, to God's people rather than a place. In Jesus' day the kingdom of Israel

---

[1] This geographic term is used without any reference to contemporary political issues in the region.

had long ceased to exist. As discussed in chapter 3, Palestine consisted of three subdivisions at the time of Jesus: Galilee in the north, Samaria in the middle, and Judea, which included the hill country around Jerusalem, in the south.

- Although strictly speaking the region in which Jesus carried out his ministry is the 'Near East' we have occasionally used 'Middle East' to refer to the much wider area.

- The Bible is traditionally divided into the Old and New Testaments, and although we continue to use the term 'Old Testament' it must be remembered that to Jesus and his contemporaries it wasn't the *Old* Testament at all; it was their Bible. On that note, we have used 'the Bible' and 'Scripture' as interchangeable terms.

- The Jewish religion is referred to as *Judaism* and non-Jews are *Gentiles*.

- When people refer to Jesus' period of public teaching and healing they generally talk about his *ministry*. Although in this sense the word may be unfamiliar today it has – or should have – overtones of service (as in *ministering*) that are helpful.

- Although there were many people who followed Jesus, he assembled around him a core group of twelve *disciples* ('disciple' means learner). After the resurrection, these, with the exception of Judas, became the *apostles* (literally, 'those who are sent').

- *Divine* is a useful adjective to do with God, so to say that 'Jesus is divine' means that he is God.

- The word *gospel* is an old attempt to render into English the Greek word *euangelion* (from which we get 'evangelist' and 'evangelical'), which means 'good news'. The word 'gospel' has two overlapping meanings. It refers to either the four accounts of the life and teaching of Jesus, or to the good news about Jesus that is proclaimed in the Bible.

- The Mediterranean culture of the time was a curious mixture of Greek culture and Roman rule and is summarised in the shorthand *Greco-Roman*.

- When we quote Bible verses in the notes at the end we adopt the standard practice of giving the Bible book followed by the chapter and then the verse: for example Matthew 5:2 is the second verse of Matthew chapter 5.

We have tried to supply references to quotations and ideas but we have to admit that in the course of all those decades of reading, teaching and preaching about Jesus, both of us have absorbed thoughts and phrases from various sources whose origin is now sadly lost to us. If we have used a phrase created by others and not acknowledged it, we apologise: attribute it please not to plagiarism but to amnesia!

LAYOUT

This book is about Jesus and we have tried to keep him central without getting too side-tracked into such fascinating topics as the origins of the Gospels, differing church interpretations, how to read the Gospels, and so on. Such material is rather like the frame to a portrait: something which, if you're not careful, can end up distracting from the picture itself. We've tried to minimise the frame of this particular portrait.

Let's get going!

1

SCENE SETTING 1:
WHAT WE KNOW ABOUT JESUS

The issue of truth is vital when we think about Jesus. As we will see, if he was – and is – all that 'traditional Christianity' has claimed him to be, then he is of extraordinary importance. If he is wholly or partially fictional then he is, at best, a curiosity of history.

Here one very important and often overlooked point needs making. It is the fact that the biblical accounts about Jesus are as much focused – indeed possibly more so – on who he was than on what he taught; on what this man did more than what he said. It's important to understand this because if the teaching of Jesus was simply about how we should live, then it wouldn't really matter if, to a greater or lesser extent, he was imaginary. If Jesus was just a teacher of morality then we could still salvage some teaching from him if he was mythical or legendary. Yet that is not the way the New Testament treats him. Ringing out from every page of the New Testament is a powerful and jubilant announcement. In Jesus, all the writers say, God has entered the world in a special way; as a result sin is cancelled, death destroyed, the devil disarmed – the Kingdom and the King has come!

Everything therefore stands on the truthfulness of the claims about Jesus. So important is the issue of truth around Jesus – and so loud the attacks against it – that innumerable books have been written defending every aspect of the claims for Jesus. All we can do here is to simply summarise the situation; at the very end of this book we refer to some of the detailed studies – often by scholars with impeccable credentials in ancient history, classical languages and archaeology – that you may read if you want to reassure yourselves further about the trustworthiness of what we know about Jesus.

Let's look at the sources.

THE BIBLICAL SOURCES OF INFORMATION

1. The Letters

The New Testament divides naturally into the narratives (the four Gospels and the book of Acts), the letters (the 'Epistles') and the visionary book of Revelation. Despite the order in which they appear in the Bible, most of the letters were written before the Gospels. They also raise the issues surrounding Jesus in the most striking manner possible so let's deal with them first.

Particularly significant here are those letters written by the apostle (or Saint) Paul. Paul's letters show him to be a profound thinker with a great knowledge of the Jewish faith and, of considerable relevance, a concern for truth.[1] What is particularly striking is that Paul (or Saul to use his Hebrew name) was closely linked with the Jewish leadership in Jerusalem within three years of the crucifixion.[2] Whether Paul ever saw or heard Jesus personally we do not know, but as someone given authority to arrest Christians by Caiaphas, the very high priest who oversaw the trial of Jesus,[3] Paul would have worked closely with people who were involved with the trial and execution of Jesus. Given that he arrested Christians he would inevitably have had close dealings with those who had personally known Jesus and in some cases he would have interrogated them. Paul is therefore a vital source about Jesus.

In general terms, three striking things can be seen when the letters refer to Jesus.

- Jesus is given extraordinary titles and astonishing reverence. Terms that an observant Jew like Paul would only use for God, such as 'Lord', 'Saviour' and 'King', are applied to Jesus. Given the fact that the Jewish faith held firmly to there being a single God this is astonishing. Equally common are such concepts as Jesus being the man who will judge the world at the end of time and someone who can be prayed to.[2] It is worth noting that crucifixion didn't just involve a slow, agonising death but intense

---

2 This is a fascinating and significant claim. To imagine that you can pray to someone, not just at a particular shrine but *wherever you are*, implies that this individual is somehow everywhere, able to hear your (unspoken) prayers in one of a multitude of languages and has the ability to handle vast numbers of prayers at the same time. This cannot apply to anybody other than God.

shame and the idea that the victim was cursed by God. Yet despite this event, Paul confers the very highest titles on Jesus.[4]

• Jesus is seen not just as a dead historic figure but as a living individual who, after having risen from the dead, has ascended into heaven and, through his Spirit, is now present and active in the lives of his followers.

• Jesus is viewed not simply as someone who *taught* things but as someone who *did* something. His great achievement is not his teaching but his death, an event which achieved the reconciliation of God and humankind.

In specific terms, we learn that Jesus was a man, descended from King David, who had disciples, taught on aspects of Jewish belief, had an extraordinary familiarity with God whom he called 'his Father', instituted the Lord's Supper and was crucified, buried and resurrected. Strikingly, Paul writes all these things in a matter-of-fact tone which clearly suggests he knew that his readers knew and believed all these things.

So we have a remarkable situation that, within no more than two decades of the crucifixion, people from a conservative Jewish faith, used to proclaiming daily that there was only one God, were, without any apology, talking about a man killed and humiliated through crucifixion as being wonderfully alive and gloriously divine.

There is uncertainty about the dating – and authorship – of the other letters and Revelation, but it is widely assumed that they were all written before the end of the first century. They do not alter the picture given to us in these early letters of a sovereign, divine Jesus elevated to the very highest heights; instead they just give him new titles.

This evidence from the letters, written to geographically separate areas; is something that needs careful consideration. When sceptics claim that all the evidence we have for Jesus comes from the Gospels, which they dismissively claim 'are written a long time after the events', they either accidentally or deliberately omit some astonishingly powerful evidence. And, of course, this has implications for how we view the Gospels. We can completely forget the naïve belief that slowly and steadily over the decades, Jesus was somehow progressively promoted from being a godly man to being God made man. The letters suggest that right at the start of Christianity Jesus was viewed as very much more than a man.

2. The Gospels

The four traditional or 'canonical' Gospels – Matthew, Mark, Luke and John – are our most detailed source of information on Jesus. They are without doubt the most examined documents in existence and have stood up to the scrutiny remarkably well.

Here we simply give a brief overview of the Gospels. In the final 'Issues' section of this book we cover in Issue 1 why they are not fictional documents, and in Issue 2 give an outline of how the Gospels came to us and why we can trust what they say. At the end of the book we list some useful books that address in much more detail other issues to do with the trustworthiness of Scripture.

What are the Gospels?

The word 'gospel' comes through the old English *godspel* or 'good news', from the Greek word *euangelion* or 'good news'. The New Testament is clear: the good news is the coming of Jesus. Note that the good news is not what Jesus said but what Jesus did.

Precisely because of this emphasis on the actions of Jesus – and in particular his trial and execution – it is not surprising that the Gospels have strong resemblances to ancient biographies.[5] Indeed Luke's Gospel makes a specific claim to being a biography or history.[6] Now this is not to say that the Gospels are biographies or histories in the modern sense of the word: for one thing there are various omissions that many people today would find puzzling. For instance, what to us would seem obvious questions remain unanswered: what did Jesus look like? What year was he born in? What exactly did he do before his public ministry? Instead, what we have is something like a compilation of word pictures of events, incidents and teaching. While in general these appear to be in chronological order, it is only when they come to focus remarkably on the last week of Jesus' life that we get a detailed and consecutive account of what happened and when.

It may be helpful to remember that there are specific differences between the Gospels and modern biographies.

- Before the printing press, ancient writers were forced to value brevity. After all, what they produced had to be copied by hand onto scrolls, something for which there was a definite length limit. The result is that, by our standards, the Gospel accounts tend to be condensed.

- First-century writers had none of the tools that we have today. For example, we often use quotation marks not just to indicate reported speech but also to indicate that some word or phrase is being used in a way that may not be strictly literal. We have brackets, full stops, commas, uppercase and lowercase letters and italics to clarify exactly what we mean, and to show where we are placing the emphasis.

- Modern readers demand a precise chronology and sequence in writing that ancient authors didn't value quite as much. So if we compare parallel Gospel accounts we may come across seeming conflicts in what order events happened. The Gospel writers were often more interested in working out themes than in sticking to a rigid chronological order.

- Ancient writers seem to have been untroubled by failing to mention matters that a contemporary reader would consider vital. So, in Mark and John there is no mention of Jesus' birth or childhood. Equally, at the end of Luke's Gospel the reader could get the impression that Jesus ascended and the Holy Spirit came down on the disciples on Easter Sunday. In fact, in his sequel, Acts, Luke is absolutely clear that this happened weeks later.[7]

It should be noted, however, that none of these differences affect the truthfulness of the documents.

Who wrote the Gospels?

Unlike the New Testament letters, where in all but one case (the letter to the Hebrews) there is a named author, the Gospels are strictly speaking anonymous. Nevertheless, the names Matthew, Mark, Luke and John appear on all the earliest manuscripts, and the idea that these were the only four 'approved' Gospels seems to be widespread from the middle of the second century. Tradition says that Matthew was the tax collector who became a disciple of Jesus; Mark, an individual mentioned in Acts who is linked with Peter; Luke, one of Paul's companions; and John, one of Jesus' closest disciples. You can read all the arguments elsewhere for authorship and we touch on them in Issue 2, but there seems little reason to reject these traditions. After all, if you were looking for a name to give authority to some fictional account it's hard to see why anybody would choose these over such 'big' names as Peter or James.

When were they written?

There is strong evidence that Matthew and Luke were written by the middle of the 60s, with Mark possibly in existence by the middle of the 50s. In particular, none of the three Gospels shows any acknowledgement that the fall of Jerusalem and the destruction of the temple in AD 70 had actually taken place. In Issue 2 we suggest reasons why very early on in church history – and certainly by the mid-60s – there would have been demands for some sort of written account of what Jesus did and said. John's Gospel was perhaps written by AD 80.

Actually, the date of the writing down of the Gospels may not be as important as has often been claimed. Unlike our world, this culture would have had an ability to accurately memorise material, and oral accounts of Jesus could have accurately been transmitted for many years. (Again, this is something we discuss in the Issues section.)

Why were they written?

The Gospels were written for a variety of reasons: they were to inform those who had come to faith in Jesus about the one they now followed; to give information to inquirers who wanted to find out more about Jesus; to provide a framework for evangelists to preach from; or to provide authoritative texts to be read out, alongside the Old Testament, in congregations where believers in Jesus met for worship.

There are many unresolved questions about the Gospels. That actually shouldn't surprise us. They are unique documents and that uniqueness doesn't simply reflect a great gap of time and culture between them and us. It reflects the fact that the one that they talk about was unique.

OTHER SOURCES

Briefly let's mention the existence of other limited but important references to Jesus outside the Bible.

There are various documents, many fragmentary and others rather cryptic, that go under the title of the 'New Testament Apocrypha'. In almost every case they are at least a century later than when Jesus lived and they reflect either attempts to fill in gaps in the Gospels or a 'spirituality' outside mainstream Christianity. Although claims are regularly made that some of them, including the so-called 'Gospel of Thomas', contain historical information on Jesus, that is questionable. In general, the old rule seems to apply: 'What's new isn't true and what's true isn't new.' Most of these documents are light on facts and heavy on mysticism. They would normally be ignored except by a subculture of scholars and others who like to claim that these books reveal an alternative Jesus who is more attractive to the modern Western mind.[8]

The Jewish historian Josephus, writing towards the end of the first century, refers to Jesus in several places. Josephus viewed Jesus as an historic figure and a teacher within the Jewish faith, who was executed under Pontius Pilate.[9]

Something that puts another firm nail in the coffin of any view that Jesus was totally fictional are a few limited but very solid references to both Jesus and first-century Christians in the historical records of the time. Given that Jesus was an insignificant character of the region close to the edge of the known Roman world, it's not surprising that he doesn't get much of a mention in the incomplete records of the period. Nevertheless, there is evidence that preaching about Christ was causing such serious trouble within the Jewish community of Rome around AD 49[10] that Emperor Claudius felt obliged to expel the Jews.[11] There are several specific references by respected

Roman historians very early in the second century that are relevant. Suetonius talks about Christians as 'a class of men given to a new and mischievous superstition' who were blamed for the fire of Rome in AD 64 under Emperor Nero.[12] Tacitus gives much more detail. He refers to the fire of Rome and describes how, in order to crush rumours of his own responsibility, Emperor Nero found suitable scapegoats among those who were 'called Christians', a name which Tacitus explains comes from *Christus* their founder who had been executed in Judaea by Pontius Pilate. Tacitus, who displays an unflattering opinion of Christians, mentions how they were tortured and refers to 'vast numbers' of them being grotesquely executed.[13] Around the same time as Suetonius and Tacitus were writing, Pliny the Younger, who was governor of a province of north-western Turkey, felt obliged to ask Emperor Trajan about what to do with what was evidently a considerable number of Christians there: he comments that they met regularly and sang hymns 'to Christ as if to a God'.[14]

From these sources outside the Bible we glimpse a clear but faint image of Jesus as an historical figure that is consistent with the picture in the biblical Gospels and the letters of who Jesus was, what he said and what he did. Let's make three observations about this 'non-biblical data'.

First, we cannot, with any sort of intellectual honesty, consider Jesus to be some sort of mythical figure. He was real and, despite being crucified 'under Pontius Pilate', soon acquired numerous followers in many parts of the Empire.

Second, this data removes any option of treating Jesus as some sort of rootless figure, isolated from any cultural background, whom we can shape and model into whatever we please. The Jesus of reality and truth is not some Indian mystic or New Age guru but is anchored firmly in a culture, a time and a place: he is a Jew of early first-century Palestine. Our views of who he was – and is – must take that into account.

Finally, consider the implications of two facts, secure from even the most sceptical attack. The first is that Jesus, a Jewish preacher, was executed in humiliating circumstances around AD 30 by Pontius Pilate, Rome's governor in Jerusalem. The second secure fact (consistent of course with the letters of the New Testament) is that within twenty years his followers were so distinctive in what they believed and so widespread that in Rome they were capable of disturbing communities and of becoming suitable scapegoats at times of disaster. This remarkable jump requires an explanation. We think the only satisfactory one is that provided by traditional Christianity, that this executed criminal was not just an ordinary man but somehow God himself in human flesh.

There is, however, one final line of evidence that the Gospels are not wholly or partially fictionalised accounts created by the early church. We have no hesitation in admitting that it's utterly subjective but it's this: *read them*. Note those extraordinary and often troubling sayings of Jesus, the way that he comforts the weak and challenges the powerful, the self-confidence in which he deals with all manner of people and the way in which he alone stays in control through the gory chaos of Good Friday. Yes, it's subjective and not objective, and impossible to pin down, but the figure that the Gospels portray carries an extraordinary and commanding authenticity. *The Bible is the only book you can read and have the author present while you read it.*

THE FOUR GOSPELS: AN OUTLINE

Finally, let's take a brief look at the Gospels themselves.

Each of the Gospels has a different style and each depicts Jesus from a different angle, with slightly different emphases, something that doubtless reflects the different audiences they were written for. The first three Gospels – Matthew, Mark and Luke – have much in common and are referred to as the Synoptic Gospels. Synoptic means that they can be seen side-by-side, and you can get books and websites showing what matches what across all three Gospels.[15]

The Gospel of *Matthew* has a Jewish flavour and contains many references to Jewish beliefs and practices. A key theme is how Jesus fulfils the prophecies of the Old Testament. In Matthew we are told that Jesus is the 'Son of David' and the Messiah, the long-promised King and deliverer. There are many echoes of the Old Testament. However, although Matthew is very focused on the Jewish aspects of Jesus, he also looks outwards and sees that through Jesus, God's plan for the whole world will be fulfilled.

In *Mark*, the shortest of the Gospels, Jesus is portrayed as the Son of God,[3] a dynamic and authoritative figure who is constantly on the move, healing and delivering people from the power of the devil. Mark says a lot about Jesus' actions, his power over the natural and supernatural world, and has an extraordinary focus on Jesus' suffering and death. It's widely assumed Mark wrote for a Roman audience and he certainly would have appealed to two well-known features of their culture: a preoccupation with action and authority, and a fear of supernatural powers.

The Gospel of *Luke* is unique in that with its sequel, *Acts*, it is part of a two-volume work. Luke seems to write for those with only a limited knowledge of the Jewish faith and emphasises Jesus as the Saviour and Rescuer sent by God to the world. Luke has a particular interest in the outsiders, those whom we would today call the marginalised: women, children, the sick and those rejected by society. In Luke, Jesus' focus is on 'the least, the last and the lost'.

These Synoptic Gospels have relationships to each other that have given rise to endless theories, a lot of speculation and little in the way of certainty.[16] There was probably a now-lost source that all three drew on. Traditionally this and other possible sources have been thought of as written documents but, as we outline in Issue 2, there may have been input from carefully memorised oral material.

The fourth Gospel, *John*, is different. Although the overall pattern of events is very similar and the account of Jesus' trial, death and resurrection in particular fits very closely with those of the Synoptics, John's style is very different. Where the Jesus of the Synoptics speaks in short phrases and parables, the Jesus of John's Gospel engages in monologues and dialogues without a parable in sight. In

---

3   This is a term – discussed further in chapter 10 – that is often misunderstood. It carries no sense of any sexual reproduction (an unthinkable blasphemy to any Old or New Testament believer) but refers to the way that Jesus possesses the full identity and authority of God the Father.

terms of his content, John makes it clear that Jesus is the one who, by his words and actions, reveals who God is. John makes much about his Gospel being eyewitness testimony, his sequence of events makes sense, and his knowledge of the landscape and culture of Palestine is accurate. There are also details in John's account that come across as eyewitness touches.[17]

Overall, John's Gospel is much more a continuous narrative and he was certainly writing for a very different audience: probably a Greco-Roman one used to a more flowing style of writing.

Looking at the Gospels together is like gazing at four photo albums for a particular year taken by four separate family members. In them we find images that are virtually duplicates, as well as others that show the same event from a different angle or with a different lens. We find some events recorded only by one or two people, and sometimes the images are in the same order whilst elsewhere they have been arranged differently. So it is with the Gospels. Yet taken together they give us a consistent and compelling account of Jesus.

NOTE: THE PERILS OF SELECTIVE READING

We have mentioned that there are many alternative versions of Jesus in existence and many of them bear a rather curious and striking resemblance to their creators. It is as if they have turned to the Gospels and reassuringly found them to be a mirror in which they see themselves.

One factor behind most of these creations is a 'pick-n-mix' attitude to the Gospels where there is a selective reading of the biblical documents. In some cases that's all that is needed to create the Mystic Jesus or the Marxist Jesus. In other cases people go further and, encountering verses that argue against their position, they then engage in 'creative reinterpretation' to try to neutralise them. Sometimes they do this by an appeal to conveniently long-lost 'Aramaic originals' or to someone somewhere making a copying mistake. One final resort is to suggest that Jesus was so radical that his followers felt obliged to add, delete or modify what he said to water down his teaching.

Actually, the peril of selective reading extends in a slightly different way even to Christians. It's all too easy to go through the Gospels and find wonderful heart-warming passages to lovingly dwell on while the uncomfortable passages get quietly overlooked.

To search for truth requires that we be prepared to be honest when we find it. In reading the Gospels we need to see Jesus for who he is, rather than who we would like him to be.

2

SCENE SETTING 2:
THE RELIGIOUS WORLD

Our modern Western beliefs and practices are so dominant that we can struggle to identify with life in other places and times. So when we encounter individuals in the Bible we must remind ourselves that these are not our contemporaries with our twenty-first-century hopes, fears and frustrations, but people with very different priorities and concerns.

Nowhere is this cultural gap deeper than when we encounter the Jewish background to the Gospels. In truth, the Jewish faith is hardly the background: it's a vast mountain range that looms high over the landscape. Here many of us find ourselves face to face with something particularly alien. For many people in the West today, religious faith is one of life's accessories, not one of its essentials. Now while there were people in the world of Jesus' day who largely ignored religion – particularly perhaps amongst the Greeks – they would have been very much the exception. Religion for Jews was something that shaped everything you were, did and said. Your faith was no lifestyle supplement; it was the foundation and framework for all you were.

When we try to find out exactly what it was like to be a Jew in Jesus' day, we must be conscious of two things. One is to remember that, as the Gospels make clear, there wasn't a single standard Jewish faith: rather like modern Judaism (and Christianity), there were many branches of the faith which involved radically different views and practices. Indeed there were 'branches off the branches' – for example, not every Pharisee was opposed to Jesus. Another is that we shouldn't assume that the Jewish faith then was identical to any sort of Judaism now. The tragic and turbulent history of the Jewish people over the last two millennia – which has included exile, dispersion and persecution – has modified the faith enormously from what it was in Jesus' time. If nothing else, it's worth remembering that no Jew has made a sacrifice on the altar of the temple in Jerusalem for nearly two thousand years. Sacrifices, the priesthood and the temple were all central features of the Jewish faith two thousand years ago: they are ancient history to all Jews today.

We can think of being Jewish at the time of the Gospels as having two aspects: having a history and holding to certain beliefs and practices.

JEWISH HISTORY

One of the most striking aspects of the Jewish people of Jesus' time is the value they placed on their history. The Old Testament is full of commands 'to remember' and the most important annual ceremony, Passover, specifically focused attention on what God had done for his people in the past. The Jews treated their history with seriousness because it shaped their identity and because it gave them hope in even the darkest of days. Their history told them that they were not just one more religious or racial group: they were special; God's own people and central to his purposes for the world. This sense of destiny underlies every page in the Gospels. It also goes a long way to explain the antagonism between the Jews and the Romans.

The history of the Jewish people is important to any reader of the Gospels. Jesus was not just dropped in from eternity into this world; he came as a Jew with deep roots in the past. In almost everything Jesus did and said he was, in some way, interacting with Jewish history. Jesus took his people's past seriously and the first Christians did the same.

Although differing groups within Judaism viewed their past with very different emphases, the tale that Jews of this time would have told went something like this.

Human history started with Adam and Eve, the first man and woman. They had been placed in the garden of Eden where they had enjoyed fellowship with the one Creator God, but had lost that blessing by disobedience and been expelled into a world of evil and suffering.

Ever since, human existence had been a long way from what it was meant to be. However, God in his mercy had intervened and begun to restore the human race by choosing Abraham as the father of a people through whom blessing would return to the world. God made promises to Abraham as part of a *covenant*.[1]

This idea of covenant is fundamental in both Jewish and Christian faiths and is of a solemn, binding agreement made by God to those who are his people. As part of the covenant God promised to Abraham that he would bless and protect his descendants – *Israel* – forever; that he would make them a great nation, give them their own land and, ultimately, do good to the world through them. The covenant was not entirely one-sided: although a gift, it brought obligations with it. To be one of God's people was a privilege but one that carried responsibility.

Over the next few generations God's promises took shape and soon Abraham's descendants had multiplied to twelve tribes. This promising start faltered as, several hundred years after Abraham, the Israelites found themselves enslaved in Egypt. From there, however, God spectacularly rescued them in the dramatic events of the exodus – commemorated every spring by the Passover festival – and liberated them under the leadership of Moses. In the course of the exodus and the wilderness wanderings that followed, God revealed himself more fully to Moses. Part of that revelation was what we might call God's personal name, *Yahweh*. This name of God, which occurs over 6,000 times in the Old Testament and which was treated as so holy that it was never spoken aloud or even fully written down, is translated in most modern English Bibles as 'the LORD'. With that invitation to a personal friendship with God came new obligations. If the people were to enjoy the blessings of the covenant then they had to have complete loyalty to the one God and follow the rules he gave. These rules were laid out in the law (the *Torah*) and are summarised in the Ten Commandments. Inscribed on stone tablets, these were carefully stored in the box that was the Ark of the Covenant and preserved as the reminder to Israel of the covenant that had been sworn between them.

One function of the rules God gave Israel was to ensure that they would be special. They were to be distinctly different from the nations – the *Gentiles* – around them: they were to be *holy*. One sign of holiness and separation for men was circumcision, an act that came to define what it was to be Jewish. Other marks of being God's people – and they are things that surface repeatedly in the New Testament – were limits on what foods you could eat and not working on Saturday, the Sabbath.

Unfortunately, almost no sooner had the Torah been given than Israel rebelled and was punished by forty years in the wilderness. Over the next millennia and a half the relationship between Yahweh and Israel proved to be somewhat dysfunctional. The way that Israel continuously rebelled against God, failed to keep the Law and worshipped other gods but was then brought back to God, is a repeated theme in the long, winding storyline of the Old Testament.

In the century or so after Moses, the Jewish people began to take control of most of the territory – the 'promised land' – that God had sworn to give them. After a long period of struggle and lawlessness, a kingship was inaugurated in Israel, and around 1000 BC, under the second king, David, the Jewish kingdom reached its maximum extent. God reaffirmed his covenant to David and added yet another promise: he would have a glorious son and be the founder of an unending line of kings. The prophecy was partly fulfilled under David's son Solomon, who built the majestic temple that came to be the focus of the Jewish religion and which was widely felt to be the earthly dwelling place of Yahweh.

The reigns of David and Solomon marked the high point of Jewish history. It was the best of times: God's king ruled over God's people in their own land, and peace, justice and prosperity prevailed for all. Nevertheless, the sun soon set on the good days and things began to slide downhill. The kingdom split along tribal lines into northern and southern kingdoms and the exclusive worship of Yahweh that was the foundation stone of the covenant began to be diluted.

The northern kingdom soon drifted into pagan practices. In 722 BC the Assyrians conquered it, took much of its population away in an exile from which they never returned, and relocated them in what is now the northern part of Iraq. To replace them the Assyrians resettled other conquered peoples in the area of the northern kingdom. One result of this was the creation of the Samaritans: a people considered ever afterwards by most Jews to be both religiously and racially illegitimate.

The southern kingdom, ruled by a line of kings descended from David and centred on the temple at Jerusalem, held more tightly to the covenant but eventually it, too, fell away from the worship of Yahweh and was conquered by the Babylonians (who had replaced the Assyrians as the regional superpower) in 586 BC. In a traumatic event that was to cast a dark shadow down the centuries and well into Jesus' day, Solomon's magnificent temple was destroyed and many of the nation's leaders were taken into exile to Babylon in the southern part of what is now modern Iraq. Many other Jews left the land for Egypt and other countries.

In 539 BC the Persians – the next superpower – conquered Babylon, and in what came to be seen as the second great deliverance in Jewish history, allowed captives from the southern kingdom to return to their homeland. Significantly for the future not all did, and a sizeable Jewish population continued to exist outside Palestine – the *diaspora* – where they became increasingly independent of how things were done 'back home'.

Despite their extraordinary rescue from Babylonian exile, things were never the same for the Jewish people. There was no regaining of independence, and rule by Gentiles continued: the Persians simply took over from the Babylonians. There were no new kings and although the temple was rebuilt it had nothing of the status of Solomon's splendid building. It was not simply a matter of architecture: there had been a certainty that God's presence dwelt in Solomon's temple, but the restored temple, in which there was now no Ark of the Covenant,[4] aroused no such confidence. This temple was empty and that emptiness was symbolic of a spiritual vacuum.

---

4   The Ark went missing during the Babylonian assault and what happened to it is one of the great mysteries of history.

The Jewish religion of this time – the so-called Second Temple period (from 530 BC to AD 70) – began to acquire a very different character to that practised before the exile. Partly as a result of the downgraded status of the temple and the experience of exile, the faith began to shift away from temple worship, with its focus on priests and sacrifices, to local meetings at what became termed the synagogue. Here there was less talk of sacrifice and increasingly more of a morality framed by a system of rules that extended into every aspect of life.

At the time of the birth of Jesus, a faithful Jew looking around at the religious landscape would have seen little that was encouraging. The rule and influence of the Gentiles seemed to be unbroken: the Persians had been replaced by the Greeks who, in their turn, had been replaced by the Romans. True, King Herod was rebuilding the temple on a magnificent scale, but he was a Roman puppet and only questionably Jewish. Of the three great offices of the Jewish faith – kings, prophets and priests – all had gone or had become tainted. The true kings had ended with the exile, prophecy had waned not long after the return (the last accepted prophet was Malachi who had spoken around 450 BC) and the priests were now Roman political appointees. In one way the exile in Babylon had ended half a millennia ago; in another, the Jewish people were still in it. They were a long way from where they were supposed to be.

One significant shift that the exile brought was to do with language. People ceased to speak the Hebrew of the Old Testament and instead used Aramaic, a related language. By Jesus' day the Hebrew of the Old Testament was probably only extensively used and understood by priests and synagogue leaders. In fact it was now common in the synagogues for the Hebrew Scriptures to be read but then translated into the more widely understood Aramaic. Greek was common in Palestine, as elsewhere in the eastern Mediterranean, and was the universal language for the marketplace, culture and for communications between Jews and their Roman occupiers. Indeed, so prevalent was Greek that many Jews, even in Palestine, seem to have used the Greek version of the Scriptures, the Septuagint.[2] Ironically, given the dominance of Roman power, Latin was probably only widely used in the context of the Roman army and administration.

In all probability Jesus was trilingual: he definitely spoke Aramaic, almost certainly read Hebrew and quite probably spoke Greek.

The sense that these were dark days for the Jewish faith forms the backdrop to the coming of Jesus. It must have taken faith for any Jew to believe that the divine commitment made to Abraham, the great covenant sealed with Moses, and the promises given to David were still valid and to trust that they would one day be fulfilled. But people did believe and to varying degrees there was an expectation, and indeed the anticipation, that one day – hopefully soon – God would intervene again as he had before in the exodus and in the return from exile.

JEWISH BELIEFS AND PRACTICES

In telling the history of the Jewish people, we mentioned some of their key beliefs and practices. If we are to understand the Gospels, we need to know something more of those things that were central to the Jewish faith.

God

One of the most distinctive features of Judaism – especially notable in a world where paganism was almost universal – was its belief that there was only one God, *Yahweh*. This God was the one universal and eternal being who had created everything and whose authority was unlimited. In Old Testament times this belief in a single, universal God distinguished the Jews from the nations around them. Given the multiplicity of gods that the Greeks and Romans believed in, it was no less a distinguishing phenomenon in New Testament times. While this unequivocal simplicity of Judaism was admirable it was also practically difficult at a time when the Romans were beginning to suggest that their emperors were divine and should be worshipped. If you worshipped Jupiter, Osiris or Artemis it wasn't too hard to tag on Emperor Augustus or Claudius as well. If, however, you worshipped Yahweh you had a problem: he did not allow any competitors.

The Jews had also discovered that having a God who is above everything else is problematic in practice. How does a holy and distant God communicate and deal with the sinful world far below him? And equally, if God is so high and exalted then how can ordinary, sinful people relate to him? To believe in such a God acknowledged an awesome gap between him and flawed, frail humanity. In response to this, the Jews of Jesus' day were cautiously exploring how Yahweh related to the world he had made. In various ways, God's Wisdom, Spirit and Word were all talked about as means by which this one perfect God could communicate who he was to the world. As these matters were discussed there were suggestions – but it seems no more – that the oneness of God might be more complex than it seemed. Nevertheless, for most Jews God was unmistakably and arguably one and, quite simply, there were no rivals.

God's grace

There has been a long-standing and troubling tradition of making a distinction between the God of the Old Testament and the God of the New. So you often hear that while the God of the Old Testament is harsh, demanding and rules by law, the God of the New Testament is, in contrast, kind and forgiving and rules by grace. It's a simple, clear and easily comprehensible distinction whose only flaw is, unfortunately, that it's wrong.

In the book of Exodus, Yahweh declares this about himself: 'Yahweh! The LORD! The God of compassion and mercy! I am slow to anger and filled with unfailing love and faithfulness. I lavish unfailing love to a thousand generations. I forgive iniquity, rebellion, and sin.'[3] In one form or another, this definition recurs many times in the Old Testament.[4] That positive self-description is matched by Yahweh's actions: he repeatedly rescued his people – whether from Egypt, Babylon or simply from themselves – because he had committed himself to them out of covenant love. The God of the Bible is a God of grace in the Old Testament as well as the New. The Old Testament laws are best seen not as rules which are intended to persuade God to be favourable to his people but as actions that are the appropriate response of God's people to his kindness to them. Good works are not the cause of Yahweh's grace, but the effect of it.

The extent to which this was understood in Second Temple Judaism is widely debated. Certainly there would have been many Jews in Jesus' day who would have readily accepted that God's grace came first and that keeping the Law was the grateful response to that kindness. Yet there were clearly others who got things upside down, overlooked grace and felt that you kept the rules in order to try to keep God happy. Much of the conflict between Jesus and the religious leaders of his day focused on this confusion between cause and effect. Sadly, the idea that God can be manipulated by our good works is not unknown within Christianity. Remember: you can never *earn* grace; if you did, it wouldn't *be* grace.

God's word

One of the distinguishing features of Yahweh was that, for all his awesome holiness and superiority, he was a God who had revealed himself to his people and had spoken to them either directly or through the prophets. What Yahweh said was recorded in his word – the Law or the *Torah* – which was, quite literally, beyond value. The Law – which could refer to everything that we call the Old Testament – was the sum of all wisdom and as such was memorised, recited, guarded and debated by the Jewish people. The dedication that the Jews of Jesus' day had to God's word is humbling; it would have been unremarkable for someone to have memorised entire books of the Old Testament. As a result the New Testament overflows with either specific quotations of the Old Testament or, more problematic for the modern reader, subtle allusions to it.

God's word was rich and also diverse. Within the Old Testament can be found not just rules of conduct but also poetry, proverbs, prophecy and laments. One genre, unfamiliar to us in the modern West, which needs mentioning is that of *apocalyptic*. Apocalyptic literature is written in symbolic, visionary language, often involving cosmic battles between good and evil.[5] It is a style of language that occurs in places in the Gospels[6] but most spectacularly in the book of Revelation.

Throughout the Old Testament we read of how 'the word of the Lord came' to someone or of a prophet beginning a speech with a phrase such as 'this is what the Lord says'. It's the idea, so commonplace that we take it for granted, that God speaks his message, the prophet hears it and then, with faithful humility, proclaims it to the people. As we will see, the absence of any such phrase when Jesus speaks is striking and significant.

God's temple

The temple in Jerusalem played a central role in the faith of most Jews in Jesus' day, especially those who lived in Palestine. Currently being rebuilt in the grandest possible fashion by Herod the Great, the temple was where sacrifices for sin were offered before a holy God. Although Herod's construction was felt to be a pale shadow of the great temple built by Solomon, the Jews of Gospel times still saw it as the spiritual centre of the world, the point where heaven and earth met and, in some way, where the one God dwelt among his people. Yet in Jesus' day the temple did not attract universal and unconditional support. It wasn't just that Herod's temple was architecturally inferior to Solomon's original; it was that it was tainted, and with a religion focused on purity, that was serious. So, the temple administration was widely assumed to be corrupt and the whole system of sacrifices contaminated by lucrative and dubious business ventures. Some Jews felt that the temple needed cleansing, others that it needed destroying. One of the certainties that clustered around the figure of the Messiah was that he would restore or renew the temple.

We have already mentioned the development of the synagogue, and at the time of the Gospels its importance for maintaining the religious life of the community was obviously enormous. Positively, the synagogue was the centre of religious education in the community. Negatively, however, it was also the centre of social control and it would have been a brave or foolish inhabitant of a village to have challenged the ruling of the local synagogue leader. The idea of the synagogue is important in Christianity because it was clearly the template around which the early Christian communities developed.

Ritual purity

An essential part of Jewish belief was the idea of ritual purity: to please God you had to be pure and uncontaminated before him. Ritual purity is one of the most difficult concepts for most Westerners to understand yet it cannot be ignored; there are a vast number of references to it in the Gospels. In fact the abolition of the entire idea of ritual purity by the first Christians was one of the main factors that led to Christianity becoming separated from the Jewish faith. (Some measure of how great a step this was can be seen in the way that it became a major source of tension within the early Christian community.)[7]

Unless you are familiar with either observant Jews or Muslims, people living in the modern West tend to think of purity and cleanliness simply in terms of hygiene. Yet in Jesus' culture purity was not primarily about avoiding disease; it was about 'holiness'. In Jewish eyes, everything was either clean or unclean, and in order to be ritually pure before God you must not be in contact with any unclean thing; if you were, you had to undergo cleansing. The Law gave precise definitions here. You became unclean by having contact with dead bodies, eating (or even touching) certain animals, having certain skin ailments, and so on. And, to make matters worse, uncleanness was contagious: touching someone who was unclean made you unclean. While some uncleanness could be avoided (for instance by shunning adultery) there were some situations (such as menstruation, childbirth and dealing with the dead) where becoming unclean was unavoidable. There was no blame attached to these unavoidable forms of uncleanness – they were not sins – but however they occurred, you had to be cleansed. There were approved rituals of cleansing in every case and many of these involved ceremonial washing.

The result of these laws – which extended into every area of life – was that people were continually reminded of the issue of holiness. The social distance that the Jews tried to keep between themselves and Gentiles was not racism but simply because the Gentiles were considered ritually impure. These rules of what was clean and unclean can be thought of as defining a series of concentric zones of increasing holiness towards the middle. Beyond the outer limits were the Gentiles with their lack of religious cleanliness. Inside the limits came God's holy people and then, at the very centre of these zones of purity, God's dwelling place, the temple. However, this zoning of holiness did not end at the temple gates. Inside the temple a succession of barriers, courts and curtains created ever purer spaces until finally, behind a great curtain, in the very inmost part of the temple, was the Holy of Holies where it was believed that God dwelt in terrifying purity. This holy core of the temple was inaccessible to everybody except when, once a year, a high priest, under conditions of strictest ritual purity, could enter it.

The Sabbath

Then, as now, observant Jews kept one day a week, Saturday, as a holy day – the Sabbath. No work could be done on that day and even non-work activities were restricted. The Sabbath was another way in which Jews demonstrated to God (and everybody else) that they had a unique relationship with him. If the rules on purity emphasised that God's people were to have a special attitude to things, the rules about the Sabbath showed that they were also to have a special attitude to time.

The fact that the first believers in Jesus, who probably still thought of themselves as Jewish, shifted the Sabbath from Saturday to Sunday is remarkable and can only be explained because of the resurrection of Jesus on a Sunday.

Circumcision

If the Kosher diet and Sabbath-keeping were open and obvious signs of being Jewish, circumcision – the removal of the foreskin, normally at eight days of age – was a private but permanent reminder for a Jewish man that he belonged to God. It was such an important distinction that the Gentiles were sometimes bluntly referred to as 'the uncircumcised'.

Feasts

The Jewish calendar was marked by a number of major feasts. These were not simply opportunities for family and food get-togethers; they were events that commemorated great events in Jewish history. Four main feasts are mentioned in the Gospels:

- The *Feast of Passover* (or *Pesach*) occurred in March or April and celebrated the liberation of the Israelites from slavery in Egypt in the events of the exodus.

- The *Feast of Pentecost* (or *Shavuot*) occurred fifty days after Passover. Coinciding with the first grain harvest, it celebrated the giving of the Law.

- The *Feast of Tabernacles* (or *Sukkoth*) occurred in October and commemorated the forty years the Israelites had spent in the desert.

- The *Feast of Dedication* (or *Hanukkah*) occurred in late November or December and commemorated the cleansing of the temple in 165 BC during what became called the Maccabean Revolt.

All these feasts could only really be properly celebrated at the temple in Jerusalem. This was particularly true of Passover, which required the ritual slaughtering of a sacrificial lamb. The feasts were a way of reminding people who they were, what they stood for and, above all, what God had done for them in the past. And of course linked with that memory of past rescues was the hope of what God might do for them in the future. Given this, it was inevitable that Passover was the most politically charged of all festivals.

As the early Christians changed the Sabbath, so they transformed the Jewish festivals and, in another remarkable transformation, the Passover became the Lord's Supper or Communion.

God's promises and purposes

For all its rules and guidance on how to live there is also a sense of promise in the Old Testament. These promises, built on the special history of the Jewish people, echo through the pages of the Gospels.

- There are promises to Abraham that the world will be blessed through his descendants. The destiny of the Jewish people is linked to the redemption of the world and there were prophetic hopes that one day all the nations would worship the God of Israel. Linked with this is the idea of God's people having peace and security within the land God had promised them. Notably, however, in some of the Old Testament prophecies the idea of God's people having land seemed to look beyond the borders of Palestine and even to extend globally.[8]

- There are promises in many places (for example Deuteronomy 30:6) that one day there would be a new covenant that would replace the old one. This finds itself most clearly spelt out in Jeremiah and Ezekiel.[9]

- There are also promises that one day there would be another monarch of the lineage of King David whose rule would be far wider, grander and more permanent. This figure would be the *Messiah*, the promised King or, to use the Greek, the *Christ*.[10] Most Jews in Jesus' day believed that the Messiah would be a political and military ruler who would utterly crush the enemies of God's people and bring justice and peace to Israel. Under the Messiah, Israel would be great and glorious and would finally bless the nations of the world. While most people seem to have assumed that the Messiah would be human, much of what was expected of him – an eternal rule, godlike wisdom and power – required that he be more than an ordinary human being.

- In addition to the Messiah, a second figure from the Old Testament is alluded to in the Gospels. This is the 'Suffering Servant' who, in the latter part of the book of Isaiah, appears as a divine figure who willingly gives himself up to an appalling death for his people.[11] Although references to the Servant are more subtle in the Gospels than that of the Messiah, there seems little doubt that this role was one that Jesus felt referred to him and that the first Christians saw fulfilled in him.

BALANCING JESUS AND JUDAISM

There are two opposing errors regarding Jesus and the Jewish faith that need to be avoided.

The first error has been, for various reasons, to ignore Jesus' Jewish background and beliefs. So some people treat him as a sort of universal human being whose Jewishness is entirely incidental. Even at its best, this diminishes Jesus' humanity and makes much of what he taught incomprehensible. The fact is that Jesus taught within the framework of the Judaism of his time: what he did with that framework is something else.

The second error is to treat Jesus as no more than any other Jewish teacher or rabbi and see him as different only in degree to the numerous other preachers who wandered around Palestine in those days. The reality here is that while Jesus was Jewish and taught much that fitted within Judaism, he claimed to be far more than just another teacher of the Law. The impact that Jesus made not just on Judaism but on the world is surely evidence that there was something very different and very special about him. We cannot – and must not – ignore the Jewishness of Jesus. But we must also be ready to accept that he was much more than just another rabbi.

JESUS AND JUDAISM: THE CONCLUSION

At the time of Jesus, Judaism was different to other religions, defining itself by unique values and boundaries. On the one hand the Jewish people valued what Yahweh had given them: the covenant, the Law, the land and the temple. On the other hand they also upheld boundaries that set them apart from other people: food, Sabbath and the rite of male circumcision.

Any Gentile who had contact with Jews at the time of Jesus, especially those in Palestine, would have found their faith irritating, baffling and intriguing. They would no doubt have been irritated and offended by the Jewish exclusivity and their view that all Gentiles were unclean. The Jewish laws would have baffled them. Yet they would probably have been intrigued by the absence of idols, the elimination of deities and the simplicity of having just one God. Indeed it was not uncommon for Gentiles to become synagogue attendees although – unsurprisingly in view of the need for circumcision in an age without anaesthetics or antibiotics – few Gentile men became fully fledged Jews.

In Judaism there was a unique history and identity. Jews were God's people and at the heart of his purposes. Yet with that sense of identity came a dilemma. Despite two millennia since the promise to Abraham and centuries since the return from exile, they were still not what they were supposed to be: God's people in God's land ruled by God's laws under God's King. The gap between the hope and the reality was enormous and frustrating.

NOTE: JESUS AND THE FULFILMENT OF PROPHECY

The Gospel writers make a great deal of Jesus being the fulfilment of Old Testament prophecy and clearly this was enormously important in the early church.[12]

Modern readers can struggle with this but let's make two points. First, some passages in the Old Testament we might be inclined to overlook as prophecies may have been widely considered by Jewish believers of Jesus' day to specifically refer to the Messiah. That they don't have the same significance to us is probably because we don't know the Old Testament well enough. One illustration here is the way that the New Testament letter to the Hebrews finds deeper fulfilments in Old Testament texts that most of us would otherwise overlook.[13]

Second, sometimes the fulfilment is more complex or deeper than we imagine. So, for instance, much is made in the Old Testament of the gift of the land to God's people, Israel. In the New Testament it is suggested that Jesus himself is the fulfilment of the land; that in him believers have everything – and more – that the Old Testament believer had in the physical land of Palestine.[14] Equally, the Old Testament sacrificial system is all about animals being slaughtered; yet the New Testament picks up the concept of sacrifice and applies it to Jesus. Here what we have is not strictly the fulfilment of the Old Testament prophecy but the 'filling-full' of it.

Christians have always seen Jesus as the direct realisation of all that the unfinished story of the Old Testament points towards. Jesus completes the uncompleted and concludes the inconclusive. He takes a story full of promises, fulfils many of them, and looks towards a final and glorious fulfilment of everything else. Paul sums it up: 'For all of God's promises have been fulfilled in Christ with a resounding "Yes!"'[15]

3

SCENE SETTING 3:
PLACE, POWERS AND PRESSURES

In discussing Jesus' world we have looked at the all-important religious aspect and now we must turn to other factors.

PLACE: THE GEOGRAPHICAL SETTING

Something that is relevant to understanding the Gospels is their geographic setting. Shortage of space forbids dealing with this at length[1] but there are some important basics.

*   The story of Jesus is set at the junction of three continents: Africa, Europe and Asia. This meant that any regional superpower felt obliged to have at least the right of access through Palestine and, if possible, permanent occupancy. Whether or not 'all roads lead to Rome' has always been debatable but certainly a lot of Roman roads went through Palestine. This strategic central location of the gospel events doubtless helped the rapid spread of the Christian message.

*   The land promised to God's people was never very big. North-south it extended from the Negev desert to the foothills of Mount Lebanon, a distance of around 400 km (250 miles). East-west it ran from the Mediterranean to the Jordan Valley, a distance of 60 km (40 miles).[5]

*   Although much of Palestine was fertile, the desert was never far from its southern and eastern borders. The result was that it took only a slight fluctuation of weather or climate to bring drought and famine to the land.[2] The fact that farming was such a vulnerable lifestyle was one of many factors that encouraged some Jews to emigrate around the edges of the Mediterranean.

---

5   For some time in the Old Testament period, some of the tribes of Israel lived east of the Jordan.

- The land was not just a convenient region that God's people happened to inhabit. It was something that had been specifically given by Yahweh to Abraham's descendants Israel by covenant: it was a cherished gift. The covenant, however, did not promise Israel the land unconditionally; it was a gift with conditions and there were warnings that unfaithfulness to the Lord would result in expulsion from the land. The Landlord could always revoke the tenancy.

POWERS: THE CULTURAL AND POLITICAL SETTING

In Jesus' day faithful Jews in Palestine would have felt their world was dominated by both Greek culture and Roman power. In very different ways both were a threat.

Greek values

By the time of his death at the age of thirty-two, Alexander the Great (356–323 BC) had created an empire that stretched from Greece to the borders of India and which included Palestine. The vision of Alexander and his followers was not just for power but for the spread of the Greek way of life. Wherever they conquered, Alexander's forces set up colonies that were outposts of Greece and all it stood for. Although Alexander's empire did not long survive his death, his vision did and Greek culture began to play an increasing part in the Middle East. This trend, called Hellenisation (after *Hellas* or Greece) was to have a lasting impact in Palestine.

After the collapse of Alexander's empire, Palestine came under the rule of Hellenistic dynasties. The last of these rulers, Antiochus IV, declared himself a god, brutally assaulted Jerusalem and outrageously desecrated the temple in 167 BC. This blow at the heart of Judaism gave rise to what became called the Maccabean Revolt after one of its leaders, Judas Maccabeus. The Maccabean Revolt succeeded through brutal but effective guerrilla warfare and lead to an eighty-year period of Jewish independence. Both Antiochus' attack and the successful Maccabean response were long remembered in Israel. The first justified hostility towards the Gentiles and the second held out the hope that occupying powers could be evicted.

Despite this bitterly won independence, the pressures towards Hellenisation continued and only increased when, in 63 BC, an expanding Roman Empire took over control of Palestine. The Romans may have wielded military and political power around the eastern Mediterranean but the language and the culture they promoted was Greek. Militarily the Romans had won, but culturally it was the Greeks who ultimately triumphed.

Hellenisation affected almost every aspect of life in Palestine, especially in the cities. Greek architecture, medicine, sport, philosophy and art became important; Greek dress became fashionable and the Greek language became widely spoken. Sometimes Hellenisation was imposed but for the most part it spread of its own accord. After all, if you were ambitious, the Greek way of doing things was very attractive: it opened up opportunities in jobs, education and trade and allowed progress up the social ladder. To a young Jewish man the choice must have seemed clear: you either stayed in a cultural backwater or you 'went Greek' and enjoyed the exhilarating mainstream of what was doubtless portrayed as 'the civilised world'.

In the time of the Gospels the influence of Greek culture was unavoidable, even in Galilee. An hour's walk north of Nazareth lay the town of Sepphoris, which was being rebuilt in Greek style in the early part of the first century. We are told that Jesus' stepfather Joseph was a carpenter,[3] and as Jesus followed his trade he may have worked there and been exposed to Greek culture and language from his youth.

Attitudes amongst the Jews to Hellenisation varied. Some aspects, such as the language, were acknowledged to be harmless; others raised serious questions. For instance, Greek athletics demanded nudity and Greek education was intertwined with pagan philosophy. To what extent could any real Jew be involved with either? Some aspects were definitely considered evil by the more religious: after all, the Greek temples and theatres depicted openly immoral pagan gods and goddesses. And the more Hellenised you became, the more you mixed with Gentiles and the harder it became to stay ritually pure. Many people must have felt that Hellenisation inevitably led to paganisation.

Roman power

When the Romans took over Palestine in 63 BC, they looked for local rulers who they could get to do their work for them. Unhindered by any of today's pressures to avoid bad press coverage and encourage democratic values, they simply chose the most effective character around, regardless of any moral failings. In Palestine this policy threw up Herod the Great (74 – c.4 BC), one of history's more unpleasant characters. Emerging as undisputed king in 37 BC, Herod reigned over a large area. Cunning, ruthless and wary, Herod was one of those people who stay alive by making sure others don't. He did, however, suit Roman purposes admirably, ensuring that taxes were paid to the Empire and that troublemakers were mercilessly removed. He was good for the economy and some people did well under his rule; others inevitably feared and hated him. Although he claimed to be a Jewish king of the line of David, Herod was actually only a half-Jew by blood and held lightly to the Jewish religion, preferring Greek culture with its more 'open morality'. He delighted in majestic building projects and his most famous achievement – still being built at his death – was the temple in Jerusalem. One result of Herod's rule which was to have positive implications for Christianity, was that the Romans granted the Jewish faith legal protection; something that the early church was able to shelter under for decades.

With advancing years, Herod's wariness slipped into a brutal, homicidal paranoia that gave rise to an epic list of murders: an uncle, two high priests, a mother-in-law, three sons (including an heir) and his favourite wife. Herod occurs in Matthew's account of the wise men, seeking to kill the infant Jesus, and the picture of him there – paranoid, deceiving and brutal enough to massacre infants – is true to life.[4]

After Herod died in 4 BC[6] his kingdom was split up and portioned out between three surviving sons: Archelaus, Antipas and Phillip. At the time of Jesus' ministry Antipas and Philip were still ruling but

6   The apparent paradox that Herod lived on beyond the birth of Jesus but still managed to die before AD 1 is a result of a miscalculation when the modern calendar was created in the sixth century by a monk, Dionysius Exiguus. It was a great idea but he got his dates wrong. The date of the Jesus' birth was probably between 4 and 6 BC.

Archelaus had been removed by Rome for incompetence. As a result, Judea and Samaria were under direct Roman control and were ruled by a series of governors, one of whom was Pontius Pilate.

Roman control

The great problem of the Roman Empire was that it was both dependent on the military and weakened by it. The army held the Empire together but at an enormous cost, which had to be met by taxes which inevitably increased Rome's unpopularity. To try to resolve this dilemma Rome preferred to rule with as light a touch as possible, consistent with maintaining stability and collecting taxes. The burden of taxation fell on the conquered states themselves and added insult to the injury of occupation. In keeping with the policy of minimising direct involvement, taxation was simply farmed out to locals who could collect as much as they wanted as long as Rome got what it needed. Those who collected the tax were naturally hated and the shock of Jesus' inclusion of Matthew the tax collector amongst his closest followers should not be underestimated.

Although hoping for an occupation that maximised taxes and minimised trouble, the Romans were well aware of the danger they faced in Palestine. Rome knew that the Jews were always going to be more loyal to Yahweh than to Caesar and that there was a danger of a re-run of the Maccabean rebellion which might encourage revolt across the Empire. The result of this was that despite the 'light rule' policy, Rome dealt with any threats with immediate severity. On the basis that the safest rebels were dead ones, anyone suspected of supporting an insurrection could expect an immediate public execution.

The Roman preoccupation with prioritising tax revenues and stability meant that issues of justice were often overlooked. The inevitable result was a great deal of unrestrained corruption at every level; something that must have contributed to the Jewish people's desire for God's King to come to rule the nation with justice.[5]

Despite its unpleasant aspects there was a plus point to Roman rule. While Alexander and his compatriots had the vision of spreading their Greek civilisation worldwide, the Romans simply wanted their security and taxes. This pragmatic approach meant that in Palestine they were prepared to allow a considerable amount of legal and religious freedom to the Jews as long as neither stability nor profitability were threatened.

The Jewish responses

The twin threats of Greek culture and Roman power produced a crisis in Judaism. The vision of God's people in God's land that the Old Testament offered was utterly incompatible with a nation militarily crushed under Roman rule and morally undermined by Greek values. How could you be a holy people when you were being openly ruled by an unholy race and subtly corrupted by an alien culture?

At the time of Jesus there were several responses to this crisis. One was that of *separation*: trying to be distinctively different from those around you. This approach was that of the Pharisees, a group who are prominent in the Gospels. The Pharisees appear to have been a pressure group within Judaism focusing on ritual purity and the correct performance of religious practices. They believed in applying the Old Testament laws to every area of life and had expanded and added to them. The Pharisees drew their support from the synagogues and the agricultural communities where they would have had a role as guardians of morality and tradition. The Pharisees' hope seems to have been that if enough people kept God's laws in the proper way, Yahweh would intervene and rescue the nation.

Although Jesus and the Pharisees had much in common, there were conflicts. Jesus criticised the Pharisees because he felt that the vast range of rules and laws they upheld, many of which were of their own making, had come to obscure what God really wanted. The Pharisees in turn objected to Jesus' practice of eating with people who had given up trying to keep the rules and whom they considered unclean. There was also an issue about forgiveness. After all, one of the most powerful weapons that any religious movement can wield is that of declaring sins forgiven. Here Jesus undermined the 'monopoly on redemption' held by the entire Jewish religious system and run out of the temple by *personally* offering people forgiveness.

Nevertheless, the picture of the Pharisees in the Gospels is not uniformly negative: for instance in John's Gospel a Pharisee called Nicodemus is shown to be quite receptive to what Jesus had to say.[6] Nevertheless, the Pharisees seem to have frequently given in to the temptation to major on minor matters and to rule with severity rather than lead with grace.

The second response to the crisis in Judaism was that of *concession*; of coming to terms with the way things were. This was the policy of the Sadducees, the group that the Pharisees saw as their main opponents. The Sadducees did not survive the catastrophe of the Jewish revolt of AD 70 so we know little about them. They seem to have been smaller in number than the Pharisees and to have had a higher social status. They had a power base in Jerusalem where they were involved in the temple, an institution not just of enormous religious importance but also of great financial power. If the Pharisees were a spiritual elite, the Sadducees were a social one. Whereas the Pharisees delighted in adding footnotes to the Old Testament laws, the Sadducees took a more minimalist approach. They believed only in the first five books of the Old Testament and held to none of the Pharisees' additions. The Sadducees were also not particularly enthusiastic about the idea that God was going to send a Messiah to save the nation. This was partly because they didn't recognise those later books of the Old Testament where the Messiah was mentioned but also because, as a social elite, they had little to gain from the overturning of the status quo. It was the Sadducees who had the best working arrangement with the Romans, a factor which, when the long-foreseen war finally broke out, ensured their extinction.

A third response to the crisis was that of *rebellion*. Many groups and individuals believed that the only solution was to repeat the heroic strategy of the Maccabean Revolt and remove the Romans by force. The best-known of such groups were the Zealots, who engaged in guerrilla warfare against Rome when, a generation after Jesus, the rebellion finally occurred. Although at the time of the Gospels a Zealot party did not really exist, a zealot philosophy certainly did. One of Jesus' disciples was called 'Simon the Zealot'[7] and if that refers to his politics then the fact that Jesus called both him and Matthew the tax collector as his followers suggests the twelve disciples were a very diverse group. Every so often someone revives the idea of Jesus being a political revolutionary but the reality is that almost every aspect of what Jesus said opposes the idea of rebellion and the teaching of his followers, as recorded in the letters of the New Testament, shows no interest in political action. And if Jesus had been a promoter of revolution, the Roman army would have made sure that he never got as far as a trial in Jerusalem.

A fourth response to the crisis was that of *isolation*. This was the policy of the Essenes, a group who, while they existed at the time of Jesus, make no appearance in the pages of the New Testament. The response of the Essenes was to withdraw from society altogether and to create alternative communities where they could wait for God to intervene. The Dead Sea Scrolls were almost certainly written or collected by an Essene group. The extraordinary outward drive of the first Christians shows a total rejection of any isolationist outlook and the influence of the Essenes on Jesus and his followers appears to have been minimal.

In fact, at the time of Jesus the vast majority of the people, those the Gospels refers to as 'the common people' or 'the crowd', probably belonged to none of these groups. The Pharisees and the Sadducees were scornful of these 'people of the land'. The Pharisees' contempt was probably due to the fact that the ordinary people were unable to devote time, energy and money to keep the rules of behaviour that they demanded.[8] The Sadducees' scorn probably arose from the fact they felt socially superior.

It is not hard to guess how the ordinary people lived. Concerned no doubt simply to have bread on the table, they kept the feasts as best they could, tried to remain ritually pure, despaired of the corruption and taxes and, when they could spare a moment from the task of survival, looked forward to the long-anticipated Messiah. If you had to characterise their lives, the best words might be *confusion* and *desperation*.

We must not overlook these ordinary people. First, much of Jesus' teaching was clearly directed at men and women who couldn't keep the standards imposed by the religious elite. Second, most of us can identify more easily with these ordinary people in their bewilderment and frustration with life and politics than with any of the other groups. They are where we are.

PRESSURES: THE SOCIAL VALUES

There has been increasing recognition of the fact that whether we are biblical scholars or merely interested readers we can make bad mistakes in understanding the New Testament if we fail to realise how society worked then. Both from reading the literature of the time carefully and looking at modern rural cultures in the Near East there is an awareness that Jesus' world functioned differently from ours and we need to take account of that fact.[9]

Here we just want to mention a few specific issues relevant to understanding the Gospels which help to explain some of the passages.

One vital social aspect was the role of shame and honour and it may be that here we find Jesus' world feels particularly foreign, especially if we live in some sort of anonymous modern city. A preoccupation with matters of honour and shame is something common to many rural cultures and is still widespread in the Middle East today. In such cultures life is a game of snakes and ladders where you need to climb up the ladders of honour while avoiding snakes of shame. You gain honour by having a high social status, influential friends, wealth, and either by having a respectable family or marrying into one. You suffer shame by not having or by losing such things and by having any sort of public humiliation such as losing a prestigious job, being snubbed by the powerful or having members of your family caught doing wrong things. Unfortunately, being ill or having some disability was also shameful. Equally unfortunate is the way that women seem to be most vulnerable in such situations; even today the victims of so-called 'honour killings' are almost entirely women. Shame is also something – like a disease – that can be transmitted. To be shamed is a fate that gets passed on to the entire family.

One major problem with honour-shame cultures is that everything focuses on appearances. So if you do something wrong it doesn't matter as long as no one finds out. Conversely, the most important thing about doing something right is that you gain honour by being seen to be doing it. Here the key factor in many decisions is not whether an action is right or wrong, it is whether it will earn you and your family honour or shame. In such cultures there is a fate worse than death: it is shame. One reason why crucifixion was a particularly effective deterrent was not that it was painful but that by exposing someone in a situation in which, half or completely naked, they died in slow, humiliating public agony, you inflicted shame not just on them but on their entire family.

These mentions of the family point to their extraordinary importance in this sort of culture. In most of the modern urbanised West we exist as individuals, often more closely linked to our friends and those we work with than to our family. This is very far from the situation that operated in the rural world of Jesus' day. People identified first and foremost with their families, something that is hardly surprising seeing as they probably lived and worked with them throughout their whole life. In such a culture the family takes on most of the roles that we have handed over to social services and other agencies. The family acts as support for the ill and the aged, and a source of financial assistance for those family members needing it. Precisely because the family is so important, 'opting out' and going it alone is extraordinarily shameful; a note sounded in the parable of the Prodigal Son.

Another key element in the culture of the Gospels (and similar cultures then and now) is what are called 'client/patron relationships'. This is the idea that powerful people (*patrons*) do favours for those who are less powerful (*clients*) in return for their loyalty and support. In such ways bonds of obligation are built within the community that, when needed, can be translated into support, action or simply silence. So, in Luke we have an account of a centurion who, having been a patron to the Jewish community, now 'calls in' those favours from his clients by getting them to ask Jesus to heal his slave.[10] It's a form of social relationship that still exists in many parts of the Mediterranean world and is chillingly but authentically exemplified in the film *The Godfather*.

A common and very public situation in which both shame and honour and client-patron relations operate are meals. In such cultures communal meals are taken very seriously and they play a major part in the Gospels. To be invited to a meal by a social superior is an open statement that you are accepted by him (and it will almost always be a *him*) and the public relationship gives you honour. Matters of shame and honour extend to the dinner table: how you are seated and your distance from the host is a way of conveying gradations of honour and something that will be widely noted. (That we are only a generation or two away from such a culture is seen in the way this idea persists in seating plans for meals at weddings and the like.) Mind you, to be invited to a meal also created a link of obligation between you and your host: you gained honour but you also incurred a debt that, at some point in the future, you could be expected to repay in some act of loyalty or obedience.

Finally – and inescapably – this is a patriarchal culture where men rule and where women know their place. The first-century Jewish philosopher Philo considered that women had different and inferior souls to men[11] and that they should be confined to the house. Jewish men praised God in their daily prayers, thanking him that they were not born a Gentile, a slave, or a woman.

With almost anybody else but Jesus, explaining such unwritten rules would normally be the preliminary to excusing them for their conformity to such social standards. In fact the opposite is true: they are explained here to illuminate the astonishing way in which Jesus ignored or subverted many of the principles of his world. He was capable of keeping his family at a distance; he ignored matters of shame and honour by being with the poor, the diseased and those considered to be immoral; he refused to be any patron's client; he was blunt to those who thought they could enlist him on their side; and he treated women as intellectual equals. (The longest theological discussion recorded in the entire New Testament is that between Jesus and the Samaritan woman which occurs in John chapter 4.) Jesus was particularly critical of the way that religious leaders sought honour for themselves and, by acting as 'patrons' in their society, wielded harsh power over the weak.

We may be very pleased that Jesus judged his culture then. We may be less so by the idea that he judges ours now.

NOTE: ROMAN RULE BEYOND THE GOSPELS

In the context of 'what happened next' two more things need to be said about the Roman Empire.

The first is that many Christians have seen the rise of the Roman Empire as part of God's way of preparing the world for the spread of Christianity. It's not hard to understand why. After all, under the Romans much of the known world knew peace. Yes, the *Pax Romana* was brutally enforced but it was a peace that this area had never seen before, was rarely to see afterwards, and doesn't see today. There was also a common language – Greek – which allowed Paul to walk into almost any marketplace anywhere and start preaching without using a translator. The Romans also gave the world an excellent travel network which would not be improved upon for at least 1,500 years. Finally, although Roman rule could be severe, it did grant freedoms and protections, particularly to individuals who were citizens and to religions, such as Judaism, that were legally permitted. The book of Acts tells how all these factors were used to advantage by the first Christians. Those of us who believe that God controls everything including the rise and fall of kings, emperors and republics, have not the slightest problem with the idea that God was able to allow the rise of the Roman Empire to make the spread of the gospel accessible.

The second is far less positive. We need to comment on what happened in Palestine after AD 30 (when we date the crucifixion) because this provides the backdrop to the expansion of the early church and is the focus of some of Jesus' prophecies about the future.

After the death of the Emperor Tiberius in AD 37, things started to go downhill in Palestine and a succession of corrupt governors provoked increasing unrest. Finally, in AD 66 the expected Jewish rebellion flared up. To demonstrate to the entire Empire that revolt could not be tolerated, Rome decided to crush Jewish resistance with the utmost ferocity. Jerusalem was besieged and destroyed in AD 70 with enormous loss of life. Josephus, who was an eyewitness, estimated that a million people were killed.[12] A hundred thousand Jews were taken captive to Rome, and Herod's great temple – which had only just been completed – was levelled and has never been rebuilt. A second revolt in AD 135 ended any hopes of a restored Jewish state.

The Jewish War, as it became known, was catastrophic for Judaism and caused changes to the way it is practised which have persisted to the present day. Its impact on Christianity seems to have been minimal: the astonishing growth of the faith meant that by AD 70 Christianity was no longer a Jerusalem-based movement but one that had spread across the Empire. Nevertheless, the disaster of the Jewish War did have one long-term effect of enormous consequence: it marked the final break between Christianity and Judaism. From then on, for better or worse, the two faiths went their separate ways.

4

BEGINNINGS AND BIRTH

We come now to the telling of the life and ministry of Jesus. Our intention is simply to sketch out the big picture and, where relevant, to apply it to how we live.

We need to be aware that none of the four Gospels in the Bible is any sort of carelessly collected assemblage of anecdotes. Each Gospel clearly has its own internal logic and agenda. And while the Gospels are biographies, they are, even by the standards of their time, strange ones. Nowhere is that strangeness seen more clearly than in the emphasis placed on different periods of Jesus' life. On the one hand we are given very little information about Jesus before he came on to the public scene in his early thirties; on the other hand there is an extraordinary focus on the end of his life. This perspective of the Gospels is important. You could tell the story of Jesus – as Mark and John do – without mentioning his birth at all; you cannot tell it without detailing his death. From the biblical perspective, Easter is of far greater significance than Christmas.

PROMISES AND PROPHECIES

Matthew's Gospel begins with a long genealogy that daunts modern readers. It's tempting to pass rapidly over this listing of fathers and sons, yet it is there for several reasons. Matthew, writing to people who were familiar with the Old Testament, is pointing out that what he is about to tell us is connected to the story they already know. Actually, Matthew is making a bigger claim than mere continuity: it is one of fulfilment. He is announcing that, in Jesus, the long-promised Messiah from the line of David has finally come. After centuries of silence, the frustratingly incomplete story of the Old Testament is, at long last, moving to its fulfilment.

Here, as elsewhere in the Gospels, there are revealing little details. There is a curious twist in the genealogy because interspersed with a typically patriarchal list of men are four women: Tamar, Rahab, Ruth and Bathsheba. Intriguingly, these are not just women but are all individuals on whom some sort of shadow falls: either of being a Gentile, of being sexually immoral or both. What seems on the surface to be the most exclusive of lists actually contains a message of inclusiveness. Matthew is here quietly announcing a theme that will be present throughout his Gospel and indeed throughout the New Testament: Jesus may be Jewish to the core but he has come for everybody from everywhere.

Luke's Gospel begins not with the birth of Jesus but that of someone else, John the Baptist. The Angel Gabriel promises an elderly and childless couple a son who will be a great figure and bring Israel back to God.[1] Given that there had been no prophets for over four centuries, the news that God was to speak again to Israel must have been astonishing.

Luke then tells how the same angel later appeared in Nazareth, a village in Galilee, to Mary, a virgin engaged to a man called Joseph. Mary is told she will become pregnant with a son who is to be named Jesus and promised that 'he will be very great and will be called the Son of the most High. The Lord God will give him the throne of his ancestor David. And he will reign over Israel for ever: his Kingdom will never end!'[2] These are momentous words: the child will rule with authority and for eternity. Mary, however, is concerned about something more basic: how is this going to happen given that she is a virgin? Gabriel's response is, 'The Holy Spirit will come upon you, and the power of the Most High will overshadow you.'[3]

Interlocking with this is Matthew's account of how an 'angel of the Lord' appeared to Joseph and told him that Mary's child would be 'conceived by the Holy Spirit'. Significantly, the angelic message goes on to say that the child will be called Jesus, for 'he will save his people from their sins'. Jesus or Yeshua ('Joshua') is highly significant because it means 'the Lord (Yahweh) saves'. Matthew records another angelic comment: this Jesus is to be 'Immanuel', which means 'God with us' and alludes back – as so many of these prophecies do – to the book of Isaiah.[4]

These prophetic statements rooted deep in the past are reminders that the New Testament is the continuation of the Old Testament. How Jesus' followers are to view the Old Testament is something that has challenged believers for two thousand years. There is a long-standing temptation to reject the Old Testament on the grounds that the coming of Christ has cancelled it, but this cuts away at the foundations of the Christian message. It is far better and wiser to see the New Testament as the culmination and fulfilment of the Old. A helpful illustration is to imagine that you are shown into a vast but poorly lit hall in a great art gallery; you can glimpse shadowy outlines of paintings that, even in the poor light, are clearly magnificent. Suddenly, the lights are switched on and now everything can be seen clearly in its full splendour. This is very much the case with the Bible. The New Testament does not change the Old Testament, but it does cast a new and brilliant light on it so that what was once hidden in shadow can now be seen with a new clarity.

THE VIRGINAL CONCEPTION

The belief that Jesus was born of a virgin is one of those issues that has become a test case for belief or unbelief. It's not helped by the fact that the common term 'the virgin birth of Jesus' is misleading. After all, it is Jesus' *conception*, not his birth, which is the issue. Both Matthew and Luke are clear that it was God, not a man, who was responsible for the conception of Jesus.

The idea that Jesus was born of a virgin is often ridiculed and assumes that the entire population of Nazareth were naïve peasants, totally ignorant of the mechanics of how babies are made. In fact we can be sure that, despite their ignorance of reproductive biology, everybody knew that the production of a baby needed a man.

Other people have suggested that this story is an elaborate cover-up for an illegitimate birth. Yet not only did Jewish law value virginity highly but this was a culture in which illegitimacy brought enormous shame on the girl concerned and the family. It's difficult to imagine how this would have happened in a small village where everybody guarded their women and knew everybody else (and what they were up to) in a way that we would probably find oppressive.

The virginal conception of Jesus is no trivial detail and it has considerable importance.

- Anyone familiar with the Old Testament story would have found this astonishingly significant. In the history of Israel there had been many cases of elderly or infertile couples miraculously granted children by Yahweh,[5] a pattern repeated once more with John the Baptist. But the virgin conception of Jesus takes the principle that God can miraculously grant conception and elevates it to an even higher level. These figures of the past were naturally conceived but with some supernatural assistance; with Jesus the conception itself is supernatural. It tells us that a new figure is about to appear in the history of Israel and he will be immensely superior to anyone in the past.

- Traditional Christianity has always held that Jesus was both God and man. Now exactly how this worked is not explained in the Gospels but if Jesus was at the same time both human and divine, then what we might call the 'divine component' had to begin at some point, and there is nowhere more logical for it to occur than at conception.

- Jesus comes to take part in a rescue mission that looks back to the first human beings. As the first Adam was miraculously created, so the idea that there was a miraculous component in the formation of the second Adam is entirely consistent.[6] Jesus marks a totally new start for the human race.

- The earthly life of Jesus ends with the supernatural events of the resurrection and the ascension. It is entirely fitting, therefore, that it begins with a supernatural event: the virgin conception. As someone has put it, the life of Jesus is bracketed by the miraculous 'from the womb to the tomb'.[7]

Christianity has always maintained that the one who was the redeemer of the world had to be both human and divine. In order to deliver humanity from the mess that we are in, any rescuer has to fulfil two conditions: they must have both the *power* and the *right* to intervene. Someone who was only human couldn't act as our rescuer: they would, by definition, be part of the problem and, anyway, they would be limited in who they could save. Equally, although someone who was 'only' God would have the power to save, they would not be eligible to save us as they would not be one of us. Jesus is the answer to this dilemma: as man, he has the eligibility as a human being to represent us and yet, as God, he has the infinite power to save us. The virgin conception allows Jesus to have 'dual citizenship': that of heaven and earth.

Finally, there is a small but significant point. It is easy – and entirely appropriate – to be intimidated by the vastness and holiness of God. Yet one aspect of the story of the coming of Christ is that, when God came to earth, he didn't come in a way that would intimidate or overawe us. God didn't become bigger to impress us; he became smaller to attract us.

THE CHRISTMAS STORY

Familiarity may not breed contempt but it certainly can breed complacency, and it's a pity that one of the few points of contact in the modern West between the post-Christian world and the Bible is the Christmas stories. They are loved: often depicted in primary colours, they have walk-on parts for animals and are rated safe for children. Besides, who can object to the birth of a baby? Yet when we give the Christmas stories the attention they deserve we find that, hiding beneath any glitter and sentimentality, are profound and significant truths.

In neither Matthew or Luke is there any sense that these are fairy-tale, once-upon-a-time stories. There are pointers in both to a time and place in the real world. But when *exactly* was the time? There's been a great deal of discussion of the dating of Jesus' life and ministry and there are some excellent summaries available.[8] It seems clear that Jesus was born during the last years of the life of Herod the Great who is normally assumed to have died in 4 BC. (As already mentioned, the reason why Jesus wasn't born in Year Zero AD was because the calculations were wrongly done when the BC/AD system was set up.) The oldest possible date is 6 BC because Luke says that Jesus was about thirty when he began his ministry and that is dated around AD 27 or 28. So a date of 6–4 BC seems most likely. Matthew's reference to 'the star' at the birth of Christ doesn't really help: what exactly it was in astronomical terms remains elusive. And, as we don't know the year, we are even less certain about the month and the day. The celebration of the nativity on 25th December goes back to Emperor Constantine in AD 336 and was chosen to replace an existing pagan midwinter festival. The key point is that even if we don't know Jesus' exact date of birth, we know that it did happen in the real world that we live in.

Both Matthew and Luke state that Jesus was born in Bethlehem, a small town about 8 km (5 miles) to the south-west of Jerusalem. Although Mary and Joseph lived in Nazareth (110 km or 70 miles to the north), their presence in Bethlehem is explained as being due to a census organised by Caesar Augustus that required registration at an ancestral town. One possible scenario is that this was not just simply 'head counting' but an attempt to sort out who owned what land for tax purposes and that Joseph had an historical right to land in the area. The significance of Bethlehem is that it is the town of David and as such crops up in a prophecy of the Messiah in Micah 5:2.

Luke tells us that Jesus' birthplace was humble. Although tradition shows Mary and Joseph turned away from an inn, modern translations suggest that the word 'inn' is better translated as 'guestroom'. This suggests a situation where the couple went to the home of Joseph's nearest relatives only to find that the only space available was in the lower part of the building, normally occupied by animals.

One of the problems with Christmas is that we follow the story but miss the significance. The Lord of all, the King of creation, humbles himself not simply to become part of humanity, but its lowest depths. The cradle in the stable foreshadows the cross outside the city.

In this most basic of settings, Mary and Joseph are visited by shepherds who have been summoned there by angels. Shepherds were close to the bottom of the social ladder at the time, and the fact that it is they and not the social and religious elite of Jerusalem who were called by the angels is significant. Jesus is to be good news for the poor and those on the margins of society.

Although three kings – exotically dressed – are an essential of any nativity play, Matthew's account[9] simply tells us that these other visitors were 'Magi' – wise men or astrologers – and makes no mention of them either being kings or representing different races. It does not even tell us when they visited the baby; although from the fact that they visited 'a child' in 'a house' their visit may have been some months later. The idea that such people should travel for months (possibly from what is now modern Iraq or Iran) to find a Messiah may seem unlikely. Yet intriguingly, the two Roman authors we have already mentioned, Suetonius and Tacitus, claim that there was a widespread belief that a world ruler would come from the Jewish people,[10] so a Jewish king could have been seen as having more than local significance.

The attitude of the Magi stands in stark contrast with that of Herod and the priests. While the strangers from afar, who presumably knew very little about the Messiah, chose to travel vast distances to show him honour, those close by – who should have recognised what was going on – failed to note what was happening just a few miles away. (And in the case of Herod, when they did, they reacted with hostility.) Here, too, another New Testament theme is announced; while God's promised deliverer comes to his own people and is rejected by them, those who are outside the faith accept him.

In a postscript that is often omitted from children's nativity plays as being 'unsuitable for infants', Matthew tells us that after the visit of the Magi, Herod ordered the massacre of all infants of two and under in Bethlehem. Its mention is a reminder that, for all its sentimentalised and sanitised retelling, the Christmas story is about a world as mad, bad and sad as our own.

In John's Gospel we find no account of the birth but instead a profound prologue reflecting on the meaning of his coming.[11] John says that the whole creation was made by 'the Word', someone who was 'with God' and 'was God'. This 'Word', says John, is not just the maker of all things; he is also 'light' and 'life', the source of everything that is essential for existence. Then in one of the most awesome statements ever written, John says, 'So the Word became human and made his home among us.'[12] In Jesus, the eternal, infinite awesomeness of God became flesh and blood.

John then says this about Jesus: 'He came into the very world he created, but the world didn't recognise him. He came to his own people, and even they rejected him. But to all who believed him and accepted him, he gave the right to become children of God.'[13] Here in the story of Jesus' birth is the heart of the matter. Jesus' coming was not an automatic blessing on all humanity. After all, many people have found it an easy matter to ignore or reject him. Yet to recognise Jesus for who he is, to accept him as the Word in the form of human flesh is, as John says, to gain the wonderful privilege of being a child of God and knowing God as your loving heavenly Father.

NOTE: ISSUES WITH ANGELS

Although they occur infrequently in the rest of the Gospels and are rarely mentioned in the letters of the New Testament, angels are mentioned several times in the account of Jesus' birth.[14]

Today the idea of angels attracts two extreme views. On the one hand we have those who are sceptical of the miraculous and scorn any idea of angels as a childish myth. Yet at the same time we have an enormous growth in mystical beliefs which often include a fascination with angels. A careful reading of what the entire Bible does and does not say on the subject of angels is an essential counterbalance to both the incredulity of the sceptics and the credulity of the mystics.

Angels appear at major events in Jesus' life; he believed in the existence of angels and he talked about them. The main role of angels seems to be to serve God as his faithful agents, acting as servants, messengers and, sometimes, warriors. Contrary to widespread belief, they are not human beings given a 'spiritual upgrade' to angelic status after death, but are powerful living creatures separately created by God. As spiritual beings they do not have physical bodies but can take on human appearance. Almost every time they occur in the New Testament those who see them find them awesome and terrifying. Normally when the Bible talks about angels, it refers to those who are good and holy. The presence of evil angels is, however, acknowledged.

Although widely overlooked, the role of angels as protectors and helpers of God's people continues. There are many reports from reliable witnesses of mysterious helpers or defenders appearing at a time of need and then vanishing: angels may have a bigger role in life than we imagine. Nevertheless, when it comes to attitudes to angels, the entire New Testament sounds the same message: it is not angels who are to be central to our faith; it is Jesus.[15]

5

THE PREPARATION FOR MINISTRY

According to the dating given by Luke,[1] John the Baptist began to preach in AD 27, with Jesus' own public ministry starting shortly afterwards. This would mean that Jesus was around thirty years old[2] and that three decades have elapsed since the events in Bethlehem. What happened during that time?

THE LONG SILENCE

The only incident recorded in Jesus' life during this period is one mentioned by Luke: a memorable visit to Jerusalem with his parents when Jesus was twelve.[3] Luke concludes that account: 'Then he [Jesus] returned to Nazareth with them and was obedient to them. And his mother stored all these things in her heart. Jesus grew in wisdom and in stature and in favour with God and all the people.' The implication is that Jesus grew up normally in a way largely indistinguishable from that of many of the children in the village of Nazareth. Like most Jewish boys raised in devout families he would have been taught to read the Old Testament and would have memorised large portions of it. Following common practice he would have learned his father's trade; in this case that of a carpenter or builder.[4]

These years of silence have frustrated many imaginative people and any number of legends and strange ideas have emerged to fill in the gap. The rather unexciting reality about these 'missing years' is no doubt that Jesus grew up, was trained in Joseph's trade, and that was that. The idea that, for a large part of his earthly existence, Jesus lived a life in which little happened ought to be an encouragement to the many people who find themselves in situations that do not change as fast as they would like. God is the master of events and also non-events.

One thing we can be certain of and one thing we can guess. The certainty is that Jesus did not waste those years. From the perception shown by what Jesus said later we can be sure that he watched carefully and learnt deeply. At the end of the thirty-year gap, when the Gospel writers talk of Jesus' family Joseph is no longer present. From this we can guess that he had died and so Jesus would have known something of a family bereavement. If so then Jesus, as eldest son, would have become the head of the family which by now included Mary and at least six other children.[5] Many people faced with the burden of family responsibilities say to God: '*You* know nothing of all this.' Yet, despite being unmarried and not having children, Jesus did know something about bearing family responsibility. Here, too, he can sympathise.[6]

JOHN THE BAPTIST

All the Gospels link the beginning of Jesus' ministry with John the Baptist, a remarkable figure who had such a great impact on the nation of Israel that people wondered if he was the Messiah.[7] There are other witnesses to his powerful influence: Josephus mentions John as 'a baptiser' and a moral reformer and says he had such a remarkable effect that Herod Antipas became concerned that he might incite a revolt.[8] Over twenty years later and far away in Ephesus, the early church found itself dealing with people who still followed John's teaching.[9] The highest testimony to John came from Jesus himself, who said that he was more than a prophet and the greatest man who had ever lived.[10]

The 'job description' of a prophet in the Bible is not so much someone who tells the future as someone who reminds God's people of their duties towards him. The way John dressed and lived marked him out as the severest form of prophet. John was outspoken in his thundering and merciless denunciations of a formal, empty religion where people relied on God's covenant without worrying about the appropriate response to it. John was plain that a right relationship with God meant there had to be right actions by his people.[11] Israel needed to repent.

Yet John was more than another old-style prophet. Two things were distinctively new. The first was that he proclaimed an urgent reason why people should repent: God was coming to his people. Invoking the language of Isaiah, John announced the imminent arrival of God's Kingdom and the need for people to be ready for it. The coming of the Kingdom was linked with the arrival of God's King: John was clear that someone was on the way who was far greater than him and who would baptise with 'the Holy Spirit and with fire'.[12] John seems to have seen the coming of the Kingdom as having a strong element of judgement and in one sense he was not wrong: judgement was to fall on Israel within a generation. Yet later, when the imprisoned John heard of Jesus' ministry, he seems to have struggled with the idea that the Messiah he had predicted was dispensing grace more than judgement.[13]

The second new feature of John's ministry was his practice of ritual washing – *baptising* – the many who came to hear him and who had been convinced by his message. Regular washing was common in Judaism to keep the laws of ritual purity, yet John's baptism was different: the sort of one-time washing that non-Jews would have undergone had they decided to convert to Judaism, but John demanded it of those who were Jews. It was a message that has parallels even today. Being born and brought up within even the very best kind of faith is not enough; there's a time when we all have to make a commitment for ourselves.

John's preaching was the great wake-up call for the nation of Israel. After centuries of silence, a prophet had at last appeared. Indeed John's resemblance to Elijah, that most uncompromising of the Old Testament prophets, would have reminded many of the prophecy at the end of Malachi: 'Look, I am sending you the prophet Elijah before the great and dreadful day of the LORD arrives.'[14] That John in fact did fulfil the role of a 'second Elijah' was confirmed by no less than Jesus.[15]

John's end was predictable. His denunciations from the Jordan Valley clearly perturbed the comfortable religious establishment in Jerusalem. Finally, after condemning Herod Antipas, the 'king' of

Galilee, for immorality, John was imprisoned and subsequently executed.[16]

John gave a diagnosis of sinfulness that had people searching for the cure of forgiveness. He pointed to Jesus as Messiah[17] and declared that he was 'the Lamb of God who takes away the sins of the world'.[18] It seems likely that many of John's disciples left him to go over to Jesus; something that the Baptist welcomed with grace and humility.[19]

John can be considered as the last of the Old Testament prophets. His was a powerful if limited ministry; he pronounced judgement and demanded repentance but offered little new teaching and, strikingly, did no miracles. He was the greatest of prophets and, by being so, he demonstrated that the Jesus he pointed to was very much more than just a prophet.

JESUS' BAPTISM

With John's baptism of Jesus in the Jordan River the spotlight swings from the prophet to the King.[20] Matthew[21] tells us Jesus was baptised not because he needed washing or purification but because he wanted to identify with God's people.

The accounts of Jesus' baptism contain much that is profound. Mark gives us a summary of what happened:

> One day Jesus came from Nazareth in Galilee, and John baptised him in the Jordan River. As Jesus came up out of the water, he saw the heavens splitting apart and the Holy Spirit descending on him like a dove. And a voice from heaven said, 'You are my dearly loved Son, and you bring me great joy.'[22]

If we look carefully at what the voice says we find that it is a combination of two Old Testament verses. The first, 'You are my dearly loved son', is to do with the coronation of God's King and comes from Psalm 2.[23] The second, 'I am pleased with him', refers to a passage in Isaiah[24] about the coming Servant who would endure pain and death to save God's people. The combination points to a

Jesus who would not just be the Messiah who would rule but also the Servant who would suffer.

One other important aspect to Jesus' baptism is the image of the Holy Spirit descending like a dove from heaven, something that suggests God has poured out his presence and power on Jesus. That Jesus was filled with the Spirit at his baptism is truly significant: it is a reminder that even God's Son did not begin his work without being empowered and anointed[7] by the Holy Spirit. It is a principle that Jesus himself endorsed later when, after the resurrection, he insisted that his disciples wait in Jerusalem until they were baptised with the Holy Spirit.

Finally, although the doctrine of the Trinity is not fully expressed anywhere in Scripture, it is implied here. God the Father confirms Jesus' authority and identity as his Son and empowers him for ministry through the Spirit. This confirmation of Jesus' vocation sees the coming together of God: Father, the Spirit and Son.

THE TESTING OF JESUS

Immediately after his baptism, Jesus spent forty days in the wilderness – the desert – where he was tempted by the devil. The precise time period is significant and is an echo of the history of the Jewish people: Moses had spent forty days and nights fasting in the wilderness before receiving God's Law[25] and the Israelites had spent forty years in the wilderness after being disobedient to God.[26] Jesus' episode in the desert marked him out not only as the new Moses, but also as the representative and pioneer of the new Israel, a people who when tested in the wilderness are obedient.

Putting aside for the moment the supernatural aspect to this event, it's not hard to see the issues facing Jesus at this time. Through his baptism, Jesus had just been commissioned as the Messiah; now, in the wilderness, he had to decide *how* he was going to fulfil that role. But to comprehend what Jesus faced in the wilderness we need to distinguish between 'being tested' and 'being tempted',

---

7   The word 'anointed' is important. The word 'Messiah' meant 'anointed one', a reference to the oil that was symbolically poured on the head of a new king (see 1 Kings 1:39).

both terms that are used of this experience. To *test* something or someone is to do something positive: the tester hopes the test will be passed so there can be a progression to some further stage. But to *tempt* someone is much more negative: the tempter desires that the one tempted will fail. Now if you take the Bible's view that there is both a God and a devil in the universe, then you can see how something can be both test and temptation. From God's perspective this time in the wilderness was a test of Jesus because he wanted his Son to succeed. From the devil's standpoint it was an opportunity to tempt Jesus because he wanted him to fail.

Linked with this is the way that all the accounts of Jesus' temptation talk of him being 'led' or 'compelled' by the Holy Spirit to go into the wilderness and face the devil. This testing was a result of God's initiative in sending Jesus to battle with the devil in his home territory, the wilderness. There are two important points here that are relevant not just to the life of Jesus but to all history. First, God – not the devil – is in charge of events. Second, Jesus was not someone who managed merely to endure the attacks of the devil but someone who challenged him, fought him and won. Jesus is not just the great survivor of evil; he is the victor over it.

The testing of Jesus involved three separate temptations.

The temptation to turn stones into bread

'If you are the Son of God, tell these stones to become loaves of bread.'[27]

This temptation addressed Jesus' physical appetite. On one level it was an attack where Jesus was weakest: he had been fasting for a long time. Yet the temptation was subtler than it seems – almost all temptations are – and the devil was surely trying to raise doubts in Jesus' mind about whether he was truly the Son of God and really did have miraculous powers. At an even deeper level there was another challenge. Would Jesus use his powers, independently of his Father's will, for his own benefit? Jesus' response was to quote the Old Testament: people need more than bread for their life; they need to feed on every word of the Lord.[28] Jesus quoted the Bible not because it has any magic power (the devil quotes it too) but because in this verse, God assures us that trusting in him is the most important thing in life.

The temptation to leap from the highest point of the temple

'Then the devil took him to the holy city, Jerusalem, to the highest point of the Temple, and said, "If you are the Son of God, jump off! For the Scriptures say, 'He will order his angels to protect you. And they will hold you up with their hands so you won't even hurt your foot on a stone.'"'[29]

The devil now took Jesus to the heights of the temple and, quoting Scripture, suggested that he throw himself down so that God will act to protect him. While this may be a temptation for Jesus to prove that he was the Messiah by some stunning and very public demonstration, it is far more likely that it was another attempt to make Jesus doubt his status as God's son. 'Prove it,' the devil is saying. 'If God really is your caring Father he will make sure you don't come to any harm.'

Jesus' reply was again based on the Bible: he points out that the Scriptures also say, 'You must not test the LORD your God.' The quote, again from Deuteronomy,[30] refers to when the Israelites rebelled against God in the wilderness. By quoting it, Jesus was announcing his refusal to do what they did: he had utter trust in his Father's loving care and had no need to test it.

The temptation to worship the devil

'Next the devil took him to the peak of a very high mountain and showed him all the kingdoms of the world and their glory. "I will give it all to you," he said, "if you will kneel down and worship me."'[31]

Finally, the devil took Jesus to where he could see all the kingdoms of the world and offered them to him. It is the most unsubtle of all the temptations; as if, having run out of options, the devil put all his cards on the table. Actually, it may not have been such a blatantly materialistic offer as it seems at first sight. After all, it's easy to imagine the devil pointing not just to all the world's wealth and glory, but to its injustices and miseries, and suggesting how much better things would be if Jesus took over running things.

However presented, it was a temptation for Jesus to seize his inheritance immediately without obedience to God's plan, which he must have known involved time and suffering. It is the temptation to take the shortcut, to try to gain power and glory without sacrifice, to seek the crown without the cross. Jesus' reply was a final and unequivocal rejection. '"Get out of here Satan," Jesus told him. "For the Scriptures say, 'You must worship the LORD your God and serve only him.'"'[32] The passage he quotes refers to exactly the sort of idolatry that Jesus is now rejecting. Jesus has determined that whatever it cost him, his ministry will be carried out God's way.

Luke tells us that 'when the devil had finished tempting Jesus, he left him until the next opportunity came'.[33] Jesus had won a victory that would determine the shape of his ministry, but the devil had not been permanently defeated. Jesus would face temptation again.

NOTE: DISCUSSING THE DEVIL

No one who reads the accounts of Jesus' temptation can overlook the fact that they are all about his encounter with a living, personal, supernatural opponent: the devil. Here, as elsewhere in the Gospels, there is mention of an evil spiritual adversary.

In thinking about the devil or Satan[8] we need to put out of our minds any ideas of red suits, forked tails and horns. There is none of that in the Bible. What we learn there is that the devil is the chief of those angelic powers who are opposed to God and human beings, and is both the great enemy of the Kingdom of God and the one who tempts men and women.

The devil is mentioned rarely in the Bible and we are wise to adopt its policy of making God our focus. However, the fact that most of the references to the devil are found in the teaching of Jesus should caution us against dismissing any idea of him as a mere superstition.

From the references to the devil in the Gospels we can learn the following things:

---

8 'Satan' comes from the Hebrew word meaning 'the adversary' and 'devil' is from the Greek equivalent, *diabolos*. The two words are used interchangeably in the Gospels. The devil also has other titles in Scripture including the 'tempter', 'Beelzebub' and the 'enemy'.

- The devil is powerful. Jesus called him the 'ruler of this world',[34] implying that the entire creation is under his influence.

- The devil is always hostile towards God's people. He is the evil one that we are to pray to be delivered from and the one who snatches away the good news from people's hearts.[35] Jesus described the devil as being 'a murderer'.[36]

- The devil's methods are deceitful. Jesus said of Satan that he hates the truth, that he is a liar and the father of lies.[37] (When faced with temptation, it's useful to remember that the devil does not keep his promises.) Elsewhere Jesus portrays Satan as being like an evil farmer who secretly sows weeds in the fields of a rival.[38]

Yet for all the portrayal of the devil as being powerful, hostile and deceitful, the Gospels also show him as someone whose authority and menace are limited. He is never seen as an excuse for human evil (as in 'the devil made me do it') but as someone who, with God's power, we can and should resist. Jesus' numerous actions of exorcism and healing demonstrate his superiority over the devil. The New Testament tells us that Jesus' challenge to the devil was far more than a few skirmishes a long time ago. Jesus taught that the devil's power would be utterly destroyed at the cross. In John's Gospel he announces, 'The time for judging this world has come, when Satan, the ruler of this world, will be cast out.'[39] The letters of the New Testament expand on the teaching of Jesus[40] and in particular make much of the fact that although the devil is still capable of doing harm, he is now a defeated foe and one whose final judgement is certain.[41] Those who follow Christ should hold a balanced attitude to the devil in which there is neither frivolous dismissal nor fearful dread.

THE MINISTRY OF JESUS

In this chapter we summarise the ministry of Jesus – that period when he was publicly teaching crowds and training his disciples.

An important issue is how long this ministry lasted. At first glance, the three Synoptic Gospels seem to pack everything into a single busy year culminating in the final fateful trip to Jerusalem. Yet their organisation of events may have been made on literary or theological grounds. (In Luke's Gospel much of Jesus' ministry is framed around his journey to Jerusalem, a theme echoed in Acts with Paul's even longer journey to Rome.) John's Gospel, however, seems to refer to a ministry of three years with several visits to Jerusalem. Following many scholars, we think that John reflects reality and that it is best to assume a three-year ministry period.

The most likely date for the beginning of Jesus' ministry is around AD 27 or 28. Its ending in the trial and crucifixion is much more firmly dated. Here there is unanimity in the Gospels (and from external sources) that Jesus died during the rule of Pontius Pilate, which can be dated as between AD 26 and 36. The mention of Herod Antipas and Caiaphas do not add any more precision to this. What is helpful is that because Jesus was crucified on a Friday before a Passover, a feast based on the appearance of the full moon, astronomical data can be used to work out when this might have occurred.[1] This gives two possible dates: either AD 30 or 33. Although 33 has its defenders, the date AD 30 seems preferable[9] partly because it allows more space for the events of the Acts, some of which can be precisely dated. Now which of these two dates is ultimately correct is not important: what *is* of profound importance is the realisation that the

---

9   Jesus prophesied the temple would be destroyed within a generation (Matthew 24:34; Mark 13:30; Luke 21:32) a time span normally taken to be forty years. On an AD 30 date for the crucifixion, the destruction of the temple in AD 70 would have been seen as a striking fulfilment of prophecy.

central event in Christianity – the death of Jesus – can be confidently marked on the calendar of history as three o'clock on the Friday afternoon of either 7th April AD 30 or 3rd April AD 33. It's another reminder that this is a story set in our own world.

In looking at the ministry of Jesus we can identify three phases and then a final dramatic week.

THE FIRST PHASE: THE EARLY MINISTRY

Covered in John 1:15 – 5:47

Probable date: late AD 27 into 28

The first five chapters of John apparently give us an account of various activities of Jesus in Judaea and Jerusalem before fully beginning his ministry in Galilee. For many years scholars dismissed this material as at best misplaced or, at worst, invented, but that scepticism seems unfounded.[2] Given that there are hints in the Synoptic Gospels that Jesus had visited Jerusalem and had friends there before his arrival on what we call Palm Sunday,[3] earlier visits seem certain. It is quite likely that John, knowing his readers would have been aware of some sort of synoptic version of the Gospels, wrote his own version as a sort of 'filling-in-the-gaps' addition.

During this period Jesus performed miracles (John refers to these as 'signs'), called some disciples to follow him but possibly only on a part-time basis, taught about eternal life, made references to his own death and resurrection, and had some interactions with Jewish leaders, Samaritans and Gentiles. We learn that Jesus found rejection and opposition among those who might have been expected to welcome him. The first five chapters of John give us an account of various activities of Jesus in Judaea and Jerusalem that seem to have taken place before the main ministry in Galilee recounted in the Synoptic Gospels.

A significant component in these early chapters of John is an account of Jesus visiting the temple and clearing it, something that stands in contrast to the confrontations in the temple at the end of his ministry described by the synoptic authors.[4] One possibility is that this first clearing is a prophetic warning that unless the temple system is reformed, judgement will follow; and the second, a sad verdict that as the warning has not been heeded, judgement is now inevitable. To use sporting imagery, in his first appearance in the temple Jesus shows the institution the yellow card of a caution; in the second, the red card of condemnation.

One interpretation of this first phase of ministry is that Jesus is exploring the nation, testing to see if it will return to God. Is restoration possible?

THE SECOND PHASE: THE MINISTRY IN THE NORTH

Covered in Matthew 4:12 – 18:35; Mark 1:14 – 9:50; Luke 4:14 – 9:50; John 6:1 – 10:21

Probable dates: late AD *28 to autumn 29*

With the imprisonment of John the Baptist by Herod Antipas, Jesus seems to have taken the decision to change the scope of his own ministry. He began to gather a new people of God based around a nucleus of twelve disciples and, largely staying in Galilee, began the next phase of his ministry.

Jesus chose Capernaum for his base, a fishing village on the shores of the Sea of Galilee, and he drew commercial fishermen from the local villages for some of his closest followers. Having access to a boat and a crew allowed him an invaluable escape route when, as was to happen, the crowds got too large or there were attempts to arrest him. A short sail eastwards allowed Jesus to leave the territory of Herod Antipas and 'cross the state line' into either the territory of Philip or that of the independent confederation of the Decapolis – 'the Ten Towns' – on the other side of the lake. We need to note that there were more than just the Twelve with him. Significantly, Luke tells us that by now – contrary to all cultural codes – his followers included women, some of whom were wealthy and were helping to support the ministry.[5]

Although if we follow John's chronology Jesus had known Simon Peter, Andrew, Philip and Nathaniel before, he now issued a formal call for them and eight others to follow him on a permanent basis as disciples. With the Twelve, Jesus began his public teaching in the synagogues but also went outside them to a public ministry that combined preaching and healing and which soon drew crowds numbering thousands.[6]

Mark tells us the theme of Jesus' preaching at this time: 'The time promised by God has come at last! The Kingdom of God is near! Repent of your sins and believe the Good News!'[7] With this proclamation of the Kingdom – and, by implication, the King – Jesus began to focus on the demands that these truths made on people.

The Gospels are clear that Jesus did not just teach but that he also performed miracles. These were miracles of healing but they also included 'nature miracles': demonstrations of power and authority over such things as wind and waves, bread and fish. These were 'signs' that gave authority to Jesus' teaching and would have aroused extraordinary attention. Contrary to what many people think, miracles are relatively rare in the Old Testament and anyone searching for any parallels to Jesus' actions would have needed to go back nearly nine centuries to the time of Elijah and Elisha. Equally, given that John the Baptist had done no miracles, they forcibly make the point that although he might have been a great man, Jesus was still greater.

At first, Jesus' ministry appears to have gathered universal support yet, increasingly, opposition mounted. We see a sequence of reactions amongst the religious authorities in Galilee: at first they are puzzled by Jesus, then become uneasy, irritated and finally hostile. Such opposition is understandable: those men who wielded spiritual and legal authority in the villages of Galilee must have been distinctly discomfited by the new arrival with his challenging words, astonishing actions and his refusal to play things by their rulebook.

At some point during Jesus' ministry in Galilee, Herod Antipas had John the Baptist executed. This event and growing antagonism from the religious authorities seems to have triggered a change. From now on, Jesus adopted a more itinerant style, constantly moving around by foot or boat. Increasingly, we find Jesus using parables as a way of teaching.

Jesus was facing two threats at this time. The most obvious peril came from his enemies. Increasingly, as he taught, healed or simply ate meals with the wrong sort of people, Jesus aroused disapproval. Sometimes that displeasure showed itself in trick questions intended to lure him into saying things that would condemn him.

The second threat came from the risk of Jesus' supporters getting out of hand and publicly declaring him to be a political Messiah and launching an uprising against Rome. On one occasion at least, matters came very close to this. When Jesus miraculously fed a vast number of people (five thousand men and an uncounted number of women and children),[8] the crowd's response was to want to make him king by force. In a telling comment in John we read: 'When Jesus saw that they were ready to force him to be their king, he slipped away into the hills by himself.'[9]

These twin threats from foes and friends help explain what Jesus said and did. He was, at this stage, careful to avoid explicitly declaring he was the Messiah, a word with so many political and revolutionary overtones that it was best avoided. Doubtless for the same reason, Jesus preferred to conceal his miracles, even telling the healed not to talk about what had happened.[10]

After a particularly serious dispute over what must have been perceived as a suspiciously lax attitude to ritual purity, Jesus took the disciples north out of Jewish areas entirely and into the Gentile regions of Tyre and Sidon.[11] In doing this he may not have just been avoiding the fate of John; he may also have been setting a precedent and pattern for the mission to the Gentiles that the disciples would undertake after the resurrection.

The turning point

Jesus' activities in Galilee came to a close after three very important and linked events which occurred within a week.

The first event took place near 'the villages near Caesarea Philippi' just beyond the northernmost limit of Galilee.[12] There Jesus asked the disciples who people thought he was and received from Simon Peter the answer, 'You are the Messiah, the Son of the living God.'[13]

It was a significant moment: after months of following Jesus, the leader of the Twelve had declared his belief that Jesus was the long-promised deliverer of God's people.

The second event followed immediately afterwards. Jesus told his followers for the first time that he would suffer. He said he would be rejected by the 'elders, the leading priests, and the teachers of religious law', be killed, but three days later, he would rise again.[14] The announcement by Jesus that he would suffer humiliation and shame rather than triumph was instantly rejected.[15] The popular conceptions of a Messiah focused on him being a glorious, triumphant king; the idea of one who would endure shame and suffering was both unfamiliar and objectionable. Isaiah might have prophesied the coming of a 'suffering servant' but, unsurprisingly, it hadn't caught the popular imagination. Even as the Twelve were attempting to adjust to this, Jesus followed it with something even worse. If his followers wanted to follow him, they must put aside their own selfish ambition and, in a phrase that time has drained of its horror, 'take up the cross' and be prepared to die.[16] Not only was Jesus going to suffer but those who wanted to follow him should be prepared to take the same dreadful road.

Over the next few days, two questions must have gone through the disciples' minds. First, in view of the gloomy words Jesus had used for his future, could he *really* be the Messiah? Second, given what Jesus had said about the cost of being a disciple, even if he was, did they want to follow him?

This atmosphere of confusion, doubt and fear provides the dark backdrop for the third event which occurred a week later. This event is the transfiguration, where Jesus took the three disciples, Peter, James and John, up a mountain to pray.[17] There, Jesus' appearance changed so that his face and clothing shone gloriously.[18] Suddenly, two figures identifiable in some way as Moses and Elijah appeared and began talking with him of how he was about to fulfil God's plan by dying in Jerusalem.[19] A bright cloud appeared with God's voice declaring, 'This is my dearly loved Son, who brings me great joy. Listen to him.'[20] The two figures departed, leaving only Jesus.

The accounts of the transfiguration look back to the Old Testament, with Moses and Elijah standing for the two great divisions of the Old Testament: the Law and the Prophets. It was an event that echoes Moses' encounter with God on Mount Sinai [21] and with a cloud like that which was associated with God's presence.[22] These references are vital in indicating a divine affirmation that the suffering that Jesus said he would undergo in Jerusalem was not a distortion of the divine design for the Messiah, but was something long planned and approved by God.

What is the significance of the transfiguration? At the time the most important thing was that it confirmed to the perplexed disciples that, for all their concerns, Jesus was indeed the Messiah and should be listened to. Yet what they saw also demonstrated what Peter had declared: Jesus was the Son of God, someone who was more than a human being. It was a lesson the disciples needed to learn. There is one other significant aspect of the transfiguration. It was not a transformation of Jesus from what he was into what he wasn't; it was the opposite – a revelation of Jesus as he really was. Of necessity the Gospels focus on Jesus as a human being; the one who lived in obscurity and died in shameful and painful weakness on the cross. Yet in the transfiguration, for a moment, that temporary identity is dropped and the disciples see something of Jesus the awesome Son of God, full of glory, majesty and honour.[23] In this it looks forward to those pictures of Jesus in glory that we get in the book of Revelation.[24]

After the transfiguration, Jesus returned with his disciples to Galilee for a brief period. Things were now different however: there was a change in emphasis in his activities. In order to teach the disciples he now sought privacy.[25] Back in Galilee Jesus gave a second prophecy of his death and resurrection, only this time there was a new and disturbing addition: 'he is going to be betrayed'.[26]

The hostility to Jesus

The growing hostility to Jesus raises an important question. Why did he meet such opposition? We will talk later about what he taught and what he claimed but it's worth giving some reasons here.

- While Jesus was dedicated to God's Law as given in the Old Testament, he either held lightly to the extras that religious leaders had added or was dismissive of them. Some of these, such as the extraordinarily numerous and detailed Sabbath rules, clearly angered Jesus because they made life so burdensome. By criticising these add-ons he became an enemy of the religious system.

- Jesus cared little about keeping those codes of social behaviour that were part of everyday life. He befriended people who had been rejected by the religious teachers, such as tax collectors and prostitutes, and had meals with them. As if to underline the point that his friendship with such people was not just at meals, Jesus had an ex-tax collector to be a disciple. Jesus' attitude to women – discussing religious issues with them, having them as followers and even teaching them – was also no doubt considered an affront to public decency. It must have been easy for those who had a vested interest in maintaining 'the way things work' to see Jesus as a danger to society. The Pharisees, who felt that it was their ministry to regulate society, found Jesus particularly subversive.

- Jesus and his disciples seemed to lack the perpetual seriousness that many people felt (and some still feel) is an essential part of following God. When his disciples were accused of not fasting, Jesus' response to the criticism was revealing: 'For John [the Baptist] didn't spend his time eating and drinking, and you say, "He's possessed by a demon." The Son of Man, on the other hand, feasts and drinks, and you say, "He's a glutton and a drunkard, and a friend of tax collectors and other sinners!"'[27] In fact the Pharisees in particular found Jesus and his disciples to be suspiciously lax in their behaviour: they were not religious enough!

- Although Jesus was careful to avoid making direct claims (at least in public) that he was either the Messiah or the Son of God until the end of his ministry, what he said and did strongly suggested that he viewed himself as more than a prophet. On one occasion Jesus healed a woman suffering from permanent internal bleeding that rendered her both unwell and ritually unclean.[28] The Old Testament clearly laid down in Leviticus 15 strict rules on how anyone who was healed should respond: they should wait seven days, offer a sacrifice at the temple and be pronounced clean by a priest. Jesus ignored all of these and simply said to her, 'Daughter, your faith has made you well. Go in peace. Your suffering is over.' In these words, Jesus was claiming for himself the authority to override the divinely instituted temple system and its rules, something that must have seemed blasphemous. In a similar way, Jesus maintained that he could forgive sins, something only God himself could do. He also claimed that God was his 'Father', another statement that could have been considered blasphemy.

- Because Jesus claimed to bring – and to be – the fulfilment of all that Israel had been waiting for, he posed a challenge and demanded either acceptance or rejection. Much of Jesus' teaching was either directly or indirectly critical of those who refused to believe in him. So, for example, when Jesus talked about the new wine of his teaching needing new wine skins,[29] the implication was that those who rejected him had a faith that was as useless as a dry, old, leathery wineskin.

- There were aspects of what Jesus taught that must have seemed deeply unsettling or even heretical. Jesus put the focus of religious life not in the keeping of the Law, nor in offering sacrifices at the temple, but in following him personally. The implications of this for the religious structure that held the nation together were obviously understood.

- There were hints in what Jesus taught that implied that the Gentiles had a place in God's great scheme of things. This went against the widespread tone of ethnic superiority that existed at the time. So, in Luke's account of Jesus' teaching in the synagogue at Nazareth,[30] what angered the congregation was not his claims to an astonishing personal authority but his reminder of how, in the past, God had instead dealt kindly with the Gentiles.

- Jesus posed a threat to the delicate 'understanding' that had been achieved between the Romans, the temple authorities and Herod. No doubt all the parties saw the situation as imperfect, but with a catastrophic nationalist uprising always possible, it was better than the alternative. It was certainly more profitable. The temple in particular provided very rich pickings: Josephus claimed that at one Passover alone the number of animal sacrifices offered was 256,000.[31] Given that these animals had to be bought at the temple, this sort of figure suggests that it was a very lucrative business indeed. It is easy to imagine how anyone with an investment in the temple system would have viewed someone who threatened the status quo. These shared concerns go some way to explain why, when it came to getting rid of Jesus, bitter enemies found themselves able to collaborate.

As is often the case, once the hostility began it acquired its own momentum and soon found new justification for its existence. So, for instance, once the verdict was reached that Jesus was a heretic then some explanation for his miracles had to be found. The obvious one was that he was doing them with demonic power,[32] something that gave his opponents the most potent of arguments against him.

There were also, no doubt, private and personal reasons why many people disliked Jesus. His moral standards were uncompromising; he challenged any sort of shallow, superficial religion; he exposed hypocrisy; and he asked for an unconditional and unlimited loyalty. Such reasons for rejecting Jesus are still with us.

THE THIRD PHASE: THE ROAD SOUTH

Covered in Matthew 19:1 – 20:34; Mark 10:1–52; Luke 9:51 – 19:27; John 10:22 – 12:11

Probable dates: late autumn AD 29 *to March* AD 30

There are two fixed points in this phase. The first is that, as John tells us,[33] Jesus made an appearance in Jerusalem for the Festival of Dedication (*Hanukkah*) in December and, evading arrest, returned to the other side of the Jordan. The second is that he came back to the outskirts of Jerusalem shortly before the beginning of the feast of Passover.

Taking all the evidence, it seems that shortly after the turning point of Peter's declaration and the transfiguration, Jesus began to make his way south from Galilee, crossing the River Jordan and going into Perea, the Jewish territory east of the Jordan. Matthew and Luke tell us that Jesus travelled south not just with the Twelve but with other followers, including the women.[34] The mood of the group was darkened by a third prophecy of his death and resurrection.[35] This was the most explicit prediction yet: Jesus referred to himself being handed over to the Gentiles, mocked, flogged and crucified. The accounts make it clear that Jesus knew what he faced in Jerusalem; they are equally clear that the disciples either did not understand or refused to understand what he was talking about.

From Perea, Jesus and his followers made periodic visits to Jerusalem. Jesus had friends in Bethany, thirty minutes' walk from Jerusalem, who during these last months hosted both him and the disciples on several occasions.[36] The impression we get of Jesus' activities at this time is that although he was still healing people and teaching in public, his priority was spending time with his disciples. When Jesus did encounter the religious authorities, the meetings were now always hostile and he faced trick questions designed to trap him.

Towards the end of this third phase of ministry, Jesus performed a miracle that focused the dislike into something more organised and lethal. John's Gospel records how Lazarus, one of Jesus' friends living in Bethany on the outskirts of Jerusalem, died and was buried. Four days after his death, Jesus visited the tomb and, in the presence of Lazarus' sisters and a crowd, ordered the stone that sealed the grave to be removed. He then summoned Lazarus to come out and, still encumbered by his grave clothes, Lazarus emerged. This was one of the most remarkable of all Jesus' miracles. It went far beyond mere resuscitation: after four days of burial, Lazarus' body would have undergone decay. Bethany's nearness to Jerusalem, the overwhelming nature of the miracle, and the fact that Lazarus was probably well known in Jerusalem, meant that what had happened was soon widely talked about.[37]

John tells us that the ruling council – the *Sanhedrin* – met to discuss the matter and concluded that Jesus posed a danger of causing an incident that would provoke the sort of brutal Roman retaliation that might threaten the very survival of the nation.[38] He records how Caiaphas said, with callous pragmatism, 'You don't realise that it's better for you that one man should die for the people than for the whole nation to be destroyed.'[39]

Here for a moment we must pause. This and subsequent passages[40] have sadly – and with terrible consequences – been used to justify anti-Semitism. This is wrong for two reasons. The first is that the worst that can be said is that these recount the bad decisions of the Jewish leadership and their supporters nearly two thousand years ago. If you were able to look at fifty generations' worth of anybody's ancestors you would uncover terrible deeds. The second reason is more subtle and deserves careful thought. What we see here in the Gospels are not the actions of cartoonish villains who love evil, but of religious leaders, fundamentally decent people, who are faced with a real and concrete threat to a religious system that they hold – with some justification – to be the most important thing in life. (They weren't even being unrealistic: the catastrophe of AD 70 was to destroy the temple, the nation and very nearly Judaism itself.) So, in order to protect what they consider to be supremely holy, they concede that it is necessary to allow bad things. When something you value intensely – and especially if it is a 'holy' thing – is threatened, the temptation to shrug your shoulders and permit a 'lesser evil' to occur is a very powerful one. It's also worth noting a warning here that we should all heed: the danger that committees can mysteriously approve deeds which individuals would reject. So when, for instance, in Mel Gibson's film *The Passion of the Christ* the Jewish leadership are stereotypically presented as *Jews*, he is not just being arguably anti-Semitic, he misses the point. The terrible reality is not that the members of the Sanhedrin were strange and utterly devoid of morals; they were *Everyman*. They were us. There, very truthfully, but for the grace of God go we.

On hearing the news that there was a warrant out for his arrest, Jesus went to a village near the wilderness until Passover.[41] The confrontation, when it came, would be at the time of his choosing not theirs.

With the approach of Passover – the most nationalistic of all the Jewish feasts – Jesus' friends and enemies were both waiting to see if he would turn up in Jerusalem. The remarkable miracle at Bethany had not been forgotten; indeed, much to the annoyance of Jesus' enemies, Lazarus had become something of a celebrity: a walking, talking testimony to Jesus' power and authority.[42]

A week before the Passover feast began Jesus and the disciples arrived in Bethany. There, probably on the Saturday night as the Sabbath ended,[10] a dinner was held in Jesus' honour with Lazarus present.[43] At the meal, Mary, one of Lazarus's sisters, anointed Jesus with an expensive ointment. Her action was critically received by the disciples and Jesus had to rebuke them. Her action, he said, was a beautiful thing. Then he sounded a sombre note: what she had done was to anoint him for burial. Jesus was clearly in no doubt about what Jerusalem held in store for him.

All three accounts of this link with it the name of one disciple: Judas Iscariot. Judas – the treasurer of the Twelve – was openly aggrieved at what he saw as the frivolous waste of the valuable ointment. Soon afterwards he began discussions with Jesus' enemies in Jerusalem.

At this point, with Jesus just about to enter into Jerusalem, we need to pause. All the players in this drama are now in place for the imminent confrontation. In Jerusalem and its outskirts we have Jesus, his puzzled followers, the would-be traitor, the excited crowds, the hostile Jewish leadership and the tense Roman authorities. Conflict is inevitable. Yet the events of the Last Week – the trial, crucifixion and resurrection – are so linked with the issues of what Jesus taught and who he claimed to be that these need to be examined first.

---

10 The Jewish day began and ended at sunset; so the Sabbath began on the Friday evening and ended on Saturday sunset.

7

FOLLOWERS AND FRIENDS

In this chapter we want to look at those men and women who Jesus gathered around him. When one thinks of Jesus' followers one immediately thinks of the twelve disciples. Although they were central to Jesus' mission, beyond them were many other followers and friends, both men and women.

THE TWELVE DISCIPLES

What does the word 'disciple' mean? It is to be much more than a follower: you can 'follow' a football team and never leave the comfort of your settee. To be a disciple carries with it ideas of dedication, obedience, effort and that related but unloved word, *discipline*. The best example of being a disciple would be the traditional one of someone becoming apprenticed to a master in a particular craft or trade. To be a disciple of Jesus is to be an apprentice or imitator of him.

There are several striking features about the way that Jesus selected the disciples.

The first and perhaps the most striking feature is that Jesus *selected* them. So Jesus called Simon Peter and his brother Andrew from the middle of their work as fishermen and did the same with James and John; Matthew the tax collector had a similar unexpected summons.[1] Ultimately all the Twelve were called.[2] While the religious teachers of the day also had disciples, the normal pattern was for disciples to choose their teachers, not the other way round. A man who wanted religious instruction would have looked at the rabbis on offer, chosen the one he felt was the best instructor of the Law and then applied to become one of his pupils. Doing what Jesus did, taking the initiative in choosing and summoning people to follow you, was as rare then as it is now.

The second striking feature is the focus of the discipleship that they were summoned to. Normally, to follow a rabbi or religious teacher was to learn from him how to study God's Law. Yet Mark says: 'Jesus went up on a mountain and called out the ones he wanted to go with him. And they came to him. Then he appointed twelve of them . . . They were to accompany him.'[3] Jesus was calling the disciples not to study the Law, but to be *with him*. In doing that, Jesus was doing what he did in many other issues: putting himself above the Law. The awesome significance of that should not be overlooked: only one person was above the Law and he, of course, was God.

A third feature is that by choosing to call twelve men, Jesus was doing something profoundly symbolic. Since its earliest days, the nation of Israel had been made up of twelve tribes and the loss nearly eight hundred years earlier of most of those tribes into Assyrian captivity had been a blow to Judaism. One of the promises associated with the coming Messiah was that he would restore the nation of Israel and the missing tribes.[4] By choosing twelve followers, Jesus was claiming to be the one who would restore and remake God's people.

WHY DID JESUS HAVE DISCIPLES?

Let's suggest three reasons.

First, the disciples were to be witnesses to who he was. They were to be people who could say that they knew him and could testify to what he had said and done. For him to turn his followers into effective witnesses involved two things: teaching them and sending them. Jesus taught his followers both directly and indirectly. In the Gospels we see Jesus directly instructing the Twelve in private, explaining his parables to them and asking them questions to make them think. Indirect learning was also important in the training of the Twelve: Jesus kept them close to him for what was, in all probability, the best part of three years, and the influence of that must have been enormous. As educationalists never cease to tell us, learning is as much caught as taught.

We see in the Gospels that early on in their discipleship Jesus sent the disciples out to be witnesses for him. As part of that task, Jesus bestowed on them his authority. The Twelve thus became his authorised representatives: they stood in his place. To accept one of them was to accept Jesus; to reject one was to reject him.[11] With the resurrection and the coming of the Holy Spirit, the role of being a witness acquired an entirely new depth and breadth. The depth lay in the fact that Jesus' disciples were now to be those who could testify that he had risen from the dead and all that this meant; the breadth lay in the fact that they would take that message to the whole world.

Second, the disciples were to help and befriend Jesus. Much of what the Twelve did was, one presumes, routine and unspectacular: they managed the crowds around Jesus (or tried to), were responsible for getting food and were in charge of making practical arrangements.[5] It would be misleading, however, to see the disciples' help as being only practical. Built into the concept that Jesus was truly human is surely that he had the universal human need for friendship and community. There are little glimpses of this side of his personality: the way he called his followers 'his friends',[6] the way he wanted companionship in Gethsemane[7] and even, it seems, the sense of outrage at being betrayed by a friend.[8] The Twelve – and the others – were not just Jesus' followers, they were also friends.

Third, as we have noted, Jesus chose the Twelve because they were to be the beginning of a new people of Israel. Much of Jesus' teaching to his followers was about how this new community was to function. So we see him teaching his followers that they are to be forgiving, showing sacrificial love and being servants of one another. So tightly knit and caring is this new community that it is no cliché to call it a family rather than an organisation. In fact, when Jesus talks about his disciples after the resurrection, he calls them 'my brothers'.[9]

This community aspect of the disciples is important. The extent to which Jesus did know about the future is a challenging question (see for example Mark 13:32), but the time and energy that he put into

---

11 The word 'apostle' – normally used for the disciples after the resurrection – carries the idea of someone being an authorised delegate.

training his disciples suggests that he envisaged a spreading and multiplying community of followers. Jesus was planning for posterity.

A PROFILE OF THE TWELVE

From the four lists in the New Testament[10] we can see that the Twelve were Simon Peter, Andrew, James, John, Philip, Bartholomew (or Nathaniel), Matthew, Thomas, 'James the Less', 'Judas the son of Jacob' (or Thaddeus), Simon the Zealot and Judas Iscariot.

Simon Peter and *Andrew* were fishermen brothers who had been followers of John the Baptist. Simon Peter, who had originally been called Simon before Jesus changed his name to Peter ('the Rock'), was the spokesperson for the Twelve from the start. In the Gospels, Peter's record as a disciple is decidedly uneven. The high point was his declaration that he believed Jesus was the Messiah; his low point came during the trial of Jesus when he repeatedly denied publicly that he ever knew him. After the resurrected Jesus had restored Peter and the Spirit had been given, he became leader of the early church. We know that Peter was married and that he took his wife with him on his later travels.[11] We know much less about his brother Andrew.

James and *John*, the sons of Zebedee, were another pair of fishermen. Jesus termed the two the 'Sons of Thunder', possibly because of their volatile tempers.[12] (If so, and if, as tradition claims, John is indeed the author of the Gospel and the three letters attributed to him, their emphasis on love suggests a truly transformed life.)

About *Philip* and *Bartholomew* we know very little. From the parallel accounts of the conversion of *Matthew*, we know that he was also known as Levi. Originally a tax collector, Matthew is widely considered the author of the Gospel that bears his name.

Thomas has, perhaps unfairly, become notorious for his initial doubt – not unnatural under the circumstances – over the resurrection of Jesus.[13] This has overshadowed his earlier determination to follow Jesus regardless of the cost and his extraordinary insight in acknowledging the resurrected Jesus as Lord and God.[14]

Of *James the Less* we know little. It is generally assumed that the 'Mary the mother of James and Joseph' who was at the crucifixion and the discovery of the empty tomb was his mother.[15] In this case a disciple's mother is more notable than he is!

Judas the son of Jacob is another obscure figure who also went under the name of Thaddeus. It seems likely that *Simon the Zealot* was so called because he held militant and even revolutionary views.

On account of his betrayal of Jesus, *Judas Iscariot* is a name that always comes at the end of all the lists of the Twelve.

While we do not know why Jesus chose the men that he did, three features stand out. One is that all the disciples seem to have been ordinary working men without any formal religious training.[16] A second is that the Twelve were a diverse group, drawn from many different backgrounds and professions. A third feature is what one can only call the 'ordinariness' of the Twelve: their only remarkable feature seems to have been that they were unremarkable. Throughout the centuries many people have been encouraged by the thought that 'if God can use these people he can use me'.

We know very little about what ultimately happened to most of the Twelve. James we are told was executed by Herod Agrippa some time before AD 44[17] and so became the first of the Twelve to be martyred. The traditions that speak of Peter being martyred in Rome about AD 64 may well be correct. Tales that talk of John living to an old age in Ephesus and being the only one of the Twelve not to be martyred, and that Thomas went as far as India to preach, are also perfectly believable. But about the rest of the Twelve there are only shadowy tales. There is a little remarked but very significant point about this silence over their fate. It is quite simply that no one considered themselves the successor to Jesus: he was, in every sense, a one-off. His followers preached about Jesus as Lord, but no one claimed to have inherited that role.

What we can be certain of is that the apostles took seriously their mission to spread the good news of Jesus to the ends of the earth. It may not be too far-fetched to imagine the Twelve clustered around the best map of the known world, deciding amongst themselves who would go where. Certainly within a few years of the resurrection, most of the Twelve seem to have left Jerusalem. Although there are gaping holes in our knowledge, the fact that by AD 60 there were many Christians in Rome and by AD 100 there were flourishing churches across most of the Roman Empire is proof that most of the Twelve did, in the end, fulfil the task they had been chosen for and entrusted with.

OTHER FOLLOWERS

Jesus had a much larger group of followers who were also considered disciples; on one occasion he sent out a group of seventy-two who are termed 'disciples'.[18] These other disciples also put themselves under Jesus' authority and obeyed his teaching. Yet there were differences:

- Whereas the Twelve were called, at least some of this group had chosen to follow Jesus.[19]

- Remarkably for first-century Judaism (and many cultures since), this larger group included women.

- The larger group of disciples was very varied socially. Some were affluent: one of the women was 'Joanna the wife of Chuza, Herod's business manager' and she and many other women used their own resources to support Jesus and his disciples.[20] Others were from lower down the social ladder. The extent of the social extremes is seen in two people who became followers of Jesus in Jericho: Bartimaeus, a penniless beggar whose sight had been restored; and Zacchaeus, the chief tax collector.[21]

- The larger group of disciples was not restricted to one age bracket. We know of three mothers who followed Jesus at least some of the time: Mary, the mother of Jesus; the mother of James and John; and the mother of James the Lesser. Jesus' mother must have been close to fifty and the other two were at least forty. That may not seem striking until you realise that if you survived the first few years of childhood, your life expectancy was around forty to fifty years[22] rather than our seven or eight decades. In other words, these women were the equivalent of our senior citizens.

- Some of the people in this larger group of followers do not appear to have left their homes or jobs. So Lazarus, Mary and Martha stayed in Bethany. John describes Joseph of Arimathea, a rich member of the Sanhedrin, as a 'secret disciple' of Jesus, a term that has been an encouragement to many followers of Jesus in cultures where the open declaration of your faith is an invitation to receiving a death sentence.[23]

Two points arise from this larger group. First, although these people are never considered 'apostles', they were not in any way 'second-class disciples'. After all, it was the women from this group who stood by Jesus at the cross and many of the resurrection appearances were to these people.[24] Second, it is this larger more varied group of followers, not the Twelve, who surely act as a model for who should constitute the church.

NOTE: JESUS AND WOMEN

The presence of women in the larger group of Jesus' followers is remarkable. In Jesus' culture, as in that of most of the ancient world (and much of the world today), the role of women was very largely limited to being home-based wives and mothers. Although Jewish culture – or at least some aspects of it – was much more pro-women than most other societies of the time, women were still treated as little more than possessions. Josephus, despite being a well-educated Jew, managed to claim that it was 'the teaching of Scripture that a woman is inferior to her husband in all things'.[25] (What 'Scripture' Josephus believed he was quoting is unknown.) That such negative values were widely held can be seen in the disciples' surprise at finding Jesus talking with a woman in Samaria.[26]

Jesus, however, was radical in his views of women.

- Jesus' followers included various women, some of whom travelled with him and the Twelve.[27] Both he and they would have risked shameful allegations of immorality.

- Women played a major role in the events leading up to the cross. The only followers who stayed with Jesus at the cross, apart from John the disciple, were women.

- Women are prominent in the accounts of the resurrection. John tells us how the risen Jesus appeared first to Mary Magdalene and instructed her 'to go and tell his brothers'.[28] Remarkably, Mary ended up preaching that key part of the good news to the apostles!

- Jesus cared for women. There are several places where we are told that he healed them.[29] When encountering a widow burying her only son – who would have been her sole means of support – we read that 'when [Jesus] saw her, his heart overflowed with compassion. "Don't cry!" he said,' and raised the man from the dead.[30]

- Jesus defended women. He lived in a world in which it was women who were considered to be the source of sexual sin. Yet in the Sermon on the Mount, Jesus blamed men, not women, for lust.[31] He publicly accepted honour from a woman who is described euphemistically as 'having lived a sinful life' and defended her against her accusers.[32] When presented with a woman caught in adultery, Jesus refused to condemn her and, forcing her male accusers to leave, let her go with a warning.[33]

- Jesus taught women with the view that they could, in turn, teach. When Luke tells us that Mary 'sat at the Lord's feet, listening to what he taught' he is using a technical expression for a student being taught by a rabbi.[34] This is in remarkable contrast to mainstream Judaism. The Mishnah, a collection of Jewish oral law from the early third century AD, dissuades fathers from teaching their daughters the Torah because they are foolish.[35]

- The longest discussion recorded in the Gospels – indeed in the New Testament – is between Jesus and a Samaritan woman.[36]

- In his parables, Jesus makes almost equal use of images from the world of women and men, and uses women as positive models. In fact in one parable about a woman who searches for a lost coin, the woman represents God.[37]

- Jesus' teaching on divorce is revealing. In the culture of the day, a man could treat his wife as little more than property and divorce was easy. So Josephus could calmly write: 'At this period I divorced my wife, being displeased at her behaviour.'[38] If a man did divorce his wife, any hurt or insult was considered to be to the woman's family, not to her. Yet Jesus taught that whoever divorced his wife and married someone else, committed adultery against her.[39]

Some people would say that Jesus should have done more for the role of women. It's a point worth considering. Normally when dealing with someone who falls below contemporary standards in such areas of concern as gender or racial equality there is a standard defence: 'Be fair: they were a child of their time.' The trouble for the followers of Jesus is that this is not an excuse that can be used: after all, we claim that in the area of morals, Jesus was *not* a child of his time.

Several responses can be made here. The first is that for us to judge someone from a distant culture and a distant time by our standards is to engage in precisely the sort of unsympathetic insensitivity that we are criticising. The second is that although Jesus stood outside his time, he did not, and could not, stand completely outside his culture. For him to have tried to impose modern standards on the ancient world would have been catastrophic for him and his mission. We would suggest that in the area of women he pushed things as far as his world allowed him to and sowed seeds for matters to be pushed even further. Jesus can hardly be blamed for the fact that his followers have so often declined to challenge their culture. And finally, it's a little bit unfair to criticise someone for not being radical enough when he was crucified precisely because he was *too* radical.

Ultimately, in a world that saw women as those who were markedly inferior to men and who ought to be submissive to men, Jesus saw them as human beings of equal worth and dignity.

8

MIRACLES

Any consideration of Jesus must examine the claims that he performed miracles. Even the most sceptical scholars will accept three things about Jesus: he lived, he was crucified; and he had a reputation as a miracle worker.[1] Miracles raise all sorts of important issues, not least the question of whether our world can be entirely defined and limited by our understanding of science. Let's start thinking about Jesus and the miracles by looking at the claims made by the Gospels.

The Gospels describe Jesus performing at least thirty specific miracles and there were apparently many more.[2] Early on in his ministry Jesus sent a message to John the Baptist through John's disciples: 'Tell him what you have seen and heard – the blind see, the lame walk, those with leprosy are cured, the deaf hear, the dead are raised to life.'[3] As recorded in the book of Acts, Peter assumes that his hearers in Jerusalem are well aware of the 'powerful miracles, wonders, and signs' that God did through Jesus.[4] No ancient historical character has as many miracles associated with them.[5] The most extraordinary miracle associated with Jesus is his own resurrection, something that from the very earliest days of the church was considered to be the foundation of its existence.

The miracles claimed for Jesus are not just numerous but also diverse. Jesus is described as having healed a range of disorders: bringing sight to those who were blind,[6] curing contagious skin disorders,[7] returning mobility to the lame,[8] ending fevers,[9] restoring a severed ear,[10] ending a long-term haemorrhage[11] and restoring a withered hand.[12] The most extreme form of healing is shown by three records of Jesus bringing people back to life:[12] Jairus' daughter, a

---

12 These events were different from Jesus' own resurrection which, as we will discuss in chapter 14, seems to have involved his body being changed into a radically new form which would never die again. These individuals had presumably to go through the whole business of death again.

widow's son and Lazarus of Bethany.[13] The character of some of the afflictions that were healed means that they cannot be explained simply as psychosomatic disorders.

The Gospels also tell us that Jesus demonstrated an extraordinary power over nature: he miraculously multiplied bread and fish,[14] changed water into wine,[15] calmed a storm,[16] walked on water[17] and gave fishermen extraordinary catches of fish.[18] The Gospels speak of Jesus having miraculous knowledge and being aware of hidden facts and attitudes.[19] Jesus also performed exorcisms with people oppressed by demonic powers.[20]

Several features about Jesus' miracles should be noted.

- Miracles are found in all the Gospels. There is no trace of any growth in number or scale of the miracles with time. In fact Mark – almost certainly the earliest Gospel – has more 'miracles per page' than the others.

- In the Old Testament, miracles are described as occurring either because God has chosen to do them or because people have specifically prayed for God to act. Yet when Jesus performs miracles he doesn't pray to God; he just does them – apparently on the basis of his own authority.

- Jesus performed miracles in an unspectacular way without ritual and with a minimum of actions and words.[21] Sometimes he turned bystanders away in order to perform miracles; on other occasions he asked that his healings be unreported.[22]

- Jesus refused to do miracles on demand to prove who he was and he had little time for sensation seekers.[23] He never did miracles for profit or publicity or even to save himself.[24] Jesus either did miracles out of compassion[25] or as 'signs' to his identity.[26]

- There are parallels between Jesus' parables and his miracles. Both communicate who he was to those who were prepared to listen and think. The miracles are, in many ways, acted parables: they challenge observers as to who Jesus is.

- Although the book of Acts records miracles being performed by the apostles in the first years of the church, it is striking that here the miracles are done 'in the name of Jesus' or attributed to the power of Jesus.

THE MIRAGE OF THE MIRACLE-FREE JESUS

People regularly try to create an account of Jesus where the miraculous is missing. So, for instance, many people consider that the feeding of the five thousand happened because Jesus encouraged everybody to contribute their own food in a spontaneous shared meal. With this comes the arrogant assumption that first-century Palestine was populated by people simple enough to cry 'It's a miracle!' at the slightest coincidence or oddity. In fact in the world of the Bible, claims of the miraculous are far rarer than many assume. There are no miracles associated with the great figures of David and Solomon, and miracles are almost entirely absent in the prophetic books that make up the second half of the Old Testament. A very significant fact in the case of the claims of the miraculous associated with Jesus is that there are none whatsoever linked to his contemporary, John the Baptist.

In reality, it is impossible to create a 'miracle-free' Jesus. Claims of the supernatural are present throughout the Gospels, not just in the miracles but in the virginal conception, the appearances of angels, the references to the devil and, of course, in the resurrection itself. The miracles are also so tightly intertwined with both Jesus' teaching and the events of his life that it is impossible to remove them. For instance, as we have noted, the Gospels record a major crisis when, just after Jesus had miraculously fed five thousand men and their families, the crowds suddenly wanted to make him king.[27] To propose there was no miracle makes nonsense of the account: it's hard to see how a bring-and-share lunch could have risked triggering a messianic uprising.

Equally, the rest of the New Testament assumes that Jesus was associated with the miraculous,[28] including the resurrection which Paul sees as being an essential fundamental of the faith.[29] Indeed to accept the resurrection and deny the possibility of other miracles is illogical. Finally, but importantly, the traditions about Jesus outside the New Testament[30] talk about him as an exorcist and a miracle worker.[13] None of the hostile references to Jesus deny his miracles; they just attribute them to him having occult power.[31]

You cannot remove the miraculous from the life of Jesus. The supernatural runs through the accounts of his life like the steel in reinforced concrete and is just as impossible to remove.

THE CHALLENGE OF THE MIRACULOUS

Many people reject the accounts of the miraculous in the Gospels because they hold dogmatically to the view that any kind of supernatural intervention is impossible.[14] On that basis they are forced to conclude that, however authentic these Gospel accounts may appear, they simply *cannot* be true. In fact that is an act of faith that needs examining. Any definition of miracles defines them as 'unusual' events and here we want to defend the possibility of such unusual events occurring with this most unusual of men.

First let's look at the objection that miracles, or extranormal, supernatural or paranormal events, are impossible.

Objection 1: 'You can't prove miracles exist'

True. But it is actually surprisingly difficult to prove anything, including the rather fundamental fact that *reality* itself exists. Certainly when it comes to the past we have to acknowledge the truth that all historical events are unprovable in the rigorous sense associated with science. We can't watch broadcasts of Julius Caesar's speeches or plant a video camera in the tomb of the buried Jesus. However, if we can't – in a strict sense – prove the existence of the miraculous, neither

---

13 Early in the fourth century, the historian Eusebius described how a man called Quadratus had written to Emperor Hadrian around AD 120 defending Christianity. The full text of what he wrote is lost, but Eusebius quotes a long sentence from it in his *Ecclesiastical Histories* (IV:3). 'The works of our Saviour were lasting, for they were genuine: those who were healed and those who were raised from the dead were seen not only when they were healed and when they were raised but were also present, not merely while the Saviour was on earth, but also after his death; they were alive for quite a while, so that some of them lived even to our day.' In other words, some of those raised from the dead and healed by Jesus around AD 30 were still alive around the end of the first century as witnesses to his power.

14 How consistent such people are here is questionable: faced with serious problems many 'sceptics' either pray or welcome the prayers of others. Ask any hospital chaplain.

can we prove its nonexistence either. To say that miracles do not happen is, rather awkwardly, to make a statement of faith.

Objection 2: 'There is no evidence for miracles'

Interestingly, this is very much an objection that arises from within the Western world. In the 'Majority World' it seems that belief in the supernatural is universal. In fact almost all cultures believe in some sort of God or gods and that there are supernatural forces of good and evil. Scepticism about the supernatural has largely been confined to individuals in Western culture from the nineteenth century onwards. Even here such scepticism seems to be superficial, as evidenced by the hunger for films and books based on the supernatural and the spread of mysticism. Of course, just because a view is held by a majority doesn't mean that it's true, but the scarcity of cultures based on total scepticism about the miraculous is very striking.

Here we need to refer to an extraordinary publication by the very distinguished New Testament scholar Craig Keener that, as he tells it, started off as a footnote to his monumental work on the New Testament book of Acts.[32] Keener felt that he ought to defend the miraculous events described within Acts by carefully documenting and detailing modern miracles. This 'footnote' grew into a two-volume work[33] running to over 1,000 pages of carefully documented 'extranormal' events, such as healings and nature miracles, that makes for fascinating reading. If even *one* of these almost innumerable accounts is true, then the rule that miracles cannot happen is broken: they can.

Keener's documentation confirms what many Christians have frequently experienced: occasions when, in answer to prayer, there has been a dramatic healing or a resolution of some problem that defies all natural explanation.

Objection 3: 'The Laws of Nature don't allow miracles'

Although you often hear such statements, they display a fundamental misunderstanding of the basis of science. In reality the 'Laws of Nature' are a provisional description of those principles by which the universe has been observed to work. They do not – and cannot – rule out the possibility of those principles changing or being modified. On this basis the 'Laws of Nature' can only *describe* what *has* been observed to happen; they cannot *prescribe* what *must* happen.

To pronounce with authority that miracles cannot occur is to make the remarkable claim that you completely understand how *everything* works. If it were possible to put the entire universe in a laboratory and examine it, as it were, from *outside* then it might be possible to state that the miraculous doesn't occur. Of course we can't do that. The possibility that there might be something – or *someone* – outside the physical universe is something that we can neither disprove nor easily prove. In the fifth century Saint Augustine wrote, 'Miracles are not contrary to nature; but only contrary to what we know about nature.'[34]

In fact much of the scepticism of miracles reflects the lingering persistence of a comfortable view of the universe that was undermined by Einstein and has since crumbled. Since the Theory of Relativity was published the universe has become so much stranger that it is unwise to be dogmatic about the impossibility of miracles. Very weird things occur in quantum physics.[15] They don't prove that miracles do occur but they do encourage caution about saying they can't happen. It is not, generally speaking, scientists who declare confidently that science proves that miracles are impossible; they know better.

Objection 4: 'To admit the possibility of the miraculous would undermine the modern world'

A widespread reason for rejecting the miraculous in the Gospels is the fear that this would open the door to an onslaught of belief in superstition and magic that would take us back to the Middle Ages. We sympathise: it might be fine to read books or watch films in which

---

15 A spectacular example is that of 'quantum entanglement' whereby two particles of light can be so interlinked that, even if separated by millions of miles, a change in one particle will instantly affect the other without there being any physical connection whatsoever between them. The whole thing so unnerved Einstein that he called it 'spooky action at a distance'.

magic plays a part, but to have it occur in reality would be unsettling. Could my ill-health be due to a curse? Is my neighbour's wealth because they used witchcraft? Will I fail my driving test because I just walked under a ladder?

Curiously, although the Christian view of the world accepts the supernatural, it acts as a defence – perhaps the only good one – against such views. The biblical position is that the universe is run by a God who firmly governs both natural and the supernatural so that everything operates on his rules. Any occurrence of the supernatural is precisely because God the Lawgiver has, on a *temporary basis*, permitted an exception to his laws. In fact, when you look at history you find that biblical Christianity was an enemy of superstition and magic to the extent that it provided a fertile soil for modern science to develop in.[35]

Now to suggest that the miracles of Jesus occurred is not to defend every claimed case of the paranormal: you almost certainly do not have fairies in your garden and you do not need to be any more concerned about taking a plane on Friday 13th than on any other date. It is, however, to point out that if Jesus was indeed God become one of us, then there is a perfect logic in him performing miracles. As 'the Word',[36] the universe's maker and sustainer, Jesus had – and has – both the authority and the power to do what he chooses with his creation. For such a unique individual to perform unique acts has a powerful logic.

THE SIGNIFICANCE OF JESUS' MIRACLES

Why did Jesus perform miracles? He certainly didn't do them for fame or fortune. Indeed some of the attention they brought him was unwelcome. For example, Luke tells us that Herod Antipas summoned Jesus before him to perform a miracle.[37]

The key to the meaning of the miracles lies in that little word used in John's Gospel: *signs*. The miracles are signposts, for those who consider them carefully, that point to the truth about Jesus. Five particular features stand out.

1. Jesus' miracles point to his identity

The fact that Jesus did miracles showed that he was, at very least, a prophet. The greatest miracle-workers of the Old Testament were all prophets: Moses, Elijah and Elisha. Indeed, some of Jesus' miracles carry unmistakable and almost certainly intentional echoes of all three. Moses oversaw the miraculous feeding of vast crowds in the wilderness; Jesus did the same.[38] Elijah brought a widow's son back to life; so did Jesus.[39] Elisha healed a leper; Jesus heals ten.[40] Many of those who thought about Jesus' actions concluded that he was a prophet.[41] The miracles demonstrated both that Jesus was a prophet and that God was with him.[42]

The miracles also pointed deeper. By showing that Jesus had the power over sin and evil that was expected of God's King, they pointed to him being the Messiah. When answering the anguished question of the imprisoned John the Baptist as to whether he was the Messiah, Jesus referred to his miracles as proof that he was indeed the one who was expected.[43] In the three miracles that involve raising the dead,[44] Jesus demonstrated that he was Lord over death itself.

Some of the miracles clearly pointed to Jesus being more than any human figure. Mark tells us that after Jesus had calmed the storm, the disciples 'were absolutely terrified. "Who is this man?" they asked each other. "Even the wind and waves obey him!"'[45] They knew the Old Testament said that the stilling of storms was something only God could do.[46] When Jesus walked on water they declared, on the same basis, that he was the Son of God.[47] Jesus also used a miracle of healing to show that he could forgive sins; another action that only God do.[48]

So Jesus' miracles were signs that pointed to him being not only a prophet but also the Messiah. Yet they went beyond even that: by doing what only God could do, Jesus showed that he was equal to God; indeed that he *was* God.

2. Jesus' miracles point to the coming of God's Kingdom

The Gospel writers link Jesus' miracles to the coming of God's Kingdom. As God's King, Jesus began to bring God's rule of peace and justice into a turbulent world that had rebelled against him. This aspect of the miracles is most dramatically seen in the encounters that Jesus had with occult powers.[49] When criticised for exorcising a demonised man, Jesus said: 'But if I am casting out demons by the power of God, then the Kingdom of God has arrived among you.'[50] Jesus was God's King who fought Satan's forces, and as he extended God's Kingdom he liberated captives.[51]

Most of us have little experience of the demonic and many people have found these reports of exorcisms problematic. There have been attempts to rationalise them, explaining them away as illnesses and psychological disturbances that Jesus, as a man of his time, interpreted as demonic. Yet several facts must be considered. First, Jesus clearly distinguished between illness and demonic possession. So while Jesus often touched the sick as part of his healing, he never laid hands on 'demoniacs' but instead ordered the evil spirit to depart. Equally, where we have any details of what happened, the demons also seem to have recognised who Jesus was. Second, the apparent absence of such phenomena in the West may be misleading. In parts of the world where occult practices, including the worship of spirits, are widespread, demonic phenomena and possession appear to be common. Indeed there are credible suggestions that, as the West becomes increasingly post-Christian, occultic activity is returning in force. Third, possession and demonic phenomena seem to be more common at some times and places than at others. Many writers have seen the apparent epidemic of open demonic activity at the time of Jesus as the response by the powers of evil to God's direct intervention in the world. After all, to preach about the coming of the Kingdom is not simply to talk about who does rule, but about who doesn't. Ultimately, the Kingdom of God is not a matter of words or concepts, but about a spiritual struggle with the human race's great enemy, the devil. Jesus' miracles demonstrated that here he was the supreme victor.

Here a strong warning needs to be issued. In the same way that saying 'the devil made me do it' is an unacceptable excuse to explain why we did something wrong, to say of some evil or personality issue that 'it's the devil at work' is almost always equally unacceptable. An awful lot that is attributed to direct attack by the demonic is no more than the results of our messed-up human nature. There have been some dreadfully misguided attempts at do-it-yourself exorcisms that have resulted in harm to all concerned and discredit to the church. Exorcism should only be conducted by church leaders who have discernment and experience in this area.

3. Jesus' miracles point to God's coming reign

Miracles also point to the future. They look forward to the day when, at Jesus' return, God's Kingdom will be fully and finally established. You can think of them as being like cinema trailers that tell you about some forthcoming spectacle: in this case the ultimate, glorious restoration of the universe. So the healing of the sick looks forward to the time when there will be no illness; the feeding of the crowds to Jesus' great banquet of eternity; and the raising of the dead to the ending of death itself.[52]

4. Jesus' miracles point to God's character

Jesus' miracles don't just show us that he is the Messiah; they show us what *kind* of Messiah he is. In the miracles we see in particular something of Jesus' compassion and mercy. Even at the moment of his arrest, when he might have been fully justified in thinking of himself, he showed his compassion by healing one of his captors.[53] In the Old Testament, God frequently describes himself as compassionate and merciful: Jesus' miracles demonstrated what that means in practice.[54] In all the miracles there is only one that is negative: the cursing of the barren fig tree[55] which is an 'acted parable' of judgement on a religious system that had promised fruit but didn't bear it.

Particularly significant is the way that the Gospels record Jesus performing miracles for people at the edges of society: a woman with a condition that left her ritually unclean; blind beggars; ostracised lepers; and demoniacs expelled from a community. Jesus didn't just heal Jews either; he healed Samaritans and Gentiles, too. Jesus' miracles demonstrate something of God's heart towards the human race and the world he has made.

5. Jesus' miracles point to the need to have faith in him

At the end of his Gospel, John wrote, 'The disciples saw Jesus do many other miraculous signs in addition to the ones recorded in this book. But these are written so that you may continue to believe that Jesus is the Messiah, the Son of God, and that by believing in him you will have life by the power of his name.'[56]

Jesus' miracles are events that demand a response. They are not curiosities of history to be debated or paranormal phenomena to be probed; they are, above all, a challenge to us to be committed to Jesus. They are encouragements to those who have no faith to look deeper and they are invitations to those on the edge of faith to take the final step.

Nevertheless, it is important to note that while miracles can generate faith, they do not compel it. Because how you treat a miracle depends on what you believe, faith is required in order to correctly understand the significance of it. So, in Jesus' time there were many people who saw his miracles but denied their meaning. Some no doubt thought they had seen an illusion, others that they had merely witnessed some bizarre marvel of nature. Still others saw the miracles as coming from the devil.[57]

Miracles should never be dismissed lightly. The Gospels make it clear that to reject the evidence of a miracle is a serious matter. Jesus gave this sad warning over two towns where he had done miracles: 'What sorrow awaits you, Korazin and Bethsaida! For if the miracles I did in you had been done in wicked Tyre and Sidon, their people would have repented of their sins long ago, clothing themselves in burlap [sackcloth] and throwing ashes on their heads to show their remorse.'[58]

Jesus' miracles are indeed best seen as signs. For those who are prepared to think about them, they point to many things: who Jesus is, the character of his Kingdom, the nature of the future, and God's character. Jesus' miracles challenged people to give their verdict on him. They still do.

9

HOW JESUS TAUGHT

Jesus sometimes referred to himself as 'the Teacher'[1] and his reputation as a teacher (or 'rabbi') was such that large crowds travelled long distances to hear him. In looking at his teaching we find a principle that we see elsewhere of him being what you might call 'familiar but utterly different'. So in Jesus' teaching we find much that clearly belongs to his culture but, at the same time, astonishing and radical differences. When temple guards were sent to arrest Jesus, they returned empty handed to the authorities with the excuse, 'We have never heard anyone speak like this!'[2]

The greatest difference in Jesus' teaching seems to have been the extraordinary personal authority that he claimed and which most people seem to have acknowledged. Most of the religious teaching of his day was based on tradition. This was passed on by a chain of transmission, so if a teacher wanted to give authority to a ruling he would always refer to the rabbis who had made it before: for example, 'Rabbi Schlomo following Rabbi Ezekiel who cited Rabbi Benjamin said . . .' Such statements may preserve teaching but they inevitably have a stale, second-hand air to them. In contrast, when Jesus taught he often began by saying, 'You have heard it said, but *I* say to you . . .' The personal authority that Jesus claimed was something that the people found remarkable, with the result that 'the crowds were amazed at his teaching, for he taught with real authority – quite unlike their teachers of religious law'.[3]

There was another sense in which Jesus spoke with authority: he came over as someone who knew first-hand what he was talking about. So, for example, he was able to talk about heaven as if he had personal experience of it. Perhaps most striking would have been his reference to God, widely felt to be a distant figure, by the familiar word 'Father'.

Jesus' authority goes even deeper and can be seen in a remarkable but widely overlooked phenomenon. In the Old Testament we find nearly a hundred occasions where, associated with some prophet, the little phrase 'the word of the Lord came to . . .' Yet although it is found in the New Testament in the context of John the Baptist[4] it is *never ever* used of Jesus. Neither do we get any mention of God in some way speaking 'through' Jesus. Quite simply the Gospels portray Jesus' teaching as if he had God's authority and indeed as if he *was* God. The description of him at the beginning of John's Gospel as 'the Word of God' seems utterly appropriate. Jesus does not speak as a prophet, but as one who is more than a prophet. No wonder people found his teaching striking.

There were other differences between Jesus and the religious teaching of his day. While the rabbis expected people to come to them, Jesus went to the people. He taught not only in synagogues and in the temple but also in homes, in fields, while travelling, and even from a boat. Where the rabbis tended to teach only a select group of male disciples, Jesus taught everybody. He also taught people that the rabbis considered unworthy to receive teaching: women, children, tax collectors, 'sinners' and even Samaritans and Gentiles.

Jesus taught wherever and whenever he could; he spoke to large crowds and to individuals. Sometimes he chose the topics, while on other occasions he let some incident or encounter act as the springboard for a lesson. Whether it was news of an atrocity or the blessing of babies, Jesus could use it as the basis for teaching.[5]

It's also evident that Jesus was a wonderful communicator. There was nothing of the formula or tradition in his teaching. He used many different ways of communicating: riddles, puns, proverbs and, above all, vivid imagery. Jesus was a great master of the most difficult task in any language: saying as much as possible with the minimum of words.

Even allowing for the double translation, from Aramaic into Greek and then into English, his words resound down through centuries.

- 'Do for others whatever you would like them to do for you. This is the essence of all that is taught in the law and the prophets.'[6]

- 'It's not what goes into your body that defiles you; you are defiled by what comes from your heart.'[7]

- 'The Sabbath was made to meet the needs of people, and not people to meet the requirements of the Sabbath.'[8]

- 'Life is not measured by how much you own.'[9]

- 'So don't worry about tomorrow, for tomorrow will bring its own worries. Today's trouble is enough for today.'[10]

- 'And what do you benefit if you gain the whole world but lose your own soul? Is anything worth more than your soul?'[11]

- 'God blesses those who hunger and thirst for justice, for they will be satisfied.'[12]

Jesus often used irony and paradox to turn prevailing wisdom upside down.

- 'God blesses those who realise their need for him, for the Kingdom of Heaven is given to them. God blesses those who mourn, for they will be comforted.'[13]

- 'If you refuse to take up your cross and follow me, you are not worthy of being mine. If you cling to your life, you will lose it; but if you give it up for me, you will find it.'[14]

- 'Those who are the greatest among you should take the lowest rank, and the leader should be like a servant.'[15]

It's important to realise that this is not just clever wordplay – the creation of elegant phrases or clever paradoxes for no other reason than to generate amusement or admiration – it reflects the truth that the Kingdom of God really does turn everything upside down. Jesus didn't just say things in a remarkable way; he said remarkable things, too. With him, content and presentation were both equally astonishing.

Whether his hearers were friend or foe, Jesus always seems to have known what to say. On one occasion he was asked whether it was right to pay taxes to the governing Romans. It was a question that carried a heavy load: to say 'no' was to invite trouble from the Romans; to say 'yes' was to guarantee the loss of popular support. Jesus' response was this: 'Give to Caesar what belongs to Caesar, and give to God what belongs to God.'[16] It's a brilliant answer that neatly puts Caesar in his place without giving cause for arrest but at the same time cleverly turns a challenge to him into one for his hearers.

Anyone remotely sceptical of the historicity of Jesus needs to consider the character of these words. Their sharpness, force and distinctive individuality are strong evidence that, rather than being the imagined sayings of some fictional creation, they are the authentic and powerful words of a striking, remarkable and unique man.

SYMBOLS AND PARABLES

One of the key elements in Jesus' teaching was his use of vivid imagery. So, for instance, we read that Jesus told his followers that they were to be 'the salt of the earth' and 'the light of the world'.[17] Sometimes the images are more extended, as in the attack on hypocrisy: 'Why worry about a speck in your friend's eye when you have a log in your own?'[18] Jesus describes himself, among other things, as 'the bread of life', the 'light of the world', the 'gate for the sheep', the 'good shepherd' and the 'true grapevine'.[19] It's worth pointing out that, as is still common in Middle Eastern and other cultures where the spoken word is more common than the written, Jesus uses exaggeration for impact. So, when he seems to recommend self-mutilation in order to avoid damnation[20] or the hating of family and even your own life in order to serve him[21] he's to be taken seriously but not literally.

An extended form of this use of imagery is the stories and illustrations that are the parables, which Jesus used extensively.[22] As one expert comments, 'As far as we know no one prior to Jesus used parables as consistently, creatively, and effectively as he did. Nor has anyone since.'[23] It's a striking fact that parables remain confined to the three Synoptic Gospels. Although John's Gospel is rich in images and metaphors, it has no parables and the early church made no use of parables in its teaching.[24]

What is a parable? They are illustrations, similes and stories that carry a meaning and have the intention of convincing the hearers.[25]

Sometimes they are as short as a sentence ('Can one blind person lead another? Won't they both fall into a ditch?')[26] and at other times they are almost short stories: for example the 'Good Samaritan'[27] and the 'Prodigal Son'.[28]

Parables generally and those of Jesus in particular have a number of distinctive features.

- Parables convey truth *indirectly*. Instead of tackling an issue head-on they tend to use an analogy or illustration instead. The English word *parabola*, which describes a type of curved path or orbit, helps us. You can consider parables as 'verbal parabolas' or curved ways of speaking.

- Parables are *brief*. It's an interesting exercise to try to condense one of Jesus' parables: it won't work. There are no unnecessary details.

- Parables are *simple*. Forget any long rambling anecdotes; these are simplified to extremes.

- Parables are *engaging and memorable*. They quite frequently have a twist in the tale. Many parables end on a note of reversal that is the equivalent to the punchline of a joke. Such teaching is not simply memorable, it gets passed on.

- Parables *are set in reality*. The stories involve the real world – there are no fantasy animals or mythical kings or queens. Almost all the parables are set in the very Jewish, agricultural world of first-century Palestine: firm evidence of their authenticity. It is striking how many parables refer to the 'woman's world' of cooking, cleaning and even widowhood.[29]

- Parables always *have a point*. Parables are like stories that begin 'now tell me what *you* would have done in this situation . . .' They demand a response whether of acceptance or rejection.[30]

Why did Jesus use parables? The fact that they were memorable and engaging ways of telling truth was no doubt important; however, the important thing was because of the way in which they conveyed truth *indirectly*. That was important in many ways.

- The curved path of the message of the parables allows them to *swing around defences*. If you were a Pharisee listening to Jesus and he had announced that he was going to attack the hypocrisy of the Pharisees, you would have immediately gone on the defensive: either gathered up your robes and stormed off or put on a pained smile and tried hard not to listen. Telling the story without saying what it was about meant that your hearers would have become involved with it and only when the punchline exploded in their face would they have realised that they'd been the target. And by then, of course, it was too late to put up defences.

- Parables *allowed indirect confrontation*. In most traditional agricultural societies there is a great deal of sensitivity to shame and honour, and the modern habit of many Western cultures of going 'straight to the point' is just too abrupt. In societies based around honour and shame, parables are common because they provide a way of saying unpopular things without inflicting public humiliation. Even today, anyone working in the Middle East or Asia soon learns to pay careful attention to any stories they are told, just in case they conceal a message intended for them. For instance, rather than directly criticising an employee publicly for being late, a manager might choose instead to tell the story about how once a late-arriving employee had missed out on being promoted. The person so targeted would recognise the warning without being publicly shamed. At times Jesus used parables for precisely this reason. So rather than directly attack those Pharisees who were self-righteous, he told the stories of 'the Pharisee and the Tax Collector'[31] and 'the Lost Son'.[32] Interestingly, in his last week, the parables Jesus told in Jerusalem (see Matthew 23) became increasingly more direct and unambiguous in their attacks on the leadership.

- Parables give the *protection of ambiguity*. Because they are indirect in their message they can provide a way of making a challenging statement without stirring up too much trouble. At the end of one exam in Beirut during the Lebanese Civil War, Chris was approached by one of his students who said with a cold smile, 'Sir, did you ever hear of the chemistry lecturer who failed a student and had his car blown up?' It was of course a parable and one with a chilling message. But expressed like that rather than as a blunt 'pass me or I'll blow your car up' it was impossible to do anything about it. (Fortunately the student got a good grade and the threat remained hypothetical.) It is possible to detect this deliberate ambiguity in many of Jesus' parables. In what is called 'the Parable of the Mustard Seed'[33] Jesus spoke of the Kingdom of Heaven being like the tiniest of seeds that grew to become a tree big enough for 'the birds of the air' to come and make nests in its branches. The 'birds of the air' echoes references in the Old Testament to the Gentiles[34] and is a prophecy that one day the Kingdom will be so great that not just Jews but all the nations of the world will take shelter under it. Had Jesus openly expressed such a view he might have simultaneously alarmed the Romans and antagonised a Jewish leadership whose only concern for the Gentiles was how to avoid them. But it's not easy to pin charges on someone on the basis of a parable.

• Parables present challenges to modern readers. In addition to the books already referred to, most modern Study Bibles (see recommendations at the end of the book) will give useful background and guidance on how best to interpret them.[35]

JESUS' TEACHING: THE POWER AND THE PASSION

Jesus spoke with authority and with compelling and involving illustrations. Yet there was more than this. Two more things come over in the Gospels: commitment and compassion.

Jesus had a deep *commitment* to his teaching. He saw himself as someone sent by God with a mission to humanity. In John's Gospel Jesus repeatedly utters a small, seemingly innocuous phrase: 'I have come'.[36] Elsewhere he talks about 'being sent'.[37] The parable of the tenants in the vineyard has the frustrated owner of the vineyard (God) finally sending his own son to deal with the rebellious tenants only for him to be rejected and murdered.[38] Jesus saw himself as come into the world with a mission to act for the human race and to communicate to it.

Jesus also had a deep *compassion* for his hearers. We read, 'When he saw the crowds, he had compassion on them, because they were confused and helpless, like sheep without a shepherd.'[39] Foreseeing the catastrophe looming ahead for Jerusalem and its inhabitants, Jesus wept over their fate.[40] Jesus loved individual men, women and children with all their hopes and hang-ups, fears and failures.[41]

Yet Jesus' undoubted compassion must not be allowed to overrule everything else. The authentic Jesus is a man who, to borrow a phrase, 'comforts the afflicted and afflicts the comfortable'. Jesus rejected all attempts to be anything less than 'the Lord'. So when someone wanted Jesus to sort out a dispute over an inheritance, he dismissed the question abruptly and instead gave his hearers a parable on greed.[42]

At times Jesus expressed anger although significantly never about treatment of himself. He was angry when he came across objections to healings on the Sabbath,[43] the temple being turned into a marketplace,[44] children being prevented from coming to him[45] and religion being turned from a blessing into a curse.[46] The anger, of course, is the inevitable consequence of a love that cares about injustice.

NOTE: THE CHALLENGES OF JESUS' TEACHING

First, we need to note *what* Jesus taught. It's all very well to confess that we truly believe that Jesus was somehow God in the flesh, the very Word of God become one of us. Excellent: but given that belief, shouldn't we treat Jesus' words with the utmost seriousness? Jesus ends the parable of the wise and foolish builders with the statement, 'Anyone who listens to my teaching and follows it is wise, like a person who builds a house on solid rock.'[47] Jesus is not requesting praise for his teaching but obedience to it.

Second, we need to pay attention to *how* he taught. Jesus was a compelling communicator: passionate, creative, authoritative and compassionate. Although there have been – and are – glorious exceptions, it has to be said his followers have not always lived up to those standards in the area of communication. We could all wish for greater gifts of intellect, knowledge or skill with language but we who are prepared to bear Christ's name should aim to communicate his truth as best we can.

10

WHAT JESUS TAUGHT

In considering how Jesus taught in the context of his world we recognised the pattern of a man who was both 'familiar but utterly different'. The same pattern applies when we consider the content of his teaching. So the Gospels present us with a roving preacher who, while teaching much that clearly fits within first-century Judaism, at the same time said things that no teacher of that culture could, or dared, say. Those who listened to Jesus' teaching might have recognised much of what they heard as familiar to them from synagogue teaching but then suddenly found themselves exposed to something utterly and shockingly unfamiliar. This principle of 'familiar but utterly different' is important. Jesus did not tear up and throw away the Old Testament. Indeed, as we have noted, it is interesting that at his trial he was not accused of wrongly teaching the Jewish faith, only of putting himself at its centre.

It is important we recognise that as a Jewish rabbi, Jesus would have held firm to the teaching of the Old Testament. The result of this is that although there are whole areas of life and morality that Jesus said nothing about, we don't need to guess what his position was. For instance, no teaching by Jesus has been preserved about idolatry, but then there didn't need to be. Idolatry is condemned in the first and second commandments and Jesus would have taken a similar position. Where Jesus did reinterpret, redefine or refocus the Old Testament teaching, the Gospels note the fact. So, they tell us that although Jesus did not condemn the Old Testament dietary laws, he pointed beyond them to the principle that it isn't *what* you eat that makes you unclean.[1] On the subject of the Sabbath – the subject of the fourth commandment[2] – Jesus again seemed to be less concerned about the practice than the principle.[3] And with respect to the temple, that focal point of Judaism, Jesus calmly said that everything that it stood for was fulfilled in him.[4]

So in considering Jesus' teaching we have to avoid the option – easy in an age where the Old Testament is an unfamiliar document – to imagine that Jesus only proclaimed what was fresh and new. We can presume that his answer to many of the questions he was given would have been 'What does it say in the Law?' Yet however much we point out the parallels in Jesus' teaching to what had already been said in the Old Testament and by other Jewish teachers such as John the Baptist, there was, from the beginning, an electrifying novelty in what Jesus taught.

THE KINGDOM OF GOD

The great theme of Jesus' teaching can be summarised in the idea that, with his appearance, God was now acting in history in a new and unprecedented way. Jesus used many ways to talk about this new intervention of God. The commonest involved the idea of the Kingdom of God. The Gospels mention the Kingdom over eighty times and it is the subject of nearly two-thirds of Jesus' parables. Together, Jesus and the coming of the Kingdom form the 'Good News' – the gospel. And although the word 'Kingdom' is far less common in the later parts of the New Testament the linked idea of Jesus ruling as King is present on every page.

The promise of the Kingdom of God

The Jewish people understood their history in terms of God's Kingdom. So the great calamity of the fall of the human race at the dawn of history was due to our rejection of God's rule, an act of rebellion against God's Kingdom. The wars, brutalities and injustices that have stained the history of the human race are testimony to how tragic and disastrous that act of rebellious independence was. Although the intention was to gain freedom from God, the result turned out not to be freedom but an enslavement under the powers of evil. God could have crushed humanity's rebellion by force, but he didn't. Instead he chose that a rebellion caused by free choice should be won back by free choice. That long, painful process of bringing humanity back into God's Kingdom is the story of the Bible.

In the Old Testament we see how God prepared the way for his Kingdom. Although rejected he remained King over his people, blessing them and disciplining them. He allowed them human kings, although they were always meant to be under his overall rule. Through the successes and the failures of these human monarchs, God's people learned the problems of having earthly rulers. The kings, however, pointed to a great and seemingly unreachable ideal: that of God's people being ruled with perfect justice under a perfect, holy King for all eternity.

Increasingly during this long period, God gave promises of a new Kingdom that would be different and far greater than any of the earthly kingships that Israel had known. One of a number of prophecies about this Kingdom in the book of Daniel says: 'The God of heaven will set up a kingdom that will never be destroyed or conquered. It will crush all these kingdoms into nothingness, and it will stand forever.'[5] It was a promise that the new kingdom created by God would be one which would challenge and defeat all other kingdoms and empires of the world and would endure forever. However, for centuries after Daniel, these other kings and kingdoms continued to brutally trample God's people underfoot. The dream of the Kingdom and of the King – the Messiah – who would inaugurate it faded, but never died. One day, the faithful reassured themselves under the yoke of Babylon, Assyria, Greece or Rome, the Kingdom would come!

Jesus and the proclamation of the Kingdom

Finally, John the Baptist came with his startling declaration that, at long last, the 'Kingdom of God was at hand'. In this mood of national expectancy Jesus began his ministry, proclaiming that the Kingdom was indeed here and that he personally had inaugurated it.[6]

Let's list some of the key things that Jesus taught about the Kingdom.

- As its King, Jesus personally represented the Kingdom.[7] To know Jesus and to follow and obey him was to enter the Kingdom. As Patrick Schreiner says, 'Jesus is the human face of the kingdom.'[8]

- At the present time the Kingdom wasn't about a sudden dramatic, political or military event. Indeed Jesus explicitly rejected a political, earthly kingdom.[9]

- The Kingdom was going to grow slowly. Like a mustard seed, it would start as something tiny that would ultimately grow into something much larger.[10] Similarly, the Kingdom, like yeast in dough, was something that by working slowly, silently and mysteriously would ultimately create dramatic change.[11]

- Whether the Kingdom was understood or not, its growth was unstoppable because God's authority and power were behind it.[12]

- Against any expectations of an imminent final and complete coming of the Kingdom, Jesus implied[13] that time would elapse before its final triumph.

- The final and complete coming of the Kingdom would await the personal arriving of the King in glory.[14]

Against the popular view that God's Kingdom would exclude all Gentiles, Jesus taught that it would know neither geographic, ethnic nor racial restrictions.[15]

The Kingdom of God would face opposition by the devil's forces.[16] Indeed the coming of the Kingdom would stir up both good and evil, and one result of this would be that not everything that claimed to belong to the Kingdom would be authentic and God-given.[17]

The importance and authority of Jesus' teaching about the Kingdom was highlighted by his Spirit-empowered miracles, which were not only a proof of his authority but a foretaste of the coming of the Kingdom.[18]

This 'phase of preparation' for the Kingdom comes to an end at the cross. If you think of the Bible as being like some big-screen film epic you can see it starting with the widest possible cosmic perspective in Genesis 1 and then, through the Old Testament, progressively zooming in ever tighter as it tracks in on a single nation and then indeed on a family line. In the New Testament the pace of our narrative – repeated four times for emphasis – slows down and stays increasingly tightly framed on Jesus until it finally fills the screen with the details of Good Friday. In doing so, the Bible seems to make the point that the horrendous event of the crucifixion is somehow the goal of the story. The unlikely destination of this greatest and grandest of tales is a man dying on the cross.

This progressively tighter perspective is dramatically reversed from the resurrection onwards. The frame of Scripture rapidly widens as the gospel spreads outwards from Jerusalem through Judaea and Samaria to – at the end of the book of Acts – Rome, the centre of the known world. In the letters of the New Testament the focus is on the spread and the eagerly anticipated ultimate coming of the Kingdom. Finally, in the book of Revelation, the biblical perspective expands to mirror the opening of Genesis, taking in all nations and the whole of creation. Here we read the great proclamation: 'The world has now become the kingdom of our Lord and of his Christ, and he will reign forever and ever.'[19]

The future of the Kingdom

This ultimate fulfilment of the Kingdom of God awaits the return of Christ and the remaking of creation. At the moment we live in the twilight of dawn. The Kingdom has been announced, the day is coming but the sun has not yet risen. Yet we know that one day the long night will end.

Although Jesus only gave limited teaching on the unparalleled events of his return and the universe's remaking, the broad picture is clear. This final event that will end earth's rebellion will involve Jesus' reappearance in a manner that is sudden, unexpected and unmistakable.[20] It will bring with it the judgement of good and evil and the final destruction of the devil and his work.[21] Jesus' followers will receive an eternal and glorious Kingdom that will be totally free from all that is evil, where people from all over the world are drawn together, finding themselves at last beyond all evil and sorrow, in unbreakable peace and joy.[22]

It's the best possible promise for the future – yet we must not overlook the fact that with it comes a solemn warning. When with Jesus' return the Kingdom appears in glory, any opportunity of accepting him as Lord will be ended. The door that lies open at present will be closed permanently.[23]

These descriptions of the final and complete triumph of God's Kingdom contain imagery that we struggle to interpret, and attempts to create a timetable for the future have proved spectacularly – and often embarrassingly – unsuccessful. Rather than focusing on what we don't know, such as dates and times, followers of Jesus should instead concentrate on what we do know. For a start, this idea that we are destined for an eternal Kingdom ought to affect every area of life. We should live out the values of the eternal Kingdom in how we think and live. In the past, Christians considered everything 'in the light of eternity' and it's a wise perspective.

The truth of an eternal Kingdom of joy also affects how we are to face death. For the followers of Jesus death is not an end; in a world where hope for the future is rare, Jesus' message here is desperately needed.

ENTERING THE KINGDOM

Jesus did not only teach about the nature of the Kingdom now and in the future, he also taught how men and women were to enter it. He repeatedly emphasised that nothing is more important than belonging to the Kingdom: to enter it is to 'gain eternal life' and it is 'to be saved'.[24] In one of Jesus' parables, the 'Pearl of Great Value', we read that the Kingdom 'is like a merchant on the lookout for choice pearls. When he discovered a pearl of great value, he sold everything he owned and bought it!'[25] The Kingdom is so valuable that no expense or sacrifice is too great to enter it and its importance is summed up in another of Jesus' sharp sayings: 'And what do you benefit if you gain the whole world but lose your own soul?'[26] If to be in this future Kingdom will be to know unspeakable joy, to miss it will be to suffer unimaginable loss. No language is adequate to express the sorrow of failing to enter the Kingdom.[27] To lose the Kingdom is to lose everything, and to lose that beyond any hope of recovery.

How to enter the Kingdom

One of the most remarkable things that Jesus taught about the Kingdom is that it is free. We cannot earn the Kingdom; we can only receive it as a gift.[28] Jesus said to his disciples: 'It gives your Father great happiness to give you the Kingdom.'[29] It is no wonder that the announcement of the Kingdom is called 'the Good News'.[30]

Nevertheless, to gain the Kingdom requires action: it may be a gift but it is not automatically given to everybody. The parable of the Pearl of Great Value does not just teach that the Kingdom is valuable; it teaches that you have to act to get in. Jesus talked about the Kingdom as having a narrow gate that needs to be searched for.[31]

So how is the Kingdom entered? The basis of entry is to have an obedient trust in Jesus, the King. The Gospels tell how, when some parents brought their little children to Jesus to be blessed, he used the children to make a point: 'The kingdom of God belongs to those who are like these children. I tell you the truth, anyone who doesn't receive the Kingdom of God like a child will never enter it.'[32] To have such faith is to have a simple, personal trust in Jesus. Luke gives an example of this when he tells us how, when Jesus was hanging on the cross, one of the criminals being crucified next to him turned to him and said, 'Jesus, remember me when you come into your Kingdom.' Jesus' reply was, 'I assure you, today you will be with me in paradise.'[33] That simple trust alone was enough for Jesus to be able to promise him forgiveness.

Yet because being in the Kingdom is to be under the rule of the King, two other conditions exist.

The first is *repentance*, the complete turning away from everything that is wrong and opposed to the Kingdom. Announcing the coming of the Kingdom, Jesus said, 'Repent of your sins and believe the Good News!'[34] To repent is to choose to reject anything that will get in the way of the Kingdom; whether it be bad actions or desires, all must be discarded. If the seeds of God's Kingdom are to grow in our lives, then all the old weeds need to be removed first.

The second is *commitment*. To enter the Kingdom also involves receiving Jesus as King of our lives. It means being committed to him as Lord and being obedient to his rule. This may sound like giving up our freedom but the Bible makes it clear that outside the Kingdom no one is free.[35] Because we are all ruled by our own desires and affected by the world, to come into the Kingdom is to be liberated. Using an image from how animals were harnessed, Jesus said, 'Come to me, all of you who are weary and carry heavy burdens, and I will give you rest. Take my yoke upon you. Let me teach you, because I am humble and gentle at heart, and you will find rest for your souls. For my yoke is easy to bear, and the burden I give you is light.'[36]

This commitment to follow Jesus in his Kingdom has to be sustained through even the severest difficulties. Jesus warned that there would be those who, although they received news of the Kingdom with joy, would fail to continue in it. Their commitment would be found to be merely one of words and inadequate to deal with life's pressures or temptations.[37] Life in the Kingdom is not a hundred-metre dash; it is more like a marathon with an obstacle course sometimes thrown in as well.

One other way of thinking about our commitment to follow Jesus is to think of how, if you become a citizen of another country, you receive not only rights and privileges but with them obligations. Those obligations will include keeping the laws, honouring the traditions and being faithful to your new country. The Kingdom of God is no different. Entry is given freely but it does come with responsibilities. It is precisely because of these obligations that Jesus cautioned those who are interested in entering the Kingdom to think things through seriously before following him. In any conflict of priorities, Jesus the King and his Kingdom must come first, whatever it costs us.[38]

LIVING IN THE KINGDOM

Jesus saw entering the Kingdom as something so fundamental and life changing that it was like being born again.[39] Like being born, entry into the Kingdom is a beginning rather than an ending, and so much of Jesus' teaching on the Kingdom centred on how to live as one of its citizens.

Two profound errors have been made about living in the Kingdom of God. The first is to think that trying to be good or imagining you *are* good will earn you entry into the Kingdom. That is wrong; the clear teaching of Jesus (and the New Testament) is that not only is no one good enough for heaven but the entry tickets cannot be earned, bought or inherited. The Kingdom is offered freely by God's grace and to offer your own good deeds as evidence that you are worthy to enter is to reject the only way of entry that there is.

The second error is to think that free entry into the Kingdom excludes the need to try to be good. It doesn't: Jesus expected his followers to live lives that were good, pure and moral. Being good is not an entry requirement into the Kingdom (and to repeat – imagining that you *are* good will exclude you) but neither is it an optional extra for those who live in it.

A new Kingdom relationship to God

Jesus taught that living in the Kingdom is something drastically new.[40] This is seen in many areas.

We mentioned earlier that when we look at Jesus' teaching in the context of his contemporaries, we discover a principle of 'familiar but utterly different'. In fact although Jesus said very little about God that was not already found in the Old Testament, he did reveal two new things about God and both were of earth-shaking significance.

First, Jesus taught that God could be known as 'Father'. He addressed God as such in his own prayers and he taught his disciples to use the same term in their prayers. In fact the Aramaic term used, 'Abba'[41] ('Daddy' or 'Dad'), was so characteristic of Jesus that the Greek-speaking early church used it.[42] This idea of God as 'Father', with overtones of affection, closeness and trust, was revolutionary. In the Jewish faith of his day, God could be known as 'Lord' or 'King' but he had become a distant figure who was rarely, if ever, addressed as 'Father'. Jesus taught that this privilege of being able to access God as 'Father' was not simply his alone: it was the privilege of all his followers, too. The prayer that Jesus gave his followers as a pattern to base their own praying on – the Lord's Prayer[43] – begins 'our Father'. All those who have come to God through Jesus are God's children and can have a relationship of trust and confidence with God.[16] This of course brings with it an implication of extraordinary significance: anyone else who is also a child of God is, by definition, our brother or our sister.

The second feature in Jesus' teaching is the awesome claim that he personally was in some way God. This is so significant that we will look at it in detail in the next chapter.

New Kingdom standards

Jesus set new standards for his people. Rather than just repeat the religious teaching of his day, he ignored all the many man-made additions and went back to the Old Testament Law, the *Torah*, and reapplied its principles. Exactly how he did this is well seen in that part of Matthew's Gospel that has become known as the Sermon on the Mount.[44]

The problem with the Law was that it was easy to treat it as something that only dealt with actions. For example, the sixth of the Ten Commandments stated 'you must not murder',[45] so most people looked at that and ticked it off as a commandment they had kept. Then, as now, few people commit actual murder. Yet Jesus took the commandment deeper than just the level of actions, applying it also to the mind and condemning anger as the root of murder.[46] He did the same with adultery, condemning lust as well.[47] Religion had been based on actions, but Jesus brought motives and desires before the judgement of God. The people of the Kingdom were not simply to perform good acts; they were to *be* good.[48] As Jesus himself taught, it is only good trees that produce good fruit.[49] With Jesus, religious purity was not about external actions; it was first and foremost about the internal attitudes that produced actions.[50] Jesus didn't just deepen the law, he also broadened it. People had decided that it was enough to be good and kind only to those who were friends and relatives. This, Jesus taught, was inadequate: you had to love even your enemies.[51]

---

16 The idea of God being our Father should not be seen as something that teaches the 'maleness' of God. Neither does it say that God is 'like your father'; something that, sadly, for many people might be *very* bad news. Its purpose is primarily to encourage us to have a close, loving and personal relationship with God.

Jesus summarised the standards of the Kingdom like this: '"You must love the Lord your God with all your heart, all your soul, and all your mind." This is the first and greatest commandment. A second is equally important: "Love your neighbour as yourself." The entire law and all the demands of the prophets are based on these two commandments.'[52]

It's undeniable that Jesus set a high standard of life. Critics have alleged that he set that standard so high that it is impossible to follow. Such a view overlooks three things. First, that Jesus and his followers considered the Kingdom 'good news', so they didn't see it as something that produces only a sense of moral failure. Second, that Jesus' followers know God as a loving heavenly Father who forgives those who acknowledge their failure to keep his standards and who encourages them to try again. Third, that God gives his people the gift of his Holy Spirit to help them live out life in the Kingdom. In John's Gospel we read how, in the middle of telling the disciples about the coming of the Holy Spirit, Jesus explained that they can only bear fruit (that is, live good lives) if they remain in him: 'For a branch cannot produce fruit if it is severed from the vine, and you cannot be fruitful unless you remain in me.'[53] The purpose of the Holy Spirit is for him to be a helper who will allow us to be related in this fruitful way to Jesus. Receiving the Spirit, obeying his guidance and knowing his empowering, is what enables us to live the sort of lives that God wants.[54]

New Kingdom lifestyle

Jesus' teaching describes the characteristics of those who are in the Kingdom.

- *Integrity*. The citizens of the Kingdom are those who are totally trustworthy. They do what they promise and do not need to make oaths or vows to strengthen those promises.[55]

- *Consistency*. Jesus' followers practise what they preach and do not concentrate on trivial matters at the expense of major ones.[56] The hypocrisy and distorted faith that characterised some of Jesus' contemporaries should be absent in the Kingdom.

- *Prayer*. Those who are in God's Kingdom pray with faith and confidence for themselves, for others and for the full and final coming of God's Kingdom.[57] Their praying is not a matter of self-glorifying public performance or of empty words but is simple and sincere.[58]

- *Forgiveness*. Because God has freely forgiven those who are in the Kingdom,[59] they forgive others. There is no place for revenge or settling scores in the Kingdom.[60]

- *Humility*. Just as no one gets into the Kingdom on their own merits, so there are no grounds for boasting and no basis for pride or self-importance. For similar reasons, there should be no critical and loveless judging of others.[61]

- *Service*. There should be no arrogance or sense of superiority among those who live in God's Kingdom; instead, there should be a desire to serve one another. Jesus saw himself as a servant and expected his followers to imitate his example.[62]

- *A right attitude to wealth and possessions.* Jesus spoke a good deal about how we handle our possessions and money. He pointed out that although both are good things, they pose dangers. They provide a misleading illusion of security and, all too easily, can become obstacles that get in the way of loving God.[63] Those in the Kingdom are to hold lightly to both wealth and possessions and be prepared to give them away.[17]

- *Love for one another.* The Kingdom is to be made up of people who care deeply for one another. On the night of his betrayal, Jesus said to his followers, 'So now I am giving you a new commandment: Love each other. Just as I have loved you, you should love each other. Your love for one another will prove to the world that you are my disciples.'[64]

- *Joy*. Those in the Kingdom should be joyful. After all, they are secure in the knowledge that God cares for them.[65]

- *Hope*. Those who are in the Kingdom can be confident about the future. The Kingdom that is already here and enjoyed is just a foretaste of that great and eternal Kingdom whose coming is

---

[17] In Acts 20:35 Paul quotes a saying of Jesus: 'It is more blessed to give than to receive.'

certain. Mixed with hope is also a longing. The Lord's Prayer has an important line in it: 'May your Kingdom come soon. May your will be done on earth, as it is in heaven.'[66]

JESUS' TEACHING: SOME REFLECTIONS

While Jesus' teaching was built solidly on the foundations of the Old Testament, four aspects of his teaching are strikingly different.

First, he deepened the moral teaching of the Jewish faith to go beyond actions and words to our internal attitudes. Jesus saw that 'the heart of the human problem is the heart'.

Second, he pushed beyond the practices of the Judaism of his day. In his teaching are indications – developed later by his followers – that rules on the Sabbath, diet, fellowship with Gentiles and even temple worship were to be superseded.

Third, Jesus put himself at the centre of his teaching. In everything he said, he proclaimed that he was 'not just another rabbi'. Where traditional teachers would have encouraged people to commit themselves to more deeply follow 'the Law' or obey the 'word of the Lord', Jesus asked for their allegiance to him personally.

Finally – and here Jesus stands above and beyond not just Jewish moral teachers but all moral teachers – he proclaimed the very highest ethical standards and lived up to them.

It has been very common to have the Ten Commandments displayed in public view with their solemn denunciations of *what we should not do*. Unfortunately, far less common has been any similar publicity of 'the Beatitudes', the memorable portrait of *what we should be like* that Jesus gave.

> God blesses those who are poor and realise their need for him,
>> for the Kingdom of Heaven is theirs.
> God blesses those who mourn,
>> for they will be comforted.

God blesses those who are humble,

for they will inherit the whole earth.

God blesses those who hunger and thirst for justice,

for they will be satisfied.

God blesses those who are merciful,

for they will be shown mercy.

God blesses those whose hearts are pure,

for they will see God.

God blesses those who work for peace,

for they will be called the children of God.

God blesses those who are persecuted for doing right,

for the Kingdom of Heaven is theirs.[67]

It is a picture of a moral perfection that remains an astonishing challenge and, ever since Jesus uttered it, his followers have found it has set standards that they must strive to meet. Yet – extraordinarily for its moral rigour – it paints a faithful picture of the one who taught it.

NOTE: SEXUAL ETHICS

Every generation and culture has struggled with some aspect or other of what Jesus taught. In our age, particularly in the West, the pressure point – and certainly the talking point – is that of sexuality. Given its sensitivity this really deserves a longer treatment but, as silence might be misunderstood, some comments are necessary.

Contrary to what seems to be popularly imagined, Christian morality is not obsessed with sex. Jesus spent far more time teaching about the sins of greed and selfishness than on sexual matters. Nevertheless, anybody who says Jesus had nothing to say on sexual morality is wrong. In this area we find that Jesus was both a traditionalist and a radical.

Jesus was clearly a traditionalist in affirming the basics of sexual ethics given in the Old Testament. He declared that human beings were made male and female,[68] that marriage between a man and a woman was a God-given institution[69] and he recognised and condemned sexual sin.[70] Yet there are radical aspects to his teaching. Jesus was, unusually for Jewish teachers, celibate, and although the Gospels record many criticisms of him, beyond the sour condemnation that he was 'a friend of tax collectors and sinners' there is no hint of sexual immorality. That radicalism is seen in the way that he was friends with not just men but women and he treated them equally.

It has been pointed out that Jesus is silent on the subject of homosexuality and this has been claimed to indicate his acceptance of it. This argument from silence is a poor one: after all, silence on a topic can be because there is nothing to argue about as it is something that everybody takes for granted. To take three topics at random, we find no teaching of Jesus against incest, idleness or idolatry. He didn't need to: that they were wrong was universally assumed within Judaism. Whether we like it or not, the Jewish faith of Jesus' time clearly condemned homosexual practice. In fact, if there is 'an argument from silence' in the area of homosexuality it lies completely in the other direction. The fact that Jesus, who was unafraid to take a radical view of moral topics, did not address same-sex relations is surely significant. It is echoed in a sad but perceptive comment by gay writer and newspaper columnist Matthew Parris: 'Jesus was never reluctant to challenge received wisdoms that he wanted to change. He gives no impression that he came into the world to revolutionise sexual mores. Even our eye, if it offends us, must be plucked out.'[71]

The fact that Jesus was unmarried and the fact that he defends celibacy 'for the sake of the Kingdom of Heaven'[72] makes the point that there is nothing wrong – and often a lot right – in choosing to be single, whatever your sexual orientation. It is unfortunate that, in legitimately seeking to defend marriage, the church has often modelled it as the only option for human existence.

Jesus' teaching on sexual ethics is demanding and there is probably no one, whatever their gender, marital state or sexual orientation, who is not challenged by it.

11

THE ISSUE OF IDENTITY: WHO WAS JESUS?

Over what Jesus did and said hangs a single challenging question: 'Who was this man?' The Christian church has long taught that, in a way that is beyond our comprehension, Jesus was both fully man and fully God. Let's consider both parts of that claim in turn.

JESUS THE MAN

The Gospels are plain that, whatever else he was, Jesus was as human as we are. We are told that Jesus was at times hungry, thirsty and tired[1] and, of course, that ultimately he died. Yet if Jesus was a real human being what *kind* of an individual was he? One indicator of who you are is how you react with others. So let's note the following.

- Jesus was a social, even sociable, person. There has been a long tradition of religious figures preferring isolation: the monk in his cell, the hermit in the cave, the guru on the mountaintop. There is no hint of any such isolationism with Jesus; although he did retreat to places of quiet for prayer he was someone who enjoyed being with people. He surrounded himself with friends and seems to have gone out of his way to make them, sometimes befriending those whom his contemporaries felt he shouldn't.[2]

- Jesus seems to have been happy being with 'common people' and, although he had wealthy followers, he seems to have had little interest in linking up with the rich, powerful and influential.

- Jesus treated children as important and valued them,[3] something unusual in cultures regulated by shame and honour.

- As we have seen, Jesus' attitude to women was remarkable and even revolutionary. In a culture in which it was perfectly permissible to dismiss or despise women, Jesus treated them with respect and valued them as equals.

But beyond his relationships with others what was Jesus like as an individual? There has been a tradition with deep roots of depicting Jesus as some sort of almost emotionless being. This is not only unfaithful to the Gospels but it deprives Jesus of his humanity. To be human is to have emotions and it is plain Jesus had those.

The commonest emotion ascribed to Jesus is compassion[4] and he was definitely someone who was deeply moved by the suffering of others. Yet at the same time we also read that when confronted with injustice and those who caused evil, he could show anger.[5] We may be uncomfortable with that idea but there are many situations – then and now – where *not* to show anger would be wrong. There is, however, no hint of any of Jesus' anger turning into the sort of rage that we all know and which does so much harm.

Jesus has frequently been portrayed as perpetually serious or even solemn. It is undeniable that there were times when, fulfilling Isaiah's prophecy that the coming Servant would be a 'man of sorrows, acquainted with deepest grief', Jesus was saddened, even to the point of tears, by human misery.[6] Equally, as Jesus drew close to the cross one senses that the burden of what he faced was crushing in its intensity.[7] Nevertheless, we cannot overlook the evidence that Jesus was frequently joyful.[8] Although there is no reference to Jesus laughing, his frequent use of humour, especially in the parables, suggests a sense of amusement and an ability to detect the ridiculous and contradictory in human life.[9] What can confidently be said of Jesus' emotions is that they were always appropriate and proportionate to the situation. We may be betrayed by our emotions; he wasn't.

One other feature of what might be termed 'Jesus the man' needs comment. It is his resolute determination. We repeatedly read of Jesus taking decisions, making choices, moving on somewhere and ultimately 'setting his face' to go to Jerusalem.[10] Two things are worth noting here. First, often when we get into difficulties we keep going because, in our ignorance, we retain the hope that somehow 'it's all going to work out right'. Jesus did not have that privilege: he knew what awaited him in Jerusalem. Second, determination or resolve is a critically important virtue. When in trying to do right we are confronted by opposition, a lot of us quit rather than keep going. Jesus didn't and neither should we.

One of the most compelling things about Jesus is the consistency he showed between words and deeds. It is an almost universal truth that those people who teach moral standards fail to live up to them. There is no harder challenge to someone teaching on ethics than to ask, 'Do *you* practise what you preach?' Uniquely, though, no shadow of contradiction falls on Jesus. 'Which of you can truthfully accuse me of sin?' Jesus demanded,[11] and two millennia of history have recorded no other response than silence.

Finally, and it's of course the secret to what Jesus was as a man, he had a profound and unparalleled spiritual life. Jesus clearly knew the Old Testament Scriptures thoroughly, not just in terms of memorisation but in terms of what they meant. In the midst of a tiring ministry and under enormous pressures Jesus rose early to find time for prayer or even spent whole nights in prayer.[12] The quality of that prayer life is clearly reflected in his relationship to God as his Father and his unshakeable sense of purpose. We may find in this area Jesus is impossible to imitate but that should not stop us being challenged by his example to be far, far closer to God than we actually are.

JESUS AS MORE THAN A MAN

So then Jesus was human and, by almost universal consent, the best kind of human. Yet Christianity has consistently portrayed him as being more than that and here we come to the very biggest of issues. If Jesus was just a man then he deserves respect; but if he was, in some unique way, God present on this planet then he deserves not just respect but worship.

In considering this aspect of Jesus' identity we are faced with two issues. First, who did Jesus claim to be? Second, was that claim true? We have already noted aspects of this – it would be impossible not to do so – in the miracles and in the authority that Jesus claimed in his teaching.

JESUS' CLAIMS FOR HIS MISSION

How Jesus saw himself is reflected in how he viewed his mission; something that can be summed up in five images.

Absolute authority

In looking at Jesus' teaching we saw the astonishing way in which he claimed authority, putting himself not just above contemporary teachers but above Moses and even the Law. In the Sermon on the Mount Jesus quoted several key parts of the Law and then added, in a seemingly matter-of-fact way, '*But* I say . . .'[13] Such an astounding view of himself and his teaching comes over clearly in the way that Jesus repeatedly begins his statements with 'I tell you the truth'. Jesus claimed not just simply to speak the truth but in some way to actually *be* the truth. He explicitly claimed, 'I am the way, the truth, and the life. No one can come to the Father except through me.'[14] The early church considered what Jesus said to be authoritative statements that could not be ignored, dismissed or modified.

Royal rescuer

For a Jew, the high point of the Old Testament was when God, through Moses, rescued his people from slavery in Egypt. Jesus saw himself as doing something very similar: he, too, was someone who had come to set people free. Jesus and the Gospel writers use such words as 'save', 'salvation', 'saviour', 'redeem' and 'redeemer' to express a series of ideas related to being rescued, whether physically or spiritually.[15]

Jesus' name here is significant: Jesus ('Yeshua') means 'Yahweh saves'.[16] At Jesus' birth we are told that he is the promised saviour and the one who will save his people from their sins.[17] Jesus himself defined his mission with the following words taken from the Old Testament:

> The Spirit of the LORD is upon me,
>> for he has anointed me to bring Good News to the poor.
> He has sent me to proclaim that captives will be released,
>> that the blind will see,
> that the oppressed will be set free,
>> and that the time of the LORD's favour has come.[18]

It's a passage that is all about rescuing and liberating and clearly central to how Jesus saw himself.

Loving leader

If the image of a 'royal rescuer' seems too military for comfort, it is balanced by another picture of Jesus as the one who lovingly leads and protects his people. Jesus came to people who had lost their way and offered to bring them back to God. We read: 'When he saw the crowds, he had compassion on them because they were confused and helpless, like sheep without a shepherd.'[19]

Jesus saw himself as the great Shepherd (a term used of Yahweh[20]); the one who came to guide, recover and protect the lost. There is no contradiction between this idea of caring leadership and being a royal rescuer; after all, shepherds fight to defend their sheep. As leader, Jesus offered his gentle rule as an alternative to those struggling with the unbearable burden of keeping the man-made religious rules and traditions of his time.[21]

Perfect provider

Jesus also declared that he was the one who provided for all his people's needs. The feeding of the five thousand, the healing of the sick, the deliverance from demonic oppression, the raising of the dead: these are all examples of how Jesus provided perfectly for every need.

The idea that Jesus is the one who completely provides for his people's needs is summed up by the seven great statements he makes about himself that are recorded in John's Gospel.

- 'I am the bread of life. Whoever comes to me will never be hungry again.'

- 'I am the light of the world. If you follow me, you won't have to walk in darkness, because you will have the light that leads to life.'

- 'I am the gate for the sheep . . . Those who come in through me will be saved.'

- 'I am the good shepherd. The good shepherd sacrifices his life for the sheep.'

- 'I am the resurrection and the life. Anyone who believes in me will live, even after dying.'

- 'I am the way, the truth, and the life. No one can come to the Father except through me.'

- 'I am the vine; you are the branches. Those who remain in me, and I in them, will produce much fruit. For apart from me you can do nothing.'[22]

These seven statements show Jesus claiming in various ways to be the complete answer to our every requirement, both now and forever. Whether there is a need for guidance, comfort, protection or simply an answer to issues of guilt and death, Jesus is the one who is able to help.

Suffering servant

A final image of Jesus in the Gospels is especially remarkable. Jesus talked about himself as being a servant and as suffering in the place of those he served. So, after rebuking his followers for their pride and selfishness, Jesus said, 'For even the Son of Man came not to be served but to serve others and to give his life as a ransom for many.'[23] Jesus claimed to be Lord and King; but he also declared that he was a lowly servant and, more amazing still, one who would willingly suffer in the place of others. Behind this saying of Jesus lies Isaiah's depiction of the Servant of the Lord, the mighty figure who would come and, despite his high rank, be rejected, suffer and die on behalf of others.[24]

The astonishing idea that Jesus saw himself as a servant who had come both to serve and save others, occurs in all the Gospels and elsewhere in the New Testament. In John's Gospel Jesus says, 'I am the good shepherd. The good shepherd sacrifices his life for the sheep.'[25] John the Baptist referred to Jesus as 'the Lamb of God who takes away the sin of the world'.[26] The idea of Jesus being a sacrifice finds many echoes in the language and symbolism of the Last Supper which looks back to the Old Testament Passover and its sacrificial lamb but also forward to the cross.[27] Paul clearly refers to this idea in the awesome passage of Philippians 2:5–11 which talks about Jesus' descent from heaven to become a servant and to die on the cross. Jesus claimed by his words and his actions that he was the Messiah, God's King, yet as part of that kingship he chose to serve and suffer for his people.

These five images, claimed by Jesus and applied to him by the Gospel writers, suggest the very highest status imaginable. In various ways they are picked up and elaborated on by the letters of the New Testament.

JESUS' TITLES

The various titles used by Jesus of himself or given to him are vital in understanding who he saw himself to be. Here are some of the main ones.

Messiah

The first Christians were so certain that Jesus was the Messiah – God's promised deliverer and King – that the names 'Jesus' and 'Christ' (from *Christos*, the Greek translation of Messiah) became almost interchangeable. Jesus, however, rarely used the title Messiah of himself; when he did, it appears to have been only where it was safe for him to do so, for example with a Samaritan woman.[28] And when Jesus did accept the title of Messiah from the disciples, he gave them a warning to keep it private.[29] Virtually identical with Messiah was the title 'Son of David',[30] a reference to the fact that the promised Messiah would be the descendant and heir of King David. The first Christian preaching proclaimed Jesus as the Messiah,[31] the Saviour not just of Israel but of the world.

Son of God[32]

Jesus directly referred to himself as the 'Son of God' and told parables that implied he accepted that title.[33] At Jesus' baptism and the transfiguration, a voice from heaven confirmed that Jesus was God's Son. In the Gospels other figures, including demons, Satan and a Roman centurion, also called Jesus the 'Son of God'. In the parable of the evil farmers Jesus clearly sees himself as God's Son.[34] But what does 'Son of God' mean? It most certainly doesn't mean – and has never ever meant in Christianity – any sense of God being Jesus' father in any 'human' way. The idea that the gods might have sexual relations with men and women was common in Greek and Roman mythology but in the Jewish faith, which proclaimed an enormous gulf of power and holiness between humanity and God, to even suggest this would have been to ask to be stoned.

To understand the phrase 'Son of God' we need to go deeper. In the cultural world of the Bible, sonship was less about biology than authority and function: what power you had and what you did with it. After all, many rulers adopted sons and passed on their authority to them. And in terms of function, most sons carried on the family trade so that there was continuity between fathers and sons over generations. What a father was, his son was.

So how was Jesus the Son of God? Let us suggest four ways.

First, *Jesus stands in the place of the Father*. Even today in many traditional cultures, especially in the Middle East, if you go to meet an important man and only meet his son, then there is no reason to feel disappointed. Traditionally, the eldest son can stand in the place of the father and bear his authority. He can be relied on to speak for his father and honour any promises that he makes. Jesus represents this situation exactly: he is one with his Father and can say, 'Anyone who has seen me has seen the Father.'[35] One vital aspect of this is that as God was King, for Jesus to refer to himself as 'Son of God' meant that he was carrying out God's kingly role.[36]

Second, *the Father loves the Son*. The Gospels clearly show there is a love between the Father and the Son paralleling that which exists between human parents and their children. It is precisely because of this love that the Father giving up his Son to death is so moving. Jesus' death was not some cold and unfeeling transaction, a view that can be misinterpreted from phrases that talk about the cross as a place where 'a price was paid' or 'an offering for sin was made' but instead an intense sacrifice of love by *both* Father and Son.

Third, *Jesus knows the Father perfectly*. In a way that we can only dimly comprehend, Jesus had such an intimate personal fellowship with God that he could refer to God as 'Abba, dear Father'. So close is this relationship that Jesus can claim to know exactly his Father's thoughts and can say, 'My Father has entrusted everything to me.

No one truly knows the Son except the Father, and no one truly knows the Father except the Son and those to whom the Son chooses to reveal him.'[37] Jesus could speak for his Father because there was a perfect unity and communication between them.

Fourth, *Jesus was faithful to the Father's will*. As the perfect Son, Jesus does exactly what the Father wants and shows perfect obedience and trust. At both Jesus' baptism and the transfiguration, God announces his pleasure at his Son's obedience.[38]

It is very significant that although Jesus taught his followers that they could know God as Father, he made a careful distinction between his unique relationship to God and theirs. He speaks of 'my Father and your Father'[39] and of himself as 'God's one and only Son'.[40]

In what precise sense Jesus was the Son of God and how he related to the Father is something that occupied the minds of some of the finest Christian thinkers for many centuries. The conclusion of the early church came in the formulation of the doctrine of the Trinity. Now *Trinity* is a not a word used in the New Testament, but conveys the sense that although Father, Son and Spirit are three distinct persons, they are united in essence and are all, at the same time, God. This idea, formalised as an item in the creed of every mainstream Christian church for nearly 1,800 years, cuts against any notion that we can separate Father from Son. So, for example, we cannot speak of the cross as an act in which God the Father punished his Son without saying that the unity between both is so great that both the choice of the cross and its agony were shared.

Son of Man

The title 'Son of Man' was Jesus' preferred way of referring to himself. At first glance 'Son of Man' is a rather cryptic phrase that seems inferior to 'Son of God' but actually it carries a great importance.[41] On one level it could simply be a way of referring to yourself as human; something that probably allayed any fears with the Roman authorities. Yet the phrase also carried the sense of a very special and unique being and Jesus' use of it clearly referred to this.[42]

Here there is a very significant passage in the Old Testament book of Daniel. There are several visions and in one of them Daniel sees God – 'the Ancient One' – sit on a throne and begin to judge the world.

> As my vision continued that night, I saw someone like a son of man coming with the clouds of heaven. He approached the Ancient One and was led into his presence. He was given authority, honour, and sovereignty over all the nations of the world, so that people of every race and nation and language would obey him. His rule is eternal – it will never end. His kingdom will never be destroyed.[43]

Because this awesome Son of Man can be worshipped, he is clearly divine. He is associated with the coming of the Kingdom in power: its universal and eternal rule belongs to him. In some places in the Gospels where Jesus used this term for himself it is unmistakably linked with this passage. So when Jesus is tried before the Sanhedrin, his declaration that he is '*the* Son of Man' who will sit at God's right hand provokes uproar, cries of 'blasphemy!' and demands for the death penalty.[44] Elsewhere, Jesus uses the term to talk about his future return in glory.[45]

Lord

The Greek word translated as 'Lord' has several meanings in the Gospels.[46] Sometimes when people call Jesus 'Lord' they are simply being respectful and the word means 'Sir'. Yet the word 'Lord' was also used as a term for Yahweh in the Greek translation of the Old Testament and, in some cases when it is used of Jesus, it clearly is a divine title. This is particularly true when Jesus refers to himself as '*the* Lord'.[47] The first Christians were in no doubt that to call Jesus 'Lord' was to give him the very highest title. Early in Acts, Peter concludes a speech with this claim, 'Let everyone in Israel know for certain that God has made this Jesus, whom you crucified, to be both Lord and Messiah!'[48] In Paul's letter to the Philippians we find a striking poem about Christ that concludes:

Therefore, God elevated him to the place of highest honour
  and gave him the name above all other names,
that at the name of Jesus every knee should bow,
  in heaven and on earth and under the earth,
and every tongue declare that Jesus Christ is Lord,
  to the glory of God the Father.[49]

In the early church, the most basic statement of belief was to call Jesus Christ 'Lord'.[50]

Other titles

Other titles are used in the Gospels for Jesus. On one occasion he is directly referred to as God. When the disciple Thomas was confronted with the resurrected Jesus, his response was to exclaim, 'My Lord and my God!'[51]

More subtle but no less powerful claims are presented when Jesus makes the seven great 'I am' statements in John's Gospel: I am 'the bread of life', 'the light of the world', 'the living water', etc.[52] If you had asked Jews of Jesus' day who it was who was these things, the unhesitating response would have been 'Yahweh'. Yet Jesus applied these words to himself.

One tiny element – 'I am' – in fact carries a great weight. During a discussion with Jesus, his hostile opponents referred to their ancestor, Abraham. Jesus responded, 'I tell you the truth, before Abraham was even born, I AM!'[53] Here Jesus was not just claiming to have existed before Abraham (which would have been remarkable enough) but the phrase 'I AM' is the name that God had used for himself when he spoke to Moses.[54] That Jesus was indeed making such an extraordinary claim is evidenced by the way that his hearers thought he was blaspheming.[55]

JESUS' ACTIONS

A number of Jesus' actions reveal that he saw himself as far more than a human being or even a prophet. We have already noted the range and style of the remarkable miracles or 'signs' that Jesus performed and how they suggest that he was far greater than any prophet. But these are not isolated: there are many occasions in which what Jesus did says a lot about how he saw himself.

So:

- Jesus summoned twelve disciples to recreate the twelve tribes of Israel. Yet as it was God who had called the original Israel, to do this was to assume an extraordinary authority.

- In the course of the Last Supper Jesus announced that he was making a new covenant.[56] However, given that the covenant was the fundamental bond in the relationship between God and his people, this action implies that Jesus put himself on an equal footing with God.

- Jesus' actions and statements to do with the temple – the 'house of God' – suggest that he felt he had the authority to determine what should (and should not) be done in it. Although the temple was considered to be the dwelling place of God, Jesus claimed that he had superiority over it[57] and even suggested that his own body was the temple.[58]

JESUS' CLAIMS

The pattern that we see in Jesus' actions is even more widespread in his words.

- Jesus clearly assumed that he was no ordinary teacher or prophet. At the end of the profound Sermon on the Mount Jesus is recorded as saying, 'Anyone who listens to my teaching and obeys me is wise, like a person who builds a house on solid rock.'[59] Any sort of ordinary prophet would have here referred to God; Jesus, however, refers to himself.

- Jesus frequently used the word 'truly' to introduce his words. This is something that seems to have been unique to him and a way of claiming his words carried absolute certainty. It suggests that Jesus believed that he spoke with God's authority.

- Jesus claimed to forgive sins.[60] Since only God could forgive sins, this was an implicit claim to be God.

- Jesus gave definitive interpretations of the Law of God,[61] reinterpreting it and redefining how it should be applied.[62] Jesus did not even justify these decisions: he simply announced 'but I say'.

- Jesus claimed to be greater than Jonah, Solomon, Jacob and even Abraham.[63] By revising – or rewriting – the covenant given to Moses, Jesus directly claimed to be even greater than him. Certainly the early church thought of Jesus as being greater than Moses: 'But Jesus deserves far more glory than Moses, just as a person who builds a house deserves more praise than the house itself.'[64]

- Jesus declared that he had authority over all other spiritual powers. He claimed that he had command of angels[65] and in his exorcisms[66] demonstrated his control over all the powers of evil. The accounts of the temptation in the wilderness claim that he had superiority over even Satan.[67]

- The Sabbath day was one of the great distinguishing features of the Jewish faith and was considered to be the gift of God. Yet Jesus, speaking of himself as the 'Son of Man', declared that he was 'Lord of the Sabbath'.[68]

- Jesus claimed that his words would outlast heaven and earth.[69]

- Jesus said that total authority on earth had been given to him.[70]

- Jesus claimed that how people responded to him would decide their eternal destiny.[71] He announced that he would be the judge on the day of judgement.[72]

- Jesus demanded that he should take complete precedence over his followers' family, friends and ambitions.[73]

- Jesus accepted worship, prayer and faith. He commanded people to pray in his name,[74] invited people to put their faith in him and praised them when they did.[75]

- Jesus taught that what people did to him they did to God.[76]

There is more. In several places in the Gospels Jesus implied that he was not limited by either time or space. So when Jesus spoke about his past, he stated that he had come from heaven[77] and, talking of the future, said that he would return to heaven.[78] He promised his disciples that he would be with them forever, even to the ends of the earth.[79] The implication is that Jesus saw himself as eternal, something echoed by John's descriptions of him as 'the Word'.[80] Given that only God is eternal and present everywhere, these are astonishing claims.

In looking at these claims we must ask ourselves the most profound of questions. Was this simply outrageous arrogance on the part of Jesus or does it reflect a genuine and staggering reality?

WHO DID JESUS THINK HE WAS?

The sheer quantity and variety of evidence that Jesus considered himself more than a human being is overwhelming. Looked at, it seems impossible to escape the conclusion that Jesus saw himself as being God; that he was God's Son, the Lord, the 'Son Of Man', the 'I AM'.

These claims to deity would be remarkable anywhere, but in the Jewish world which was dogmatic that there was only one God, they are particularly remarkable. There's a story of a modern Jewish scholar who having looked at length at what Jesus claimed about himself, shook his head and in a moment of utter exasperation said aloud, 'Who does this man think he is? *God*?'

Considering the claims of Jesus

Jesus' claims are so awesome and significant that they cannot simply be ignored or overlooked. If Jesus was, in some way, God come to earth, and if our eternal happiness is dependent on giving him our total loyalty, then we are faced with an issue whose truth or otherwise is the most important thing not just in this world but in the next.

Equally, if the claims of Jesus to be God's unique and supreme intervention into our world are to be rejected, then some alternative explanation for their challenge must be found. Those alternatives are very limited. One assessment of Jesus eloquently made by C. S. Lewis in the 1940s and endlessly repeated since is that, because of Jesus' claims, there are only two alternatives to him being Lord: he was either a liar or a lunatic. Although profoundly influential, this has been criticised because it overlooks the possibility that he is a fourth L: *legend*.

Nevertheless, Lewis' principle of forcing us to choose amongst limited options is sensible. Extending these options we would suggest that if Jesus was not God's Messiah, then he must be *mythical*, *misunderstood*, *mistaken*, *mad* or someone who *misled* his followers. Let's deal with these one by one.

Was Jesus mythical?

This view bluntly assumes the Gospels are unreliable and that the divine figure they portray is legendary. Here, because Jesus is fictional, any claims about him are, of course, meaningless.

Yet this view is hard to hold. As we have pointed out, the Gospels are not written as myth but as biography and history. They show none of the characteristics of myth: they are matter-of-fact narratives set in a real-world context of history, involving definite places and dates. There is not the slightest hint of 'once upon a time' in the Gospels. The data from classical historians is consistent with the existence of a real flesh- and-blood Jesus crucified under Pontius Pilate in Palestine. The remarkable nature of the Gospel accounts with their claims of a Jewish preacher who considered himself equal to God, have a high degree of consistency. The idea that they are complete inventions seems very difficult to hold.

Furthermore, a mythical Jesus invites an obvious question: how did such a mythical figure arise? Propelled by little more than preaching, an alternative lifestyle and some miracles, the Christian church had, within twenty or thirty years, spread out around the Mediterranean. This remarkable sociological phenomenon surely requires either: a) real events that were extraordinary; b) a real individual who was extraordinary; or, better still, c) a combination of both. It's also difficult to see how the belief that 'this Jesus was a good man' could have been transformed into 'this Jesus was God' in the presence of people who'd actually known him. There are no remotely similar parallels with this sort of development elsewhere and none at all in Judaism with its remote and incomparable Yahweh.

Was Jesus misunderstood?

This alternative suggests that, in reality, Jesus never claimed to be God. Rather, despite having spent three years with him, his disciples spectacularly misinterpreted what their teacher said and turned his reverent claims to be a faithful spokesman for God into assertions that he was an incarnation of God. This view might have some merit if Jesus' claim to be divine rested on one single statement. Yet, as we have seen, there is a portfolio of evidence that makes such a view unacceptable. It is also difficult to believe that Jesus' disciples were so inept that they misunderstood what Jesus said about who he was. The charge of profound incompetence can also be extended to the leaders of the early church for never thinking to check whether the disciples had got it all wrong. Given that so many of the first Christians were martyred, their incompetence was not only profound but fatal.

Was Jesus mistaken?

Here the alternative is that it is Jesus himself who was wrong. He genuinely thought he was God but in reality was sadly mistaken about his own identity. This would mean, however, that, far from Jesus being a reliable and authoritative interpreter of God's Law, he was breaking the first commandment – 'You must not have any other god but me' – in the most breathtaking and blasphemous way. The implications of this view are devastating. If Jesus was wrong about who he was then nothing else that he said can be trusted. If he was wrong here, Jesus could be wrong about everything else.

As we will see, the Christian church has seen the resurrection as the great defence against this argument. It is felt, with some logic, that God would hardly have raised from the dead a man who mistook himself for the Messiah.

Was Jesus mad?

Another alternative is that Jesus suffered from a delusional psychological disorder. For example, the writer George Bernard Shaw considered that Jesus must have suffered from megalomania. The sole virtue of this explanation is its acceptance that Jesus made astonishing claims about himself. Yet there is little to support it. In the Gospels, Jesus does not come over as the slightest bit delusional or disturbed. It also seems very hard to believe that those who travelled closely with Jesus for years somehow overlooked the unfortunate fact that he wasn't the Messiah at all, but mad.

To hold this view also requires you to accept that the greatest moral influence the world has ever seen was a man who was mentally disturbed. Even allowing for the fact that the human race is a seriously messed up species, this is a conclusion so bizarrely unsettling that few people have felt comfortable even considering it.

Did Jesus mislead his followers?

The final alternative is that, in making his claims, Jesus deliberately misled his followers, knowingly lying to them. This faces a veritable army of problems. It is hard to imagine any motive for Jesus wanting to mislead people in this way; far from leading to fame or glory, his claims led to his death. And lying seems to be utterly inconsistent with everything else we know of Jesus including the fact that he started many of his statements by saying '*truly*, I say to you'. To know you are a man and accept worship from your followers as a God would be an extraordinary act of evil. To say that it doesn't fit with the character of the author of the Sermon on the Mount is a major understatement!

Here, too, the resurrection is important. Again it's difficult to imagine God raising from the dead someone who could easily be considered to be the greatest con-artist of history.

CONCLUSIONS

Jesus made astonishing claims that he was, in some way, God. If those claims are true then they have awesome life-changing implications. In Jesus, every search for God comes to an end. In Jesus is found everything that our heart truly desires. In Jesus, we have hope for the darkest days of life and death.

No other explanation seems feasible. One of Sherlock Holmes' comments to Watson is helpful here: 'It is an old maxim of mine that when you have excluded the impossible, whatever remains, however improbable, must be the truth.'

In presenting the claims of Christ about himself here, we have in effect jumped ahead of the story. We have still to consider the vital matter of the resurrection. Yet placing Jesus' claims here rather than later is deliberate. It has been unfortunately common to focus entirely on the resurrection and say that *on that basis alone* Jesus is the Son of God and worthy of trust and worship. In fact the early church did not believe that Jesus was divine because he rose from the dead but because his resurrection confirmed the claims he had already made. The resurrection was the utterly unexpected but overwhelming confirmation by God himself that Jesus was, despite the shame of the cross, everything he said he was. The resurrection rules out every possibility for this man apart from what he and his followers have always claimed: he was God in the flesh.

A final but vital point is this. Simply saying 'I believe Jesus is God' does not even begin to exhaust the significance of Jesus' identity. It is too easy to limit the idea that Jesus is the divine Son of God to an answer to some theological test question that sets out the boundaries of authentic Christianity. To be a Christian does not mean to obey doctrine or faithfully recite a creed; it is to live within a transforming relationship with Jesus. After all, as James (traditionally assumed to be Jesus' brother) points out, 'Even the demons believe this, and they tremble in terror.'[81]The reality is that the idea that Jesus is God is a truth that should sustain us every day. Jesus was not just the Absolute Authority, Royal Rescuer, Loving Leader, Perfect Provider and Suffering Servant for his people two thousand years ago; he is all those things for us today.

NOTE: HOW COULD JESUS BE BOTH MAN AND GOD?

The traditional Christian view of Jesus is that he was both perfectly God and perfectly human. It's easy to say but it raises an important issue: how can God and man coexist in the same body? Two drastic attempts to solve the problem have been to either deny the fact that he was truly man or to deny the fact he was truly God. Both come with more problems than they solve. Theologically, the church has always argued that he had to be both man and God. In order to be *eligible* to save us, Jesus had to be truly human; in order to have the *power* to save us, he had to be truly God.

Given that human beings have limited power and knowledge and God has unlimited power and knowledge, it is surely a legitimate question to ask how this works. Did the young Jesus never get the wrong answer at school? Did he never become frustrated trying to learn another language? Did he never forget a name? Did he never look up at the stars and wonder how far away they were?

Now these are difficult questions and there is no way we can fully understand how it all worked because we are not God. But the problem is some people assume that incomprehensibility means impossibility. In fact some helpful suggestions have been made and we repeat them here because they may help those who find such matters troubling.

The issue of God's power is easier to deal with than God's knowledge, so let's start there. The Bible presents Jesus as someone who was able to exercise divine power and authority, in that he could do such things as still storms, raise the dead, heal the sick and turn water into wine. Yet it seems obvious that for Jesus to be truly human, he could not be an invulnerable and all-powerful being. This is not simply something that we deduce from theoretical arguments; the fact is that the Gospels portray Jesus as being totally and completely human: he was tired,[82] hungry,[83] thirsty[84] and ultimately he was tortured and killed. So presumably, although Jesus had access to God's power, there were times when he did not choose to use it. There is a hint of this when Jesus stops his disciples defending him at his arrest: 'Don't you realise that I could ask my Father for thousands of angels to protect us, and he would send them instantly?'[85] Presumably again, Jesus could only use such power as he knew his heavenly Father would want him to use. There was therefore a continuous voluntary obedience to the will of his Father and this restricted what Jesus did.

Such a principle no doubt also applied to the issue of how much Jesus knew. Clearly Jesus was aware of many things that ordinary people cannot know[86] yet there were some things that he did not know.[87] Luke's reference to Jesus growing both 'in wisdom and in stature'[88] implies that Jesus learnt as we do. It seems, therefore, that while Jesus always had a right to divine knowledge and, had he chosen to, he could have accessed it, he only made use of such knowledge as he knew his heavenly Father wanted him to. Jesus allowed his obedience to his Father to limit both his power and his knowledge.

This suggestion not only helps us make sense of how someone who was God could at the same time be totally human, it also points us to a Jesus who is a helpful model of obedience. Genesis tells us how the human race's rebellion began with disobedience against God and the desire to take what had been prohibited. The Gospels and the Epistles tell us that the answer to this rebellion came when Jesus lived out an entire life in obedience to God. The second Adam succeeded where the first failed.[89]

The New Testament does not try to answer how Jesus is God and how he relates to the Father; the answer – like a problem in five-dimensional geometry – is probably beyond our comprehension. For the Gospel writers, the mechanics of how the incarnation worked are not the issue. All they want to tell us is that, in Jesus, God came to this world to reach out to us. And that really is all we need to know.

12

THE LAST WEEK

In a biography of any other person what we have done would be bizarre: to pause just before the final week of their life to consider all that our protagonist did, taught and claimed to be. No less bizarre would be to then spend two whole chapters describing nothing more than the six days prior to and including their death. After all, in very few cases does someone's death affect the significance of their life. Yet here, as elsewhere, Jesus breaks the rules.

Traditionally the church has termed the period from the entry into Jerusalem on 'Palm Sunday' until the Easter Sunday of the resurrection as 'Passion Week' (from the Latin *passio*, 'suffering') and in covering it in detail we are simply echoing the emphasis of the New Testament. All the Gospels spend an amazing amount of space dealing with this period: in John's Gospel, while chapters 1 to 12 seem to cover three years, chapters 13 to 20 cover just the Passion Week. Mark's Gospel has been famously described as 'a passion narrative with an extended introduction'.[1] The importance of this last week is not simply represented by the number of words used. The way the Gospels are written puts these 'final days' not as the last pages of a biography but as their climax. Luke, for instance, structures his Gospel around the idea of Jesus making a journey, with Jerusalem and the cross as a destination.

The accounts of Passion Week are not just more detailed than the earlier parts of the Gospels, they differ in style. Whereas elsewhere the Gospels can give the impression of being almost a scrapbook compilation of events, here things are much more ordered. Statements are placed in context, allusions are explored, locations are mentioned and individuals are named. Above all, these accounts of the last week are reflective: they bear all the hallmarks of profound contemplation. This, the reader senses, is a story that has been deeply and repeatedly thought about. To return to the language of cinema used earlier, the pace of our fourfold film here slows down. The camera lingers, the framing is tighter, the focus sharper. We see now not just simply Jesus and the disciples but cross-cuts to those plotting against him. In fact, the detail of these four accounts is such that we can reconstruct what happened on this final week on a daily basis and, by the time we come to the Thursday night and Friday, we know what happened almost to the hour.[2]

There are other notable features in the Passion narratives. Their tone is striking: they record grief, but do not express it; there is no evoking of tragedy here, no tearful claims of 'a life cut short', no lament for a promising career unfulfilled. In fact, the contrary is true: underlying the drama is a solemn and awesome sense of deliberate purpose. The tone is less of a tragic march to an execution than the procession of a king to the throne of coronation. Strange to recount, the narratives ring with a sense of triumph: this is 'mission accomplished'. Indeed, the high point of John's account is the cry from the cross, 'It is finished!'[3]

This sense of purpose must not be overlooked. The Gospels indicate that this is an event which Jesus deliberately sought and even prompted. Passion Week is increasingly full of people – mostly men – who, pressured, driven by fear and a need for self-survival, make the worst choices for the worst reasons. We read of crisis meetings behind closed doors, of whispered threats, deals and bribes, of unhappy compromise and political intrigue. Yet at the core of this angry and fearful vortex of tumultuous activity we see, still and calm, one person who remains in control: Jesus of Nazareth. Remarkably, the only person who is not a victim of circumstance in Passion Week is the victim.

PALM SUNDAY

All four Gospels[4] describe Jesus' entry into Jerusalem on what the church calls 'Palm Sunday'. Although this event is often called the 'Triumphal Entry', a more attentive reading of the texts show that while it is an event full of symbolism, there is little note here of triumph.

At Passover, Jerusalem overflowed with pilgrims. The population of what might be called 'Greater Jerusalem' was normally around a hundred thousand but this figure would have been multiplied several times over during Passover.[5] Jerusalem wasn't just crowded, it was also tense. Given that Passover celebrated a past liberation by God from foreign oppression and looked forward to a new liberation in the future by the Messiah, it was the most potentially explosive festival of the year. The Roman authorities increased the military presence; the governor came up especially from Caesarea to provide 'hands-on crisis management' if needed. On the Jewish side the concern that everything would pass off smoothly would have been shared by those with vested religious and financial interests in the temple system. Everybody knew that Rome would deal with any trouble swiftly and savagely.

That Jesus was going into Jerusalem was apparently known and expected; while in the past he had hidden his actions and avoided confrontation, that time had now ended. Jesus' very public entry into Jerusalem was carefully prepared beforehand and had a deep symbolism. He arranged, presumably with friends from those previous visits to Jerusalem, to ride in on a young and unridden donkey. It was fulfilment of an important prophecy about the Messiah in Zechariah:

> Rejoice, O people of Zion!
> Shout in triumph, O people of Jerusalem!
> Look, your king is coming to you.
> He is righteous and victorious,
> yet he is humble, riding on a donkey –
> riding on a donkey's colt.[6]

In this conscious and public action Jesus was making a double statement. There was an unmistakable claim to be the promised Messiah, yet at the same time a deliberate rejection of any role as a military or political king. All the trappings of a conquering monarch – the stallions, the swords and the soldiers – were missing. Like all occupying powers throughout history, the Romans would have had a network of informers and collaborators and would no doubt have been aware of the arrival of a potential Messiah. Nevertheless, Jesus' underwhelming entrance on a young donkey, in gentleness and humility, would have quickly undermined any sense of threat. The geography of Jerusalem may be significant here: the governor and his soldiers would have entered by the west gate but Jesus entered from the east.

News of Jesus' entry into Jerusalem seems to have become well known and crowds had gathered to welcome him. Their welcome was enthusiastic and revealed an expectation that Jesus was going to declare that he was the Messiah and the one who would liberate God's nation from the Gentiles. In acts of homage the crowd threw their cloaks and palm branches before him and, using verses from Scripture, shouted out, 'Praise God! Blessings on the one who comes in the name of the LORD! Blessings on the coming Kingdom of our ancestor David! Praise God in highest heaven!'[7] John tells us that they also shouted, 'Hail to the King of Israel.'[8] These verses, the references to 'the coming Kingdom' and, above all, 'the King of Israel', reveal the people's hopes. The palm branches, too, were significant: two centuries earlier, when the victorious Judas Maccabeus had entered Jerusalem after liberating it from the Greeks, palm branches had been used during processions.[9]

Any expectations of a spectacular inauguration of the Messiah's reign as king were disappointed. Instead of confronting the Romans, Jesus simply went to the temple, looked around with a careful scrutiny and then returned to Bethany outside Jerusalem where he and his followers were staying. By the end of that Sunday there may already have been many in Jerusalem who were feeling disillusioned. It's a universal phenomenon of the human race not just to want a Messiah, but to want one on our terms.

MONDAY TO WEDNESDAY

After lodging in Bethany, Jesus re-entered Jerusalem on the following day. On the way he saw a fig tree that already had a show of leaves, normally a sign that small, edible shoots could be found on it.[10] Yet despite the promise, the tree bore none and Jesus pronounced judgement on it: 'May no one ever eat your fruit again!' Later, it was seen to have withered. The link that both Matthew and Mark make between this – the only miracle of destruction in the Gospels – and the clearing of the temple highlights that this is an enacted parable: the fig tree was often a symbol of Israel.[11] Despite being intended for blessing and offering promise, the nation and the temple system had failed to deliver. Judgement loomed: as the fig tree had withered at Jesus' word, so would the temple system.

Jesus then returned to the temple and taking dramatic action drove the merchants and their customers from the outer court of the Gentiles.[12] This 'clearing of the temple' is seen as the fulfilment of one of the last Old Testament prophecies found in the book of Malachi: '"Look! I am sending my messenger, and he will prepare the way before me. Then the Lord you are seeking will suddenly come to his Temple. The messenger of the covenant, whom you look for so eagerly, is surely coming," says the LORD of Heaven's Armies.'[13]

Here in the temple it is not just what Jesus does but what he says that is important: 'The Scriptures declare, "My Temple will be called a house of prayer," but you have turned it into a den of thieves!' This is a compilation of two Old Testament quotations: the first from Isaiah referring to God wanting to bless the Gentiles through the temple; the second a passage where the prophet Jeremiah announces judgement on the temple of his day because of the people's corruption.[14] Jesus was pronouncing a solemn verdict on the temple: greed and complacency had kept it from serving its appointed task as a place where all people, including the Gentiles, could find God.

The context of these passages in Isaiah and Jeremiah brings a chill to these words: originally they had announced the destruction of the First Temple, and by quoting them Jesus was passing sentence on the Second Temple. His action was not that of a reformer warning that change was necessary lest judgement fall; it was of a prophet declaring guilt and pronouncing judgement. What we see here and elsewhere in these final chapters of the Gospels is not simply the prophecy of the destruction of the temple and the priestly system in AD 70, but of its replacement. Jesus will be temple, priest and sacrifice, and not just for the Jewish people but for the world.

On the Tuesday, Jesus returned to Jerusalem for a full day of teaching. The day was marked by confrontation. Jesus appeared again in the temple where he was soon involved in controversy. A delegation from the Jewish ruling council – the Sanhedrin – turned up[15] and questioned Jesus about the source of his authority. Jesus answered that it came from the same place as that of John the Baptist. As the religious leaders did not dare to admit – or deny – that John's authority was from God, they were forced into a humiliating silence. Jesus faced trick questions designed to evoke answers that would discredit him with the faithful or incriminate him with the Romans. His skilful evasion of the traps set for him in a way that publicly humiliated his questioners would only have served to enrage his opponents.

Jesus also told parables which openly challenged or threatened the religious leadership. Some of them talked of impending judgement on the religious establishment, others taught unmistakably that Jesus saw himself as 'God's Son'.[16] In these encounters we see Jesus becoming increasingly open about his identity and in turn being given an ever more hostile response from the authorities. The growing intensity of the attacks on Jesus suggests a change in attitude from the authorities: he has gone from being an annoyance who they wished would go away to being an opponent who had to be removed.

On this day Jesus also talked about the near and distant future.[17] As they were leaving the temple, the disciples drew Jesus' attention to its monumental grandeur. Jesus response was startling. 'Do you see all these buildings? I tell you the truth, they will be completely demolished. Not one stone will be left on top of another!'[18] Later, sitting on the Mount of Olives looking across at the majestic edifice of the still uncompleted temple, the disciples, evidently still perturbed by Jesus' words, asked him, 'When will all this happen? What sign will signal your return and the end of the world?'[19] Although it seems that they assumed the temple's destruction and Jesus' return would occur together, Jesus separates these two events in his answer. Referring to the destruction of the temple Jesus said that there would be warning signs and warned his followers to flee the area.[18] Then speaking of his own return, Jesus implied that it would not be immediate: there would be a long and turbulent period when the good news about him would be proclaimed in the face of bitter opposition. There would be rumours of his return and false messiahs would appear, but his followers should ignore them: when he did return it would be an event that was unexpected, unmistakable and unavoidable. As for the time of his return, Jesus said that it was something that only the Father knew.[20] The key issue for his followers was to be faithful and ready at all times for his return.

While we do not know what Jesus did on the Wednesday, Mark tells us that the Sanhedrin – or at least part of it – met then to consider their options.[21] Monday's symbolic clearing of the temple and the further confrontations on Tuesday would have confirmed their decision that Jesus was someone who had to be eliminated. He was undermining their authority, making blasphemous claims and, worst of all, threatening the stability which gave the Romans their security and taxes and the Sanhedrin some measure of control.

In seeking the death of Jesus, the Sanhedrin had a problem because the Romans had removed their authority to impose capital punishment.[22] Doubtless they could have arranged a spontaneous and unofficial stoning – as was to happen to Stephen only a few years later[23] – but Jerusalem was too volatile to risk it. The best solution would be for Jesus to be executed by the Romans themselves. For one thing, this would allow the Sanhedrin to avoid blame by portraying it as an action by the occupying powers. For another, the mode of death would be crucifixion and not only was that particularly shameful but the Scriptures stated that anyone who was 'hung on a tree' was cursed.[24] What surer way could there be of destroying Jesus' claims to be the Messiah than by having him both publicly shamed *and* divinely cursed?

Yet there were two problems. The first was that the Romans needed to have evidence that Jesus was indeed a threat. Given Jesus'

---

[18] Early church writers claimed that, just before the siege of Jerusalem began, many Christians acted on prophetic warnings and fled Jerusalem, crossing the Jordan River to safety.

popularity it is almost certain that the Romans had already checked on him and his teaching. Had they felt Jesus posed a threat to Rome he and the disciples would simply have been rounded up by the military and executed on the spot. The fact that not only had the Romans not done this but had ignored Jesus' very public entry on Palm Sunday suggests that he was not considered a serious threat. The second problem was the practicality of arresting a man who retained great support among the crowds. Organising any arrest would have involved unpredictable risks and so the Sanhedrin resolved to play safe and act after the feast when people had gone home and the atmosphere was less politically charged.

These plans were overthrown by the unexpected intervention of Judas Iscariot.[25] By offering to betray Jesus, Judas made things easier: with inside knowledge, Jesus could now be safely arrested without risk of disorder.

Why Judas betrayed Jesus has been the subject of endless discussion. Unless it was a down payment, the money offered him – the infamous 'thirty pieces of silver' – was not a great amount. It is far more probable that Judas had become bitter and disillusioned. Indeed it may be that, perhaps alone of the disciples, Judas had realised that Jesus had rejected the idea of becoming a political and military king in order to become 'a suffering servant' and that wasn't something that he wished to be part of. Ultimately, though, Judas' motives elude us. One significant result of this is that it leaves him as an anonymous, universal figure who challenges all who follow Jesus. Followers of Jesus need to stay close to him lest, in the outline portrait of Judas, they find their own face staring back at them.

THE LAST SUPPER

Towards the evening of the Thursday, Jesus and his followers gathered for a meal, the 'last supper', in an upper-floor room in Jerusalem. Jesus made the arrangements in secret, presumably to prevent his arrest there. Although Jesus clearly knew that his arrest and execution were near, we see no hint of urgency or desperation in his attitude or actions at the meal: he remains in complete control of events.

In Luke's Gospel we learn that despite having spent so long with Jesus, the disciples were still rather childishly squabbling with one another over rank and status.[26] That issues of pride and position existed is alluded to in John's Gospel where we read that, before the meal began – and amid embarrassed protests – Jesus took it upon himself to wash the dust and dirt off the feet of the disciples.[27] By performing a task so humble that it was only done by the lowest ranking servants, Jesus demonstrated that the only model for leadership was one of being a servant. Although some Christian denominations do perform a ritual of foot-washing at Easter, the principle of a 'servant leadership' is something that constantly needs to be remembered.

While there have been attempts to understand the last supper in different ways, it seems clear that it was the standard Passover meal. This was traditionally a family meal and Jesus presided over it in the manner of the head of the household. Traditionally, symbolic actions and ritual questions were part of the meal to bring out the meaning of the Passover as a commemoration of God's deliverance and the inauguration of the covenant. During this particular Passover meal, however, Jesus departed from the normal time-honoured patterns. Suddenly, his followers found they were no longer commemorating the old covenant; they were now celebrating the inauguration of a new one.

The idea of a new covenant for 'the forgiveness of sin' is something that God had promised long ago through Jeremiah[28] but how Jesus referred to it now was both unprecedented and shocking. Taking the bread, Jesus broke it, saying, 'This is my body which is given for you.'[29] Then, taking the cup of wine, he said, 'This is my blood which confirms the covenant between God and his people. It is poured out as a sacrifice to forgive the sins of many.'[30] Jesus' words here are full of deep significance. In establishing the first covenant, Moses had sprinkled the blood from sacrificed animals over the people, saying, 'This blood confirms the covenant the LORD has made with you in giving you these instructions.'[31] The first covenant had also involved a meal: immediately after Moses had sprinkled the blood, he and the leaders of Israel had ascended Mount Sinai and shared a meal together in God's presence.[32] By echoing those words, Jesus was indicating the new covenant that he was inaugurating would also be put into effect with blood, but that the blood involved would be far more precious than that of any animal.

Through the simple but unforgettable images of bread to be eaten and wine to be drunk, Jesus was teaching his followers that his torn flesh and his shed blood were given 'for you'. He was indicating that his impending death was not going to be an accident or a meaningless tragedy, but something deliberately done for his people. Jesus saw himself as going to stand in the place of his followers and to bear the judgement that was theirs. Like the Servant prophesied in Isaiah, Jesus would suffer *for* others. His death was going to achieve something; it was to be a sacrifice, the ransom, the payment of a penalty that would allow the forgiveness of sins.

By telling his followers that they were to 'do this in remembrance of me',[33] Jesus was also declaring that this meal was not a one-off action. As the Passover had been a yearly reminder of the first great deliverance by God and the giving of the first covenant, so the sharing of the bread and wine was to be repeated regularly to act as a reminder of God's great deliverance in Jesus and the new covenant. One of the most remarkable features of how the Christian community distinguished itself from Judaism was the replacement of the Passover by the new ritual that Jesus instituted. Under various names – the Communion, the Breaking of Bread, the Eucharist, the Lord's Supper, the Mass – Christians have re-enacted this taking of bread and wine ever since. It is – or should be – a reminder of three things: forgiveness is given to those who have received Jesus; this forgiveness is blood-bought; as saved individuals we are part of God's people with whom we must share fellowship.

At some point in the meal Jesus talked about his betrayal and told John that he knew it was Judas who would betray him.[34] With Jesus' permission Judas left, taking to the priests the information they needed: Jesus would be spending the night in Gethsemane, an isolated walled garden, where he could be arrested.

Immediately after Judas' departure Jesus predicted that all the disciples would desert him. Peter, however, was boastfully confident:

'others' might abandon the Lord but he would follow him even to death. Jesus replied that before the cock crowed Peter would have denied him, not just once but three times.

In John's Gospel we are given an account of what Jesus said to his disciples following Judas' departure.[35] Jesus told them that he needed to go away, but this was not some disaster that should trouble them; his departure would be for their benefit. Jesus promised to return and also to send them another helper, the Holy Spirit, who would guide and empower them and do for them what he himself had done so far. Jesus warned his followers that they had a mission which would not be easy; the world would be hostile towards them. He also instructed them to show love to one another. Yet the final note he sounded was that of encouragement: they could rejoice – in Jesus they had overcome the world.

Jesus followed his teaching with an extraordinary prayer which gives an unsurpassed glimpse into his relationship with his Father.[36] We see in this prayer the unity and love that exists between Father and Son, and Jesus' desire to complete the task he has been given. Finally, Jesus prayed for all who follow him – present and future – and particularly that they would be united in a way that would show who they were to the world.

Jesus and the disciples then left for Gethsemane.

GETHSEMANE

Gethsemane lay at the foot of the Mount of Olives and it seems to have been a private garden that was well known to Jesus and the disciples. What happened here is something that is both revealing and profoundly moving.[37]

At Gethsemane we see an astonishing change of mood. Jesus, so far the master of events, the confident leader without a hint of fear or indecision, suddenly became overwhelmed by events. He summoned Peter, James and John to go with him and walked away from the rest of the disciples. He then left the three a short distance behind him with instructions to stay alert. Then he began to grapple with the appalling immensity of what was to happen to him. Here the Gospels describe Jesus as falling on the ground and 'being anguished and distressed', 'crushed with grief'; in Luke we read that 'he was in such agony of spirit that his sweat fell to the ground like drops of blood'.[38]

The focus of Jesus' intense anguish was what lay ahead. 'He prayed that, if it were possible, the awful hour awaiting him might pass him by. "Abba, Father," he cried out, "everything is possible for you. Please take this cup of suffering away from me. Yet I want your will to be done, not mine."'[39] In the darkness of the garden, Jesus clearly faced a final and almost overwhelming temptation to reject what lay ahead. He saw fully what the cross would cost him and was given a foretaste of the physical, mental and spiritual agony that he would suffer. The reason for the extraordinary depths of Jesus' distress here was no doubt not a realisation of the physical suffering of the crucifixion but the awareness that on the cross he, the Son of God from eternity, would know for the first time a separation from God the Father. Paul, writing to the Galatians, gives us an indication of what Jesus must have seen facing him: 'When he was hung on the cross, he took upon himself the curse for our wrongdoing. For it is written in the Scriptures, "Cursed is everyone who is hung on a tree."'[40]

The temptation for Jesus literally to walk away from the trial and the cross must have been overwhelming. Yet he resisted it and his praying ended with 'I want your will to be done, not mine'.[41] This act of profound obedience by the one who was seen as the 'Second Adam'[42] in this garden has long been seen as being the counterpart to the act of disobedience of the first Adam in the garden of Eden. What was lost there is now to be regained, but at an appalling cost.

Twice Jesus went to see the three disciples who were keeping watch with him but on both occasions he found them asleep. Jesus had never failed them but now, when he needed them, they failed him. Finally, he returned a third time to awaken the sleeping three but now it was too late for recriminations or apologies: the arrest party had arrived. The calmness that characterises Jesus throughout the Gospels has now returned; the storm that almost overwhelmed him has passed. Gethsemane was, it seems, the moment of final temptation. Here Jesus confronted all that lay ahead and irrevocably chose to commit himself to the horror that he must now face.

13

THE TRIAL AND THE CROSS

This entire chapter covers little more than twelve hours. It is a thought-provoking fact that with their four separate descriptions of what happened, we have here the most detailed account of any event in ancient history. Returning to our cinematic analogy, it is as if the pace of film has now slowed down almost to a stop, with focusing and framing lingering on every grim detail. This, every writer of every Gospel says, is the heart of the story that they are telling. Indeed, to use the revealing Latin word for cross, this is the *crux* of the matter.

The accounts of what has become known as Good Friday do not make pleasant reading. It's not just the blood and gore. In fact the Gospel writers skip over that: after all, their readers would not have needed reminding of the horror of crucifixion. It's more subtle. With few exceptions other than the victim himself, we see here humanity at its worst. There is large-scale evil – the big sins of hatred, envy, mockery, cowardice, injustice and brutality. Yet there is also a swarm of petty evils – the passing of blame, religious hypocrisy, the chaotic rage of a mob, the shameful reluctance to intervene on behalf of an innocent man. In one sense Jesus is judged on Good Friday: in another sense it is the human race which is judged. We don't come out of it very well at all.

The dreadfulness of the day is highlighted by the fact that Jesus was totally innocent. For a day that has become known as 'Good Friday' there seems precious little good about it.

THE ARREST

A large, armed crowd sent from the religious leadership and led by Judas arrived in Gethsemane in the early hours of Friday morning to arrest Jesus.[1] It included soldiers, probably from the temple guard but possibly with some Roman elements to keep an eye on things. The use of overwhelming force here was intended to utterly crush any opposition and to prevent Jesus from slipping away in the darkness. Those responsible for the arrest were clearly anxious that nothing would go wrong.

Aware of the danger of misidentification in a darkness lit only by flickering torches, Judas identified Jesus with the customary kiss of greeting. The Gospels tell us that Judas' act was, in fact, pointless: Jesus readily declared who he was and asked that his followers be spared. There was a faint eruption of resistance as Peter lashed out with a sword and then, rebuked by Jesus, he and the other disciples fled.

Jesus, now on his own, was arrested, bound and taken away.

THE TRIALS OF JESUS

Each of the Gospel writers reports that, following his arrest, Jesus underwent a succession of legal examinations and procedures at the hands of the Jewish authorities, Pilate and even Herod Antipas, the ruler of Galilee.[2]

Although the religious authorities had managed to arrest Jesus relatively easily, their difficulties were far from over. Originally the plan had been to delay arresting Jesus until after the feast when the pilgrims were all heading back home, but Judas' offer had abruptly advanced matters. It had, however, created problems.

One of the chief problems involved time. Sunset Friday evening would mark the start of the Passover Sabbath and once it began nothing could be done until the Sunday morning. Jesus clearly retained support both among the people and also it seems within the Sanhedrin, where at least two figures, Nicodemus and Joseph of Arimathea, were opposed to the execution.[3] If Jesus were to be simply locked up pending trial, there might be the possibility of him being released or trouble from his Galilean supporters. Plainly, the whole process of accusation, trial and execution needed to be completed within hours in order that the fragile peace of Passover could be kept.

To complicate matters Jesus had to be judged by two separate systems. At the very least the formalities of the Jewish religious system had to be kept: Jesus needed to be found guilty by the Sanhedrin of a religious offence worthy of death, such as blasphemy. However, while the Sanhedrin might pass the death sentence they did not have the power to inflict it, so it would be necessary to hand Jesus over to the Romans. But given that the Romans had not the slightest interest in any charge of blasphemy against the Jewish faith, here the accusation needed to be different. Accordingly, Jesus of Nazareth was to be presented to the governor, Pontius Pilate, as someone who had claimed to be a king and as such was a rebel against Rome, a charge that carried the penalty of death by crucifixion.

The accounts of the processes through which Jesus was judged and executed can be followed simply as a judicial narrative: a grim and sad tale of false accusation, unfair judgement and brutal punishment. Yet the authors of the Gospels saw beyond the superficialities of court procedures and we need to do so too. They plant their careful narratives with double meanings and deep allusions. For instance, when Pilate presents Jesus to the crowd with the simple announcement, 'Behold the man!'[4] we are doubtless meant to hear something deeper: this is the 'true man', the 'authentic man', the 'new Adam'. Equally, the constantly re-echoed theme of 'king' and 'kingship' is something that carries the most profound level of meaning.

One feature of these trials that should trouble all who consider themselves religious is the way that although intent on seeing Jesus killed, the authorities are careful to maintain the superficialities of faith. They are anxious not to break the Sabbath or to become unclean by entering the palace of the Gentile Pontius Pilate.[5] There is a warning here: it's easy to fall into the trap of keeping the niceties of religion while overlooking the truly important matters.[6] People with clean hands may still do dirty deeds.

The preliminary hearing before Annas

From John's Gospel we learn that Jesus was first taken to the house of Annas, the man who had been high priest from AD 6 to 15 and who was probably still considered to be the 'proper high priest'.

Annas retained a vast influence on Caiaphas, the current high priest, who was his son-in-law.[7] On the verge of a problematic trial, the Sanhedrin needed to make sure that they had the backing of the highest religious authorities. This informal first hearing may also have been intended to probe any defence that Jesus would offer. Annas asked Jesus about his followers and what his teaching had been. Jesus' response, that what he said was public knowledge, earned him a blow to the face: the first of many physical attacks.

The formal trial before Caiaphas

Shortly afterwards, while it was still night, Jesus was brought before Caiaphas, the man who was officially the high priest.[8] With him were enough of the Sanhedrin to make any verdict valid. Witnesses were summoned against Jesus, apparently with the intention of showing that he had threatened the temple, but they could not agree on their statements and Jesus remained silent.

Throughout the various trials Jesus is either silent or gives the minimum response. In this, the first Christians saw a fulfilment of one of the prophecies about the Suffering Servant in Isaiah 53.

> He was oppressed and treated harshly,
>> yet he never said a word.
> He was led like a lamb to the slaughter.
>> And as a sheep is silent before the shearers,
>> he did not open his mouth.[9]

Finally, apparently frustrated, the high priest resorted to putting Jesus under solemn oath: 'I demand in the name of the living God – tell us if you are the Messiah, the Son of God.'[10] No faithful Jew could ignore such a charge. Jesus answered, 'You have said it. And in the future you will see the Son of Man seated in the place of power at God's right hand and coming on the clouds of heaven.'[11] By applying Daniel's great prophecy[12] to himself Jesus was not simply claiming to be the Messiah but also to be equal to God. Inevitably there was uproar. 'Then the high priest tore his clothing to show his horror and said, "Blasphemy! Why do we need other witnesses? You have all heard his blasphemy."'[13] The verdict was inevitable: Jesus was guilty and should die.

We should note in Jesus' declaration another remarkable and ironic claim. Jesus stood in the court accused of breaking the Jewish law but claimed that one day he himself would be the judge of all people.

Dawn was breaking as Jesus, mocked and struck yet again, was led away. The first phase of his trial was over: he had been convicted of blasphemy.

Peter and Judas

The Gospel writers weave together the fate of two of the Twelve into their accounts of Jesus' trial before the Sanhedrin. Peter, his natural bravado returning and no doubt feeling bound by his oath of faithfulness, followed Jesus into the courtyard of Annas' house.[14] There, as he stood around in the darkness, Peter found bystanders and servants challenging him. Wasn't he a Galilean? Hadn't he been with Jesus? Hadn't he been in Gethsemane? Peter denied each question with increasing force, finally swearing with an oath that he didn't know Jesus. After his third denial, the cock crowed: Peter remembered Jesus' prophecy of his betrayal and broke down in tears. Far from following Jesus to death, as he had promised, Peter had disowned him at the merest hint of danger.

On hearing that Jesus had been condemned to death, Judas was struck with grief and guilt. He returned to an unsympathetic temple leadership, threw away the money he had been paid and then in utter despair went and hanged himself.[15] There has been speculation ever since that had Judas repented then, like Peter, he might have been restored.

The Roman trial

Jesus was now brought before Pontius Pilate, the governor, and the one man who could approve a death sentence. The historical reports we have of Pilate[16] paint him as a man who was insensitive, brutal and probably disliked Jews.

The Sanhedrin presented Jesus to Pilate as someone who, by claiming to be 'King of the Jews', had committed the capital offence of high treason. They were presumably hoping that Pilate would just rubberstamp their request for an execution. But, as everybody other than Jesus was to find out that Friday, nothing would work out as they anticipated. Pilate turned out to be reluctant to agree to their demands. Had perhaps mention of Jesus' kindness to a centurion[17] found its way to Jerusalem? As already noted, the Roman security must have known something about Jesus and if some of his soldiers had been present at the arrest, Pilate might not have been in total ignorance about the prisoner. Pilate questioned Jesus as to whether he was the 'King of the Jews'. As the questioning of Jesus continued Pilate seems to have become increasingly convinced of the innocence of the accused man. Finally, he announced to the priests and the crowd gathered outside the palace that he saw no basis in the allegations.

The angry response of the crowd that Jesus had stirred up trouble all the way from Galilee showed Pilate that they wanted nothing less than a death sentence, but it also suggested a way out. Herod Antipas was in town for the Passover and as ruler of Galilee had the authority to pass judgement on Jesus. Trying to dodge responsibility, Pilate sent Jesus to Herod. He may have hoped that Antipas would take Jesus back with him to Galilee where, as had happened with John the Baptist, he would disappear in some way or other. Luke's account of Jesus' interrogation before Herod – the man who had John the Baptist executed – suggests that the ruler was not only brutal but also shallow.[18] While the religious leaders shouted theological accusations, Herod treated Jesus simply as a conjurer, posing question after question in the hope of seeing a miracle. Jesus stayed silent and Herod's frustration turned to mockery. Finally, dressing Jesus in a royal robe – perhaps one of his castoffs – he had him returned to Pilate.

Pilate, reluctant to either sentence Jesus or risk the crowd's anger by freeing him, now resorted to a new ploy. He offered to release a prisoner as a Passover gesture of goodwill in the hope that the crowd would choose Jesus. Here, again, he was thwarted. The crowds, prompted by the priests, demanded instead the release of Barabbas, a criminal guilty of murder and rebellion.[19] Again we hear the echoes of a deeper theme: a guilty person is set free because the innocent Jesus takes his place.

Increasingly frustrated and not wanting to bow to pressure from the religious leadership, Pilate resorted to yet another tactic. He had Jesus flogged, presumably hoping this would be enough to appease his enemies. Then, amid more blows and mocking, Pilate's soldiers placed a crown of thorns and a purple robe on Jesus. Pilate now presented this battered and bleeding figure to the crowd. Any hope that this brutal and mocking humiliation might satisfy them was dashed as the priests and temple guards began shouting, 'Crucify! Crucify!'[20]

Pilate, by now utterly exasperated at the turn of events, declared that he found Jesus not guilty. The sharp response by the religious leaders that Jesus ought to die because he called himself the 'Son of God'[21] merely stiffened Pilate's reluctance by frightening him: like most Romans, Pilate was probably intensely superstitious. Once more he made another attempt to have Jesus released but this time the leadership played their strongest card, telling the governor, 'If you release this man, you are no "friend of Caesar." Anyone who declares himself a king is a rebel against Caesar.'[22] It was an unsubtle threat that if Pilate released Jesus they would send a delegation to Rome to tell the Emperor Tiberius that he was disloyal. After all, Rome could only have one Emperor.

For Pilate this was the deciding factor. He made one more feeble attempt for Jesus to be acquitted. 'What? Crucify your king?' he asked the crowd, only to get the reply from the leading priests, 'We have no king but Caesar.'[23] It was probably meant to be ironic but it was utterly tragic. The covenant demanded that Israel had no king except Yahweh and this was an act of betrayal.

Pilate, recognising that he had been outmanoeuvred, yielded to their demands. He pronounced the formal sentence of death and, in an action that has echoed down the ages, washed his hands publicly as a gesture that he personally was not guilty. Jesus was sent to be flogged and then executed.

The flogging that Jesus now suffered was almost certainly the most severe form, using cords with metal tips which ripped open the skin, tearing muscles and even exposing internal organs.[24] It was a punishment so severe that it alone was sometimes sufficient to cause death. In this case it was associated with further intense mockery from the Roman soldiers.[25]

THE CRUCIFIXION

When it comes to describing Jesus' death by crucifixion, the Gospel writers make no attempt to arouse our emotions: they simply state what happened.[26] Yet what happened was horrific. For the Romans, the point about crucifixion was not that it was an appropriate punishment for criminals but that it deterred crime. One first-century Roman author Quintilian writes, 'When we crucify criminals the most frequented roads are chosen, where the greatest number of people can look and be seized by this fear. For every punishment has less to do with the offence than with the example.'[27]

Although there were variations in the details the basic principle of crucifixion was the same. A man – almost all victims were men – had his arms fixed by rope or large nails hammered through the wrists[19] to a crossbeam which was then raised and slotted into a vertical post. The feet were then nailed to the upright and the victim simply left to die. With his weight supported largely by his legs, the victim found breathing agonising, with every breath forcing him to push down on his nailed feet. For all the pain caused by being fixed to the cross the process caused no wounds to vital organs so that death often occurred slowly. A crucified man could survive for days, suffering dehydration and sunstroke and increasingly becoming food for birds, animals and insects until, eventually, exhaustion set in. Finally, unable to lift his head from his chest to breathe, suffocation and death would occur.

It was characteristic of Roman practicality that they had perfected the methods of crucifixion and could hasten or extend the duration of suffering. Giving the victim a peg or ridge to sit on delayed death and kept the victim alive in agony as long as possible. Breaking leg bones – which made breathing harder – hastened death. The deterrent effect of crucifixion was enhanced by the way that it

---

[19] The artistic image of Jesus being nailed to the cross through the palms of his hands is incorrect: the soft tissue there is not strong enough for such a purpose. The word translated in the Bible as 'hand' included the wrist.

exposed the victim to public humiliation: stripped naked, unable to move, unable to control either bladder or bowels. Crucifixion was the most appalling of deaths.

Under Roman guard, Jesus was led to the place of execution. As was customary for convicted criminals he was made to carry the crossbeam himself.[20] Weakened by the floggings Jesus stumbled under the weight and the Romans ordered a passer-by, Simon of Cyrene (a Roman colony in Libya), to carry the wooden beam.[28]

The site of the crucifixion at Golgotha ('the place of the skull'[21]), would have been somewhere prominent just outside the town walls, possibly at a crossroads where the maximum number of people could see what happened. There, in the late morning, Jesus was nailed to the cross.

The Gospels are more interested in why Jesus was on the cross than describing what happened but they do provide some details. Jesus was crucified between two other criminals and the procedure was supervised by Roman soldiers, who passed the time gambling for Jesus' clothes.[29] Almost all of Jesus' followers had now deserted him: only the women and one disciple, John, remained. A crowd gathered, including the curious and some of the religious leaders. It is an horrific but authentic insight into human nature that the mocking that had been directed at Jesus continued as he was pinned helpless to the cross.[30] Soldiers, bystanders, the religious leaders, even the criminals now next to him, all ridiculed him.

Above the cross Pilate had arranged for a title to be fixed: 'Jesus of Nazareth, the King of the Jews.'[31] It was written in Hebrew, Greek and Latin. Tradition has seen in these the languages of faith, culture and government and thus the significance of this crucified man to every area of life. It was a petty and spiteful gesture by Pilate intended to infuriate the religious leadership who had outmanoeuvred him but,

20 The idea that Jesus carried the whole cross is another product of artistic imagination. The Romans found that the whole process was much more efficient and less time-consuming if you kept the vertical beam permanently in the ground. This had the incidental benefit of creating a permanent reminder of the penalty of rebellion.
21 Older English Bibles translated 'the place of the skull' by the word 'Calvary'.

in yet another instance of a hidden significance, it allowed Jesus to die with his true identity proclaimed to the world.

The Gospel writers are well aware of the fulfilment of prophecy and their accounts are interwoven with references to the Scriptures, particularly Psalms 22 and 69. There seems little doubt that they also saw what happened that day was a remarkable fulfilment of prophecies of the 'Suffering Servant' in Isaiah. Here are some of the relevant verses from Isaiah 52:13 – 53:12.

But many were amazed when they saw him.

His face was so disfigured he seemed hardly human,

and from his appearance, one would scarcely know he was a man . . .

He was despised and rejected –

a man of sorrows, acquainted with deepest grief.

We turned our backs on him and looked the other way.

He was despised, and we did not care.

Yet it was our weaknesses he carried;

it was our sorrows that weighed him down.

And we thought his troubles were a punishment from God,

a punishment for his own sins!

But he was pierced for our rebellion,

crushed for our sins.

He was beaten so we could be whole.

He was whipped so we could be healed . . .

He was oppressed and treated harshly,

yet he never said a word.

He was led like a lamb to the slaughter.

And as a sheep is silent before the shearers,

he did not open his mouth.

Unjustly condemned,

he was led away.

No one cared that he died without descendants,
>   that his life was cut short in midstream.
But he was struck down
>   for the rebellion of my people.
He had done no wrong
>   and had never deceived anyone.
But he was buried like a criminal;
>   he was put in a rich man's grave.
But it was the LORD's good plan to crush him
>   and cause him grief.
Yet when his life is made an offering for sin,
>   he will have many descendants.
He will enjoy a long life,
>   and the LORD's good plan will prosper in his hands.
When he sees all that is accomplished by his anguish,
>   he will be satisfied.
And because of his experience,
>   my righteous servant will make it possible
for many to be counted righteous,
>   for he will bear all their sins . . .
He was counted among the rebels.
>   He bore the sins of many and interceded for rebels.

This passage, which the Dead Sea Scrolls confirm was written long before the crucifixion, interprets the cross. The early Christians were certain that, for all its dreadfulness, what happened on the cross was no accident but the awesome culmination of God's age-old plan. It was a death *for* God's people.

SEVEN SAYINGS FROM THE CROSS

The four Gospel writers record in total seven sayings of Jesus from the cross, what the church came to call 'the Seven Last Words'. In these statements uttered under such pain that every syllable must have been agony, we see something of the meaning of the cross.

'Father, forgive them, for they don't know what they are doing.' Luke 23:34

Jesus' first recorded words from the cross were a prayer for forgiveness for his persecutors. The hardest teaching Jesus ever gave was for his followers to love their enemies, but here Jesus practised what he preached and he showed exactly how far forgiveness should go. By doing this Jesus revealed the forgiving heart of God as well as establishing a tradition of forgiveness that has continued through Stephen, the first Christian martyr,[32] to the present day.

'I assure you, today you will be with me in paradise.' Luke 23:43

Although both of the criminals hanging either side of Jesus began by mocking him, one changed his mind. He rebuked the other, declared that Jesus was innocent and asked Jesus to 'remember me when you come into your Kingdom'.

Jesus' answer is a powerful statement of his own authority and power to save. In it there is not even a hint of a 'maybe' or 'I'll try to put in a good word', there is only a majestic certainty: 'I assure you, today you *will* be with me in paradise.' Jesus' answer is also a tremendous expression of God's grace: it is an active, free forgiveness given to someone who deserved nothing, who could do nothing to save himself and most certainly was going to do nothing to earn his salvation in the future. This incident has always been seen as an encouraging demonstration that last-minute conversions are possible if there is genuine repentance.[22]

'Dear woman, here is your son.' 'Here is your mother.' John 19:26–27

Turning to his mother and to John 'the disciple he loved', Jesus said to her, 'Woman, here is your son', and to him, 'Here is your mother.' John's Gospel tells us that 'from then on this disciple took her into his home'.[33] Assuming that Joseph had died, Jesus as the eldest

---

22 That salvation at the last minute is possible doesn't justify postponing a decision to follow Jesus. After all, who of us knows when our last minute will be?

son would have been responsible for his mother and, with his other brothers still hostile to him, he now passed that responsibility onto John. Honouring parents was one of the Ten Commandments and Jesus' action here is a reminder that throughout his life he perfectly obeyed God's Law. It also shows that even in the most appalling pain, Jesus cared for those who were dependent on him.

'My God, my God, why have you abandoned me?' Mark 15:34

Mark tells us that at noon a darkness descended on the land that lasted until three o'clock and as it fell Jesus cried out in Aramaic, *'Eloi, Eloi, lema sabachthani?'* meaning 'My God, my God, why have you abandoned me?'

The darkness and Jesus' anguished cry are linked. The cause of the darkness is unknown; it couldn't have been an eclipse. Whatever its origin the darkness was deeply symbolic of what was happening. In the Bible darkness is a symbol of judgement[34] and now judgement was falling on the land and also on Jesus.

Jesus' cry, a quotation from Psalm 22:1, is the only recorded instance when he does not pray to God as *'Abba*, Father'. The prayer shows that although Jesus still trusted in God, he sensed that he was now separated from him and felt abandoned by him. For the first time in eternity, the unique fellowship between God the Father and God the Son was broken.

The Gospel writers do not attempt to explain the meaning of Jesus' experience of abandonment and separation but in the letters of the New Testament we find Paul saying, 'God made Christ, who never sinned, to be the offering for our sin, so that we could be made right with God through Christ.'[35] At the very hour when Passover lambs were being slain in the temple, Jesus, 'the Lamb of God who takes away the sin of the world',[36] was dying on the cross as a greater and ultimate sacrifice for sin.

'I am thirsty.' John 19:28

Jesus' statement of his thirst is a reminder of the physical pain of the crucifixion. Again we are given a thought-provoking irony. He who had supplied all needs now suffers the most basic of human desires; the one who had offered 'living water' to the thirsty is now thirsty himself.

'It is finished!' John 19:30

In the original Greek 'it is finished' is a single word which, in this context, means that something is fulfilled or completed and was often stamped on a bill to show it was paid. Jesus was not saying '*I am finished*' but something very different: he had completed all that he had come to do.[37] He had paid the price and offered the needed sacrifice.

'Father, I entrust my spirit into your hands.' Luke 23:46

The very last words of Jesus as he died were a simple prayer committing himself to his heavenly father. The spiritual darkness was over; he had surfaced from the terrible depths and could now call God 'Father' again.

AROUND THE CROSS

John's Gospel tells us how the Jewish leaders, not wanting to have the crucified men still hanging there on the Sabbath, asked Pilate for the deaths to be hastened. The soldiers duly broke the legs of the criminals either side of Jesus but found that Jesus was already dead. To make sure, one soldier pierced Jesus in the side with a spear and 'immediately blood and water flowed out'.[38] Whatever the medical explanation it was clear evidence that Jesus was dead. Jesus appears to have died unusually quickly for someone who was crucified, perhaps because he had already been flogged heavily and subjected to other physical abuse. Ultimately, however, Jesus is portrayed as laying down his life; even as he submitted himself to death, he retained control over it.

The Gospels tell us about two other incidents that occurred as Jesus was crucified. The first was an earthquake; the second was that as Jesus died the great curtain in the temple was torn from top to bottom.[39] The temple curtains were symbols of the separation that existed between sinful human beings and the Holy God. The miraculous tearing of this curtain speaks of how men and women can now come to God directly through Jesus. It also carries with it an implication of awesome significance: the temple and the temple system are now redundant.

THE BURIAL

Normally, the corpse of someone who was crucified was thrown into a common grave, but if there was a request from the family, the body might be released to them. With Jesus, such an intervention came not from the family but from Joseph of Arimathea, a man who while being a member of the Sanhedrin had not agreed with its verdict.[40] Joseph, courageously identifying with Jesus, asked Pilate for the body. After ascertaining that Jesus was indeed dead, Pilate allowed the body to be taken down and handed over to Joseph.

With the Sabbath due to start around six that evening, Joseph did not have much time. Aided by Nicodemus, another sympathetic member of the Sanhedrin, he had Jesus' body taken down from the cross. It was taken to a tomb that, as was common practice for the wealthy, had been cut into the rock nearby for later use. There Joseph and Nicodemus wrapped the body in grave clothes, packed a large quantity of spices around it and placed it in the cave-like tomb. Finally, they had the large round stone rolled back across the entrance of the cave. The first three Gospels mention a significant detail: namely that the women who had followed Jesus from Galilee stood nearby watching the burial.[23]

Night fell.

On the following day, the Sabbath, only one event is recorded. A delegation from the Sanhedrin visited Pilate and asked for the tomb to be guarded in order to prevent his disciples from coming and stealing his body and then telling everyone he had come back to life. Pilate gave orders that the tomb be sealed and authorised a guard to be placed at it.[41] The religious and political powers in the land had collaborated to see Jesus dead and buried; they now collaborated once more to ensure that he stayed that way.

23 There are some eyewitness touches here. The women are carefully named in the Gospels, quite probably because they were well known in the early church. The fact that they did not help out with the burial is doubtless because, in this society, unaccompanied women from a rural background in Galilee would certainly not dare to lend a hand to unknown wealthy Jerusalem men. Even amid the bitterest tragedy, cultural rules must be kept.

THE GREAT EXCHANGE

Christianity has always declared that the cross was not a meaningless tragedy but instead something profoundly filled with meaning. The passage from Isaiah 52 and 53 quoted earlier says repeatedly that the suffering of the Servant would be *for* something or someone.

Some modern writers have criticised this idea of Jesus acting as a substitute for others as being fundamentally immoral. This reflects modern Western concepts of individualism and quite overlooks the fact that in many – possibly most – cultures, people do not exist simply as individuals but as *family*. And within a family it is legitimate, indeed expected, for one member to bear the burdens, whether financial or even legal, of other members. Significantly, the letter to the Hebrews invokes this idea of family solidarity: 'So now Jesus and the ones he makes holy have the same Father. That is why Jesus is not ashamed to call them his brothers and sisters.'[42] If becoming a Christian is to be adopted by God[43] then there is a legitimacy in Jesus bearing our punishment: we are his brothers and sisters – we are family.

One way of looking at the cross is to see it as the place where everything becomes overturned or reversed. At least five of these reversals can be identified and all are vital.

Innocence and guilt

The Gospel writers detail the trials of Jesus not to show the guilt of the judges but to show the innocence of the defendant. All that Jesus had done wrong was to declare the truth: that he was the Son of God, the Messiah. No other charge was made against him. Nevertheless, in being crucified Jesus was judged a criminal and executed between criminals.

Yet if innocence becomes guilt at the cross so here can guilt be exchanged for innocence. Here, if we choose, our guilt can be taken off us and Christ's innocence offered us in return.

Power and weakness

In the Gospels, Jesus is a man of extraordinary power and authority; all things – wind and waves, fevers and fish, demons and death –

yield to his command. Jesus is the King of nature. On the cross, however, Jesus lays all this aside: he becomes helpless, unable to move even his own hands and feet. 'He saved others,' jeer the leaders, 'but he can't save himself.'[44]

Yet if power becomes weakness at the cross so here can weakness become power. Here, if we choose, our weakness and frailty can be taken from us and God's power through the Spirit offered us in return.

Fellowship and separation

All through his life Jesus had perfect fellowship with God the Father, yet on the cross he becomes separated from him. Jesus knows God intimately as 'Abba, Father' and rejoices in the access that he has to God, but on the cross a terrible barrier descends between them.

Yet if fellowship becomes separation at the cross so here can separation be exchanged for fellowship. All human beings have distanced themselves from God, but at the cross that gulf of separation can be closed. Here, if we choose, our separation from God can be ended and fellowship offered us in return.

Light and darkness

The Gospels note that there were three hours of darkness at the cross.[45] When you consider that Jesus frequently described himself in terms of light and claimed he was the 'light of the world' (John 8:12) this phenomenon acquires the deepest of meanings. No explanation of this darkness is offered in the Bible but over the centuries many people have seen the cross as the place where Jesus drew the darkness of the world's evil onto himself. Here, uniquely, is the one place in history where the darkness of evil is neutralised and replaced by light.

Yet if light becomes darkness at the cross it also indicates that it is a place where, if we choose, we can exchange our darkness for the light that Jesus offers.

Life and death

Jesus was the one who raised people from the dead, the one who declared that he was life. Now he submits to the death of the very worst kind. He of whom John could say he 'gave life to everything'[46] dies.

Yet if life becomes death at the cross, so here can death be exchanged for life. Here, if we choose, our lives, doomed to eternal death, can be taken from us and Jesus' life offered us in return.

This idea of reversal is implied in the words of Jesus at the Last Supper when he declared the bread was his body 'broken *for you*' and the wine was his blood 'shed *for you*'. It is that repeated phrase '*for you*' that ultimately explains both the purpose of the cross and indeed Jesus. What happened at the cross was, as Isaiah foresaw in his prediction of the Servant, *substitution*. It is where Jesus descended to the depths so that we might ascend to the heights. It is where Jesus, out of love, became everything that we human beings are – guilty, weak, separated from God, darkened by sin and evil and subject to death – in order that we may *if we choose* share in his innocence, his power, his fellowship with God, his light and his life. But choose we must.

And when you understand that, referring to the worst day in the history of the world as 'Good' Friday makes sense.

14

THE RESURRECTION

By every precedent of history, by every law of nature known then and now, by every experience of everybody, the story of Jesus should have ended with his burial. Not only was he dead but he had been brutally and publicly killed in such a humiliating and disgraceful manner that it was obvious to all that he was not God's promised Messiah. Jesus' followers had been shamed, scared and scattered. It is hard to imagine a more definite, public and final closure to the story of Jesus. It was the end.

But it wasn't.

Something happened.

A *something* that transformed Jesus' followers and ultimately transformed the world; a something that made Passover AD 30 not the disappointing end of a sad story in an obscure part of the world, but the beginning of a vast and unsurpassed epic that has shaped and shaken history on every continent and that remains unfinished. That this *something* was a single event – the bodily resurrection of Jesus from the dead – is the foundation of all Christian belief, past and present.

It cannot be emphasised enough that without the resurrection Christianity would not exist. As we noted when we looked at Jesus' teaching, what he taught repeatedly focused on who he was. Most teachers would say 'this is the truth for you to have' but Jesus said '*I* am the truth for you to have'. If Jesus had died a criminal, abandoned and cursed by God and *stayed dead*, then the authority and validity of everything he said would be fatally and finally undermined. That is not just today's verdict but, significantly, it was also the verdict at the time. Around AD 53 Paul wrote to Christians in Corinth: 'And if Christ has not been raised, then all our preaching is useless, and your faith is useless . . . And if Christ has not been raised, then your faith is useless and you are still guilty of your sins.'[1] Barely two decades after the crucifixion, Paul, who as we have seen knew personally some of the people involved in the trial and crucifixion, was making the astonishing statement that the Christian faith stood or fell on the reality of the resurrection of Jesus.

We must clarify what resurrection means. The Jews, along with almost everybody in the Middle East and Mediterranean areas then and, indeed, most people since, believed in ghosts, spirits and visions. So the idea that after the crucifixion Jesus' followers might have 'had a vision' of the dead Jesus or even 'seen his spirit' would not have been surprising. Such things were a fact of life or – more precisely – death. Yet this sort of thing is exactly what Christianity has always said was *not* what happened. It has always claimed that far from being spiritual or visionary experiences, what did happen was something radically different. It is that, after his death, Jesus' body was physically 'raised from the dead' and he appeared to his followers for several weeks in a solid, material form that could, among other things, eat food, be touched and – how matter-of-fact can you get? – make breakfast.[2] When twenty years or so later Paul preached about Jesus to the Athenian philosophers, it was this idea of a physical resurrection that aroused their scepticism and mockery.[3] A *bodily* resurrection was as head-shakingly outrageous to them as it is to us.

In this chapter we want to look at the resurrection. We want to examine whether it really happened[24] but also to look at what it means. The first Christians preached about the resurrection of Jesus not as an utterly remarkable, attention-grabbing event but as something full of significance with implications that are both breathtaking and life changing. Everything Jesus claims about himself and for his teaching is true: God can be known as 'Father'; forgiveness

---

24 There is no shortage of full and detailed discussions of the resurrection. One accessible treatment of the issues can be found in the 70-page chapter 10 of Josh and Sean McDowell's *Evidence That Demands a Verdict* (Authentic, 2nd edition, 2017). At a more scholarly level the traditional Christian view of the resurrection has been examined and supported in different ways in the very substantial studies of N. T. Wright, *The Resurrection of the Son of God* (SPCK, 2003) and Michael R. Licona, *The Resurrection of Jesus: A New Historiographical Approach* (Apollos, 2010).

is possible; heaven is attainable; and death for the believer is just a short sleep before eternal joy. If the resurrection of Jesus didn't happen, then the implications are equally breathtaking but in the most devastating way: Jesus' teaching cannot be trusted; God – if any such being exists – is a remote deity; there is no certainty of forgiveness; no assured hope in life; and no confidence in the face of death. Whether or not the resurrection happened is something that changes how we view every aspect of our past, present and future.

THE ACCOUNTS

Detailed information about the resurrection comes from six places in the Bible: the four Gospels, the book of Acts and a summary that Paul gives in 1 Corinthians 15. The resurrection is assumed in all the letters of the New Testament; their talk about Jesus in the present tense and their constant references to him as 'Lord' only makes sense if he was risen from the dead.

The 1 Corinthians passage reads:

> I passed on to you what was most important and what had also been passed on to me. Christ died for our sins, just as the Scriptures said. He was buried, and he was raised from the dead on the third day, just as the Scriptures said. He was seen by Peter and then by the Twelve. After that, he was seen by more than 500 of his followers at one time, most of whom are still alive, though some have died. Then he was seen by James and later by all the apostles. Last of all, as though I had been born at the wrong time, I also saw him.[4]

This statement is important as it is almost universally agreed that 1 Corinthians was written no more than twenty-five years after the crucifixion. Actually Paul's reference to this truth having 'been passed on to me' suggests that it is what Paul was taught after his conversion, when perhaps around AD 36–37 or even earlier he met the other apostles in Jerusalem.[5] In other words, it is a statement of belief in the resurrection that can be traced back to within a few years of the event itself.

Paul is a highly significant witness. As we noted in chapter 1, he had been a zealous persecutor of Christians and played a key role in the trial and execution of Stephen (probably within two or three years of the crucifixion) and had then been commissioned by the highest religious authorities to round up believers in Jesus.[6] In the course of his duty, Paul would therefore have heard both the claims by the persecuted about the resurrection of Jesus and inevitably the explanation by the Jewish leaders in Jerusalem of what had happened just a few years ago and only a short distance away. But whatever this 'official party line' was, Paul ultimately found it inadequate.

The Christian belief that Jesus was raised from the dead centres on three lines of evidence: the empty tomb, the appearances themselves and the very existence of the Christian church. The first two lines of evidence come from the Bible; the second from outside it.

EVIDENCE 1: THE EMPTY TOMB

All the Gospels report that on the Sunday morning Jesus' tomb was found to be empty, Jesus' body gone and the grave clothes left behind.[7] What seems to have happened is something like this.[25]

Just before dawn on the Sunday morning, the women returned to the tomb with spices. Although they had observed the burial of Jesus by Joseph of Arimathea and Nicodemus late on the Friday afternoon, they wanted to pay their own last respects to him. Given that the entombment had been in haste, they may have wanted to be sure that the burial rituals were properly carried out. Arriving at the tomb, they found the guards had fled and the large gravestone had been rolled away. Concluding that the tomb had been robbed, Mary Magdalene ran back to tell Peter and John. The other women peered into the empty tomb and were greeted by two angels, one of whom made the statement that Jesus was not there: he had been

---

25 One classic attempt at harmonising when and what happened over Easter is to be found in John Wenham's book *Easter Enigma: Are the Resurrection Accounts in Conflict?* (Paternoster Press, 1984, reprinted 2005). A more recent attempt at a reconstruction is to be found in Andreas Köstenberger and Justin Taylor, *The Final Days of Jesus: The Most Important Week of the Most Important Person Who Ever Lived* (Crossway, 2014).

raised, 'just as he had promised'. With feelings of joy, amazement and fear, the women ran away from the tomb. Alerted by Mary, Peter and John ran to the tomb and found it empty apart from the linen grave clothes[26] and the cloth that had covered Jesus' head which was 'folded up and apart from the other wrappings'.[8] The two then left – Peter bemused, John apparently beginning to conceive of the idea that Jesus had risen.

From this point on the tomb disappears from history although it may well be that the very ancient Church of the Holy Sepulchre in Jerusalem was built on the site. The emphasis on the *empty* tomb is interesting. With most prophets there is a great deal of interest amongst their followers in preserving the memory of where they lay buried. Yet however far back you go in Christian history there is no evidence of any veneration for the tomb of Jesus of Nazareth as the place where his body lay, just a statement that it was found empty.

Of course, on its own the empty tomb does not prove the resurrection took place. After all, there could be other reasons for a missing body. But it is strong indirect evidence. Given that the only resurrection Jews believed in involved the physical restoration of the body back to life, no one could have possibly held that Jesus had been resurrected if his body was still in the tomb. Joseph was a wealthy and well-known man; his tomb was probably in a private garden that he owned and its location was no doubt public knowledge. There had been guards and the tomb had had some sort of official seal placed on it. All the Sanhedrin or the Roman administration had to do was have a public exhumation and the tales of a resurrection would have collapsed. But they didn't do that and the reason is very simple: they couldn't. The body wasn't there.

---

[26] Although the Shroud of Turin has been claimed to be the burial cloth of Christ it does not seem to fit with the biblical description of the grave clothes and there is strong evidence, particularly from Carbon-14 dating, that it is a medieval forgery. Nevertheless, how anyone produced such a remarkably lifelike and anatomically accurate representation of a crucified man currently defies explanation.

EVIDENCE 2: THE APPEARANCES

The records of the appearances

In the narratives the empty tomb is far less significant than the central feature of the resurrection accounts: the appearance of Jesus to numerous people over a period of forty days. Around a dozen appearances of the resurrected Jesus are specifically mentioned. We list them here.

- **The appearance to Mary Magdalene** (John 20:11–18). According to John, the very first resurrection appearance was to Mary Magdalene. After telling Peter and John that the body had gone, Mary returned to the tomb. There she encountered Jesus, mistaking him for the gardener until he addressed her by her name. Jesus told Mary to go and tell the others.

- **The appearance to the women** (Matthew 28:8–10). Jesus also appeared to the rest of the women as they left the garden. He told them not to fear and confirmed the message they had been given by the angel at the tomb.

- **The appearance to Peter** (Luke 24:34; 1 Corinthians 15:5). There are two references to a private encounter some time on the first Easter Sunday between the risen Jesus and Peter, the man who had so badly failed him.

- **The appearance on the Emmaus road** (Luke 24:13–32). Luke tells how, in the late afternoon of Easter Sunday, two of Jesus' followers, Cleopas and an unnamed companion (possibly his wife), were walking away from Jerusalem and talking about what had happened when they were joined by a stranger. In response to the man's enquiry they told him what had happened to Jesus. Rebuking their disbelief, the stranger began to explain the Scriptures to demonstrate that the Messiah must suffer before entering his time of glory. Arriving at their destination, Cleopas insisted that the man join them for a meal and when the stranger broke bread, prayed over it and handed it to them, they suddenly realised it was Jesus.

- **The appearance to the disciples** (Luke 24:33–43; John 20:19–23). The disciples, still afraid of the religious leaders, met behind locked doors on the evening of Easter Sunday. Cleopas and his companion arrived and, as they were telling their story, Jesus appeared to all of them. Their immediate reaction was to be terrified because they thought they were seeing a ghost. Jesus reassured them of his identity, encouraged them to touch him and then, as a final proof that he was not a ghost, asked for some food, which he ate. Jesus explained that what had happened to him had been predicted in the Scriptures and promised the coming of the Holy Spirit.

- **The appearance to all the Eleven** (John 20:24–29). Thomas, who had been absent from the Easter Sunday evening encounter, expressed quite understandable scepticism about the accounts of the resurrection. Eight days later, as he and the disciples were again meeting behind closed doors, Jesus came and stood among them. Thomas, invited by Jesus to touch him, now believed, declaring, 'My Lord and my God!'

- **The appearance by the Sea of Galilee** (John 21:1–23). After these events the disciples returned to Galilee and seven of them decided to go fishing overnight. Early in the morning Jesus met them and ate breakfast with them. It was at this meeting that Peter was finally and publicly restored to fellowship.

- **The appearance to the disciples in Galilee** (Matthew 28:16–20). Matthew ends his Gospel with Jesus meeting his disciples in Galilee and giving them instructions. There he told his disciples, 'I have been given all authority in heaven and on earth. Therefore, go and make disciples of all the nations, baptising them in the name of the Father and the Son and the Holy Spirit. Teach these new disciples to obey all the commands I have given you. And be sure of this: I am with you always, even to the end of the age.'

- **The appearance to more than five hundred followers** (1 Corinthians 15:6). In his list of resurrection appearances in 1 Corinthians, Paul records an appearance to more than five hundred of Jesus' followers at one time, most of whom he claims were, at the time of writing (around AD 53), still alive.

- **The appearance to James** (1 Corinthians 15:7). Paul also says that Jesus appeared to James, his brother. This helps explain the otherwise puzzling fact that although James had previously not believed in Jesus he soon became a leader in the early church,[9] something noted by Josephus.[10]

- **Another appearance at a meal** (Acts 1:3–5). Close to the end of the forty-day period of appearances, Jesus showed himself again to the disciples in Jerusalem. At a meal with them he told them to stay in the city until they were baptised with the Holy Spirit.

- **The Ascension** (Luke 24:50–53; Acts 1:6–11). Luke tells how, at the end of the forty days, Jesus went a short way out of Jerusalem with the disciples to the Mount of Olives, where he ascended into heaven. This event, which the church calls the Ascension, was a visible illustration of two truths. The first is that the time of the resurrection appearances was now over, Jesus' earthly ministry was completed. The second is that, from this point on, Jesus is enthroned as King and rules in majesty in heaven.

The nature of the appearances

There are a number of notable features of these appearances that are worth thinking about.

- The appearances are very varied. They occurred outdoors and indoors, to one, two or more than five hundred people at different times of day and in different places.

- The appearances are repeatedly – almost insistently – described as physical events rather than visions. The Jesus who appears can be touched and felt and prepares and eats food.

- The appearances are dynamic rather than static. The Jesus who appears walks with people, does things with them and engages them in conversation.

- The appearances of Jesus are lasting rather than momentary. His followers didn't just get a fleeting glimpse of him; there was time for meals and conversation.

- The appearances are undramatic and unsensational. There are no fanfares of trumpets or flashes of lightning: the risen Jesus just appears and then talks or eats with his followers.

- The appearances are unpredicted and unexpected.

- The Jesus who appears is still recognisably the 'old Jesus'. Physically he still bears the scars of the crucifixion (not many people had those!). After their initial shock, the disciples relate to him with the same intimacy and familiarity that they did before the crucifixion.

- In other ways, however, the Jesus who appears is different from who he was. He is able to appear and disappear at will: locked doors pose no barrier to him.

In summary, these appearances are described as being of a real, physical but somehow transformed Jesus who was very much alive.

EVIDENCE 3: THE FACT OF THE EARLY CHURCH

For someone searching for the truth about the resurrection, the first two lines of evidence that we have been discussing are somewhat problematic. After all, the empty tomb is no longer available for study and the appearances ended forty days after they had begun. Yet there is a third piece of evidence – the existence of the church – and that is one that has convinced many people that the resurrection did occur.

If you think about the situation on the evening of Good Friday it is clear that Jesus' followers had been totally shattered by what had happened. After the highest of hopes Jesus had been crucified, an event that carried with it the implication that God himself had delivered an overwhelming condemnation of his claims to be the Messiah. The catastrophe was deepened by the uncomfortable fact that Jesus had been betrayed from within the Twelve and that Peter, their leader, had himself denied Jesus. In this totally miserable situation without the least ray of hope, there is not the slightest indication that anybody among Jesus' followers expected any miraculous overturning of the disaster. From the account in Luke of Cleopas heading out to Emmaus with his companion, it seems likely that the crushed disciples were beginning to disband, leave Jerusalem and return home.

Yet seven weeks later everything was astonishingly different. According to the book of Acts, Peter and the other disciples were back in Jerusalem, openly and confidently declaring to crowds that the Jesus who had been crucified was indeed the long-awaited Messiah. Something had transformed the dispirited, disillusioned and discredited followers of Jesus into a dynamic, confident and expanding movement. The disciples claimed that what had transformed them was the appearance of the risen Jesus to them and the sending of his Spirit on them. It's difficult to think of a more plausible alternative.

The rise of the church poses a problem to even the most sceptical. That Jesus existed and died on a cross around AD 30 are facts beyond dispute, but equally indisputable is the fact that, within twenty years of the crucifixion, there were groups of people across much of the eastern Mediterranean worshipping the crucified Jesus as Lord and Messiah. Within thirty years there were enough of them in Rome for Nero to grotesquely execute a 'vast number'. Within seventy years Christians were, despite brutal persecution, widespread across most of the Roman Empire and beyond. Explaining this explosive growth from the most discouraging start imaginable – a humiliated Jewish manual worker, a handful of very ordinary people and a message of peace with God – requires some sort of explanation. The only satisfactory solution for this otherwise inexplicable expansion of the church is a combination of three remarkable things: the extraordinary person of Jesus himself; the extraordinary phenomenon of the resurrection; and the extraordinary power of the Holy Spirit.

SUPPORTING EVIDENCE

In any legal case you will have the main body of evidence and then also supporting evidence. This is exactly the case with the resurrection. Let's briefly mention some of the supporting evidence.

1. The nature of the resurrection accounts

One significant factor is that there is no indication in the language of the resurrection accounts that we are dealing with anything other than real events. So, for example, if you look at the way in which

John describes the trial and that in which he describes the resurrection appearances, you find his style of writing remains the same. There is no evidence that we have suddenly shifted from remembered history into invented fantasy.

The most detailed account we have of the first resurrection appearance is to be found in John 20:1–18 which is well worth a careful examination. It tells how Mary goes to the tomb on the Easter Sunday morning and, finding the stone rolled away, runs back to the disciples, two of whom come back with her. They look at the tomb, note the folded grave clothes and then go back to where they came from. Mary stays and meets two angels who do nothing more than ask her why she is crying. Then, evidently having concluded that the body has been stolen, Mary turns round to see the risen Jesus who she immediately assumes is the gardener. Only when he calls her by name does she realise who it is. After the briefest of encounters she is told to return to the disciples with the news of Jesus' resurrection.

Now, consider the following aspects of the account.

- There are incidental and even trivial elements that are entirely irrelevant to the story but which appear to be details remembered by eyewitnesses. So, for instance, we read that the beloved disciple (normally assumed to be John) outran Peter and got there first where he stooped and 'looked in and saw the linen wrappings lying there, but he didn't go in'.[11] These are precisely the sort of irrelevant details that occur only in genuine eyewitness accounts or in realistic fiction. And no one had invented realistic fiction.

- The focus on a woman as the first witness of the resurrection is unlikely to have been invented because women were not trusted to be legal witnesses.

- The chief female character is identified not just as Mary but as Mary of Magdala; in other words a figure who is specifically identified, probably someone who was known in the early Christian community and who could verify the story.[12]

- It's all very embarrassing for the church leadership. Peter, the leader of the early church, runs to the tomb, sees the grave clothes and then, apparently completely baffled, *goes back home, leaving a woman behind at what he must presume is a crime scene.* It's neither bold, wise nor chivalrous.

- Mary turns around and – further embarrassment – sees Jesus and mistakes him for the gardener. (You can hear her, can't you, years later, recounting the story for the thousandth time? 'And – I still blush to think about it – it was *quite* the stupidest thing I ever did in my life . . . I honestly thought he was the gardener!')

- There are also curiosities in the account that, had the accounts been invented, would surely have been edited out. So was it one woman or several? Why was Mary Magdalene told by Jesus, 'Don't cling to me, for I haven't yet ascended to the Father'?[13]

- When Mary recognises Jesus, John tells us that she cried out '*Rabboni!*' the Aramaic for 'my teacher' and a word so alien to his Greek-speaking readership that he has to explain it.

- Jesus rebukes Mary for trying to cling onto him and then gives her instructions to go back to the disciples and tell them that she has met with him. So a *woman* is told to go back to tell the *disciples* about the most important event in history?

No, a modern novelist might well conjure up something like this using imagined realism, but not a first-century writer. Interestingly we do have a good idea of what a 'fictional' treatment of the resurrection might have been like in what is called the 'Gospel of Peter', a pretty sensationalised reworking of the crucifixion and resurrection that almost certainly comes from the middle or late second century.[14] Here there is the full Hollywood treatment: a loud voice from heaven, descending gigantic angels, a stone that rolls away by itself and, finally, a walking and talking cross.[15] This, in the Gospels, is what we *don't* have.

2. The place and time of the claims

It's easy to believe remarkable things if you are separated by either time or space: distance truly does lend enchantment. Yet the first preaching of the resurrection occurred within a few weeks of the events of the first Easter, within a mile or so of the place where Jesus had been buried and in front of people who had witnessed everything.[16]

3. The role of women as witnesses

In Jewish culture of the time women were not allowed to be legal witnesses. The Talmud, a compilation of Jewish law, states that 'though the woman is subject to the commandments, she is disqualified from giving evidence'.[17] Josephus also says that a woman's testimony should not be admitted.[18] Had the resurrection accounts been invented, or even heavily rewritten, they would not have made so much of the witness of women.

4. The unexpected nature of the resurrection

It seems clear that no one was more surprised by the resurrection than the disciples. That there was a logic to the resurrection is something that had to be explained to them. It's difficult to see how the disciples would have manufactured the evidence for something they weren't expecting.

5. The early church's belief in the resurrection

However deep people dig into the history of the Christian church, no level has ever been identified in which the resurrection of Jesus was not an utterly central belief. In early Christian preaching there is no hint of any apology or unease about the resurrection, nor any suggestion that it was an invented explanation for the embarrassing fact of the crucifixion. Every sermon recorded in the book of Acts focuses on it. Throughout Acts and the letters there is an unshakeable and universal certainty that the resurrection of Jesus really happened. The triumphant tone of the early church, whether persecuted or not, suggests a confidence that the resurrection really did happen.

6. The shift in the Sabbath

The keeping of the Sabbath on Saturday was not an optional extra in Judaism: it was one of God's Ten Commandments and one of the most distinguishing features of the Jewish faith. Yet within a few years of the crucifixion, Jesus' followers, who had been devout Jews, had changed celebrating the Sabbath from Saturday to Sunday. It is hard to imagine anything capable of causing such a shift other than the resurrection.

7. The rituals of communion and baptism

The early church clearly regularly held meals, derived from Passover, with a ritual involving bread and wine that we have given various names to such as Communion or the Lord's Supper.[19] With the language and imagery of shed blood and broken body these were inextricably linked with the death of Jesus. Bizarrely, however, the tone of such meals was celebratory, something that is difficult to explain unless Jesus' death had indeed been followed by a resurrection. In a similar way the imagery of baptism – of descent into water linked with death and of coming back up out into a new life – only makes sense in the context of belief in the resurrection.[20]

8. The logic of the resurrection

The resurrection of Jesus may be unexpected but it has a logic. It is like some extraordinary twist in a novel or film that takes you by surprise, but when you think about it later you realise that actually it all makes sense. So the Old Testament teaches that death is the inevitable consequence of human beings having sinned against God. One interesting implication of this (which no one seems to have explored before the resurrection) is that if someone who had never sinned actually did die, death could have no hold on them. They might, as it were, sink down into the deep waters of death but then they would have to inevitably bob up again into life.

ALTERNATIVE EXPLANATIONS

No one who has been at the funeral of a loved one finds the idea of the resurrection of the body easy to believe. Yet the claims that Jesus rose from the dead cannot simply be dismissed. As with the issue of Jesus' deity, to simply say 'I can't believe in the resurrection' is not an adequate response. To be intellectually honest, we need to have some alternative explanation that fits the facts.

Such alternatives are hard to find and there are barely a handful of options. They include such suggestions as the idea that Jesus didn't die, the resurrection was 'wishful thinking' or some sort of hallucination, the body was stolen or his followers got the wrong tomb. We list these briefly here: they are analysed and refuted in several books.[21]

The chief problem with finding any alternative to the resurrection is that it has to explain multiple issues. It has to deal with the empty tomb and the curiously folded grave clothes, the multitude of very physical appearances of the crucified Jesus of Nazareth and to explain the transformation of the disciples from fearful failures cowering from everything to assertive evangelists confronting everybody. None of the alternatives explain either the joyful triumphant tone of the early Christian writings or that sense of the presence of the living Jesus that so many Christians have claimed to have known (including us) for the last two thousand years. No, the best solution is the traditional one: Jesus really *did* rise from the dead.

1. Jesus didn't die

Obviously the whole issue of the resurrection is avoided if you can argue that Jesus never really died but simply fainted on the cross and recovered in the tomb. Such a theory, however, demands not just one improbability but an entire succession of them. It requires that the Roman soldiers failed to kill Jesus, that the burial party didn't notice that he wasn't dead, that the tomb, wounds and the weight of spices didn't finish him off and that somehow – after tidying up his grave clothes – Jesus managed to escape from the tomb and then, most improbably of all, present himself convincingly as the risen Lord of Life and the victorious conqueror of death to his followers. Understandably, this view attracts little support.

2. It was all wishful thinking

Other people hold that the belief in Jesus' resurrection came about through wishful thinking; the desperate triumph of hope over grim reality. Here, after Jesus' death, some sort of tragic desire and longing within the disciples slowly crystallised into the confidence that, after all, he had been raised from the dead. This too, however, stumbles over many inconvenient facts, not least that there are limits to what wishful thinking can do. We have all experienced things that we wish hadn't happened – embarrassments, tragedies, accidents and mistakes – but we all know from our own experience that no amount of telling ourselves that they didn't happen can undo them. Reality is remarkably immune to the effects of wishful thinking. After all, if wishful thinking worked then why aren't there more stories of resurrected martyrs? The bitter, sad fact is that, however hard we may wish, the dead stay dead. *Normally*. The sheer physicality and the extent of the occurrence of the resurrection appearances also speak strongly against this view.

3. It was a vision or hallucination

Similar objections arise to a related idea: that the resurrection appearances were some sort of 'collective vision' or 'mass hallucination'. It's difficult to find any serious parallels to this sort of event. There are many problems with such a view: the defeated psychology of the disciples, the varied nature of the appearances and, again, their clearly solid and physical nature.

4. The body was stolen

Some people have claimed that Jesus' body was stolen either by his followers or by someone else. Again this is difficult. The body could not have been stolen by a casual thief because removing the stone that guarded the entrance would have required several people, and the neatly left-behind grave clothes renders the theory of theft improbable. And exactly why the body should have been stolen, or by who, has never been explained. Suitable candidates are hard to find. It was hardly the disciples, who had clearly gone into hiding. If the body was stolen by Jesus' enemies why didn't they produce it once the tales of the resurrection started? And why did Paul, once so close to the religious leadership, know nothing of it? If the idea of the resurrection was based solely on the empty tomb then this explanation might have merit but of course it fails to explain the appearances.

5. They got the wrong tomb

As an alternative to theories based on conspiracy we have those based on confusion. Here we have the women finding the wrong tomb, bumping into a Jesus look-alike, mistaking gardeners for angels and mishearing what is said. And the rest is done by the power of suggestion and that eternally useful standby, wishful thinking.

Yet to explain even the empty tomb as history's greatest blunder is incredibly hard. The Gospels make it clear that the women had been at the tomb on the Friday afternoon, so they knew the place. It would hardly have been a mass graveyard either: given Joseph's status, the tomb would have been in some small, walled garden. And, of course, tombs that contain empty shrouds are a fairly rare occurrence. Presumably, too, one of the first people to be told was Joseph of Arimathea who would have pointed out a misidentified tomb. (One would love to know his response to the news that, after brief use by one careful owner, he could have his tomb back.)

Significantly there is no sceptical consensus as to what happened. None of these views seems to have attracted more than limited support. As we note in the main text, the centrality of the resurrection in early Christian thinking demands some sort of explanation. We are convinced that the most satisfactory explanation is the simplest one: it really happened.

THE RELEVANCE OF THE RESURRECTION

As noted earlier, the resurrection of Jesus is not just one of the most awesome facts of history; it is something that overflows with significance. Let us suggest three things that are profoundly relevant.

The resurrection is a vindication

Imagine a good man or woman being punished for what they didn't do. He or she is publicly humiliated and their reputation, and all they stand for, is dragged deep into the dirt. If justice is to be done then they must be vindicated: the verdict must be reversed and they must publicly be declared free of guilt.

This principle applies to Jesus. The cross saw an utterly innocent Jesus treated as a guilty man, and so in the resurrection we see God reversing that decision and vindicating him to his followers. By raising Jesus from the dead God was declaring Jesus innocent and saying through an action what he had said before in words, 'This is my dearly loved Son, who brings me great joy.'[22] Mind you, it is only a partial vindication; Christ's full, final and public vindication will be given when he comes again in glory and the whole world sees him.[23]

The resurrection is an authentication

As we have seen, Jesus made extraordinary claims about who he was. Those claims require our trust and demand action. Inevitably, when we are asked to trust someone we must ask whether we can indeed put our faith in them. In raising Jesus from the dead, God is authenticating who Jesus is and what he said. The resurrection is God's signature of approval written on Jesus' claims: we can trust him with our lives. The resurrection shows that God has accepted Jesus' payment for our sin on the cross, that the power of evil has been decisively broken and that our own personal resurrection from the dead can be assured.

The resurrection has implications

We have noted repeatedly the contrast between a secular worldview that denies the miraculous and the biblical view that accepts it. So we pointed out that to really make sense of the miraculous we needed to step back from any materialistic worldview that rejects everything and anything beyond what can be observed or touched. In rejecting the medieval idea of a heaven 'up there' somewhere above the birds and the clouds, people have also rejected the idea of a heavenly realm beyond what they can observe. In doing so they have thrown out the very biggest of babies with the bathwater.

The resurrection has important implications in at least two ways. The first is that the only real explanation for resurrection involves God's direct miraculous intervention. Because nothing is as bad or final as death, the resurrection is God confronting the very worst that can happen and spectacularly dealing with it. This is a big God solving a big problem in a big way. The resurrection represents a God who sustains the whole cosmos and sees all of time and space before him, taking the corpse of Jesus and remaking it into a body in a way that both represents the simultaneous renewal of an old life and creation of a new form of life.

To understand the second way the resurrection is important requires we see it in its theological context. The fact is that there is a great deal of logic in the resurrection. We have already mentioned that as death is the punishment for sin, death can have no hold on a sinless being. Yet there is more. In one sense what the disciples claimed had happened to Jesus in the resurrection was not a theological novelty within the Jewish faith. Apart from the Sadducees, Jews of that period believed that, at the end of time, the dead would rise in glory. But that was in the future: they didn't believe it would happen in the present. Now remember what Jesus had claimed to be: the Messiah, the Son of God and also the One who would be Lord of the great day when death would be overturned and the cosmos remade. The resurrection of Jesus is the essential preliminary to that great event. The One who, at the end of what we call history, will summon the dead to life, has already risen. In the New Testament Jesus is called 'the Morning Star',[24] a reference to that heavenly body that announces the imminent rising of the sun in its glory. It is no wonder that with Christ risen, the New Testament talks about us being in 'the last days';[25] the King is already risen and ready to appear. The resurrection is not a bizarre, unique, one-off event. It is a foretaste of the final great and universal resurrection that will occur at the return of Jesus, Saviour and Lord.

This idea of Jesus being the prototype and pioneer of the great future event lies behind more of Paul's verses in 1 Corinthians 15.

> But in fact, Christ has been raised from the dead. He is the first of a great harvest of all who have died. So you see, just as death came into the world through a man, now the resurrection from the dead has begun through another man. Just as everyone dies because we all belong to Adam, everyone who belongs to Christ will be given new life. But there is an order to this resurrection: Christ was raised as the first of the harvest; then all who belong to Christ will be raised when he comes back.[26]

The resurrection of Christ must be seen in this context of the future. The very physicality of the resurrection is a reminder that heaven, not earth, is the place of true reality. The common view of heaven is that it is an utterly insubstantial place: a faint, transparent world of shadows and spirits. The authentic Christian view is the exact opposite: heaven is a place that is more real than real, more solid than solid. The resurrected Christ demonstrates this: he can enter rooms with locked doors, not because he is less substantial than matter, but because he is *more* solid. This world is, to use C. S. Lewis' memorable phrase, 'the shadowlands'. The resurrected Jesus is not simply the human race's first survivor of mortality; he is the King of a glorious, eternal Kingdom that will, in every respect, be better than anything we know or can conceive of here. Above all, the resurrection looks ahead to the promised renewal of the universe. The risen Christ is the pioneer from beyond the grave who tells us that one day, perhaps sooner than we imagine, this world with its griefs and pains will be put behind us.

CONCLUSION

The resurrection is an astonishing and unparalleled event with the most profound significance. It is also an event which for all its uniqueness and remarkable nature is supremely well attested. There are no other parallels in history but then there are no other parallels to Jesus of Nazareth.

Finally, there is an area of evidence which we have not yet mentioned, an area where the resurrection of Jesus can be personally tested. At the heart of the idea of the resurrection is the astounding belief that Jesus himself is alive, not just as an historical figure but as a present reality: a living person who we can communicate with and relate to. The testimony of Christians over the centuries is that this continues to be true: Jesus is alive and can be experienced as someone who transforms lives. Those who truly want to find the risen Jesus, not out of idle curiosity but ready to make him Saviour, King and Lord of their lives, can still find him.

These implications of the resurrection apply not just to our heads but also to our hearts. For the disciples, the resurrection was not simply an historical fact; it was also a personal experience. After Jesus had left them, the two on the road to Emmaus said to each other, 'Didn't our hearts burn within us as he talked with us on the road and explained the Scriptures to us?'[27] Since that day billions of people have experienced a similar 'warming of the heart' as they have encountered the risen, living Jesus. Indeed, it is that personal experience of the presence of the resurrected Jesus that lies at the very heart of the best and most complete Christian faith.

To believe in the resurrection of Jesus is not just to put a tick against a box on a list of 'things I believe in'; it is to let it change how we live.

15

NOT THE LAST WORD

The Jesus we see clearly portrayed in the Gospels is a man of outstanding power, wisdom and authority; an individual unlike anybody before or since; a figure who towers above both his own time and all history; someone who puts all others – including his followers – in his shade.

One of the most telling summaries of who Jesus was is to be found in the book of Acts, when the apostle Peter speaks to the Roman centurion Cornelius.

> You know what happened throughout Judea, beginning in Galilee, after John began preaching his message of baptism. And you know that God anointed Jesus of Nazareth with the Holy Spirit and with power. Then Jesus went around doing good and healing all who were oppressed by the devil, for God was with him.

And we apostles are witnesses of all he did throughout Judea and in Jerusalem. They put him to death by hanging him on a cross, but God raised him to life on the third day. Then God allowed him to appear, not to the general public, but to us whom God had chosen in advance to be his witnesses. We were those who ate and drank with him after he rose from the dead. And he ordered us to preach everywhere and to testify that Jesus is the one appointed by God to be the judge of all – the living and the dead. He is the one all the prophets testified about, saying that everyone who believes in him will have their sins forgiven through his name.[1]

Here there is the focus on the past: the miracles, the healing, the exorcisms; the death on the cross and then the resurrection to life on the third day. Here, too, there is also the focus on the present and the future: Jesus is the one appointed by God to judge the world, the one who fulfils prophecy and the one who can forgive sins. It was all there then and it's all there now.

In considering the truth about Jesus we are compelled to admit that he is unique. So we must accept that Jesus is a genuine figure of history, a man who existed in reality to the extent that his execution can be pinpointed not just within decades or years but within hours. Yet if Jesus is a figure of history, he is also *uniquely* above and beyond it. After all, nearly two thousand years after his death, his followers still refer to him using the present tense: they don't just say Jesus *was* but Jesus *is*.

That uniqueness is not just to do with his existence then and now: the Gospels tell us of a Jesus who is unique in four areas.

Jesus' *teachings* are unique. What he taught was simple, authoritative and of universal significance. Those who have taught morality to the world subsequently have either ignored his teachings, copied them or rewritten them – they have not surpassed them. Two thousand years of astounding cultural change and remarkable technological advances has not reduced the towering dominance of the Sermon on the Mount by a hair's thickness.

Jesus' *claims* about himself are unique. He considered himself God's Son, took the titles for God on himself and assumed God's authority. He claimed implicitly and explicitly to be one with God. His followers then and now have believed him.

Jesus' *actions* are unique. He showed an unsurpassed control over the natural and supernatural world, and demonstrated a total mastery of people, things and spiritual powers. His actions confirmed that he had God's power and authority even over death itself. Jesus' own resurrection is the validation of all his teaching and the confirmation of his claims.

Jesus' *character* is unique. On any sort of close examination even the best human beings are flawed by weaknesses, inconsistencies and excesses. Yet in Jesus we see no such defects. In him the virtues are balanced, complete and consistent: we see strength without hardness, gentleness without frailty, courage without recklessness, authority without arrogance. In Jesus we see a man whose forgiveness never becomes permissiveness, whose friendship with even the worst people never slips into compromise, whose deep personal faith never becomes a weapon to crush others. When we look at Jesus we see the human being we were meant to be and the person we wish that we were.

Yet for all the remarkable features of Jesus that the Gospels portray, what they depict is not some fantasy figure but a picture of a real, coherent and credible person. The figure they portray is an utterly extraordinary individual. He is someone simultaneously of his time, place and culture and yet so alien to it that his assertion that he came from heaven is perfectly believable. The claim that he was both perfect God and perfect man is plausible.

Yet ultimately, where it really matters, we see Jesus as exactly who two millennia of Christians have always claimed him to be: the One who is Lord, Saviour, Redeemer and the Living and Eternal King who will return one day to remake the cosmos.

It is not enough, though, to simply sum up Jesus as one of 'history's most remarkable characters' and leave it at that. Uniquely he is not a man whose biography you can close the pages with the thought 'I wish I could have known him'. After all, if we believe in Jesus' resurrection, then he is not just an historical figure; he is alive and active in the world. To return to the book of Acts, Luke opens his account by addressing Theophilus and in doing so writes one of the most extraordinary statements ever penned: 'In my first book I told you, Theophilus, about everything Jesus began to do and teach until the day he was taken up to heaven after giving his chosen apostles further instructions through the Holy Spirit.'[2] In all that he did in his life on earth, says Luke, Jesus was only *beginning* his actions; those actions continued after his death and they continue today. You cannot just close the book on Jesus. There can be no last word about someone who claimed to be *the* Word.

Jesus' question to his followers, 'But who do *you* say I am?'[3] still challenges and provokes us today. We need to reflect on, and respond to, that question.

To choose to follow Jesus is not a trivial decision: it is one that has consequences for every part of our lives. To say 'yes' to Jesus is to be prepared to have your life changed and to accept responsibilities and obligations. It is significant that in many of his miracles, Jesus asked others to help him: other people filled the jars with water at the wedding in Cana; other people served the bread and the fish to the five thousand; other people rolled the stone away at Lazarus' tomb. Where he could, Jesus gave his followers the privilege of being involved in his work. Ultimately, Jesus left those who trust in him the task not just of obeying him but of telling the entire world about him. Those who decide to follow Jesus must be prepared for him to give them responsibilities that will stretch them to their limits. To their limits indeed, but not beyond because he himself has promised to be with his followers through his Holy Spirit.

To say 'yes' to Jesus is to open the door to being challenged. Jesus never disguised the fact that following him was far from easy and he warned that it would involve hardship. In the darkest days of 1940, with his nation facing, almost alone, a powerful and seemingly unbeatable enemy, Winston Churchill promised 'nothing but blood, toil, tears and sweat'. Jesus' promise to his followers in their battle against a far greater darkness is similar. The great difference is that, unlike Churchill, Jesus can guarantee his followers an ultimate victory and an infinite reward. After all, he has written the future. But before those days of eternal glory we who follow Jesus must be prepared to accept hardships.

There are only two responses to Jesus' demand that we follow him now: acceptance or rejection. (Postponing a decision to follow him *now* is, of course, rejection.) It is a terrifying truth that he gives everybody the right to say 'no' to him, both for this life and the next. Yet to reject Jesus is the most serious thing any of us can do; it is to reject all the good he offers us now on earth and all that he promises us in eternity. To accept Jesus, to put following him before everything else, is to have your life transformed permanently. It is to accept his forgiveness, blessing and guidance and at the same time to take on willingly whatever obligations and challenges he gives us.

For all the struggles, pain and losses we may suffer in following Jesus we can know both times of inexpressible joy and an inexhaustible peace in this life and an eternity of it in the future.

Let us remind you of the prayer that Jesus gave his followers to say. Why not pray it yourself and begin your journey of faith in Jesus?

> Our Father in heaven,
>> may your name be kept holy.
>
> May your Kingdom come soon.
>
> May your will be done on earth,
>> as it is in heaven.
>
> Give us today the food we need,
>
> and forgive us our sins,
>> as we have forgiven those who sin against us.
>
> And don't let us yield to temptation,
>> but rescue us from the evil one.
>
> For yours is the kingdom and the power and the glory forever.[4]

Let me end with some words of blessing from Saint Paul: 'The grace of our Lord Jesus Christ and the love of God and the fellowship of the Holy Spirit be with us . . .' *Amen*.

ISSUES

ISSUE 1: CAN WE TRUST THE GOSPELS?

Let's be frank: the simplest way to disregard the challenge of Jesus is to consider him as fictional. Yet this is a response of intellectual laziness and should be challenged.

Unless you adopt the iron rule of the sceptic that anything that speaks of supernatural events is, of necessity, fiction, there is little in the Gospels to suggest that they are not factual. In fact, were there no miracles in the Gospels then they would no doubt be held by everybody to be some of the most authentic documents of the ancient world. (Of course, in reality, had there been nothing beyond the ordinary about Jesus, then there would have been no Gospels.)

Let's briefly consider the possibility that the Gospels are fiction. Novels did exist in the ancient world but such works are obviously recognisable as not belonging to the world of reality. They are, by our standards, rather unsophisticated: they shun realistic dialogue, play fast and loose with geographical and historical facts, include extraordinary and fantastic events and often have utterly implausible happy endings.[1]

As we noted in chapter 1 the Gospels fit firmly in the category of biography. The one Gospel author to talk about what he has written, Luke, specifically states in his opening words that he has produced a careful and accurate report through what we would call 'doing research'.

Let's briefly look at some of the evidence for the Gospels being authentic and factual accounts of what happened nearly two thousand years ago. Perhaps the strongest argument for authenticity is that the Gospels are, for the most part, set in an utterly credible world of rural Palestine (often specifically that of Galilee). This is one of the isolated, rural and closed village communities where people living at little more than subsistence level, are bound strongly together by family bonds, tradition and an unyielding and controlling faith. It is a place where the community sticks together, holds tightly to strict social codes, knows exactly what everybody is doing, and which views the outside world with suspicion.[27] Yet, and here's the striking thing, this is not the world of the early church – faithfully reflected in the Epistles – which, by within a few decades of the crucifixion, had become centred on the much more urban, open, cosmopolitan Gentile and Greek-speaking regions around the northern shores of the Mediterranean. It's impossible to imagine someone in Rome or Athens writing up an imaginary life of Jesus of Nazareth decades later and a thousand kilometres away without generating a multitude of agricultural, geographical and cultural inconsistencies.[2]

There are other pointers to authenticity in the Gospels.

- There are 'untidy' elements in them that, had they been invented, would surely either never have been included or would have been swiftly edited out. Take for instance the verses where Jesus says he doesn't know the time of his return and others that are, at least superficially, puzzling.[3]

- Equally, the various letters of the New Testament give us a very good idea of the 'theological language' that the early church used, yet the language of the Gospels is very different. So the Gospels talk about 'the Son of Man' and 'the Kingdom of God', terms that are almost totally absent from the New Testament letters. Yet for all the difference in language there is a real match between the picture of Jesus in the letters and that of him in the Gospels.

- The Gospels talk a great deal about worship in the context of the temple in Jerusalem and contain sombre warnings by Jesus about a looming judgement on that temple. There are even prophetic messages that seem to instruct believers what to do when the temple is besieged.[4] These 'the temple is doomed' references make perfect sense if the Gospels were written in

---

[27] Such rural communities have persisted in parts of the Middle East with little change. Chris, who has spent a lot of time in Lebanese villages just over the border from Galilee, finds the social and cultural setting of the Gospels immediately recognisable.

the context of Palestine *before* the catastrophe of AD 70 when the temple was indeed destroyed, but it's hard to see why anyone would have invented them *after* the event.

- The letters of the New Testament indicate that the early church grappled with all sorts of issues: circumcision, eating food offered to idols, the role of women, the gifts of the Spirit, how to relate to Roman authority, and so on. If the Gospels were wholly or partially invented, it would surely have been irresistible for the church leadership to have produced a Jesus who gave an authoritative judgement on these and other appropriate issues. One looks in vain for statements in the mouth of Jesus such as 'Truly I say to you, obey your leaders and pay them well' or 'Avoid dancing, amphitheatres, temples to pagan gods and non-kosher butchers'.

- One surely authentic feature is the way in which the Gospels portray the disciples – the very men who were the leaders of the early church – in an unflattering manner. For example, Peter, the chief of the apostles, is depicted in the Gospels as a man of limited comprehension, who is impetuous, inclined to speak before thinking and, worst of all, someone who, when it came to the test, denied Jesus.

- Some very striking work by the distinguished scholar Richard Bauckham has suggested that the considerable number of personal names which appear in the Gospels, and the way they are mentioned, is highly significant. Not only are these authentic names for Palestine at this time but there are indicators that readers would have known these individuals and recognised their names as testimony to the authenticity of the account.[5]

There are other and very serious problems with the 'fictional account' hypothesis. The sceptical proposal is that the early church wrote the Gospel accounts to somehow justify its existence. Yet this raises all sorts of questions. What sort of organisation creates one of the most uncomfortably radical and anti-organisation figures in history for its followers to imitate? There is also the interesting chicken-and-egg question: which came first, Jesus or the church? If the church created Jesus then who created the church? As we have seen, it is an unassailable fact that within two decades the improbable belief that a crucified Jewish carpenter (it's not hard to imagine the shudders and sniggers here) was someone you could pray to, had spread around the Mediterranean. Which is the most likely hypothesis? That someone came up with 'the greatest story ever imagined' or in Jerusalem that Passover something astonishingly remarkable happened to an astonishingly remarkable man?

We can't prove that the Gospels are 'true'. But it's difficult to imagine that they are in any way fictional. To believe that one or indeed several first-century authors were able to imagine a Jesus with such rich and detailed authenticity requires more faith than we have.

All the evidence suggests that the Gospels are what they claim to be: reliable accounts of what this extraordinary Jesus did and said.

ISSUE 2: HOW DID THE GOSPELS COME TO US?

When archaeologists or museum specialists in ancient artefacts are given an object, the first question they ask is, 'What is the provenance?' In other words, what is the history of this object? How has it come to us? This is a wise rule and it is entirely appropriate in the case of the Gospels. The best way of treating this is to trace the history of the Gospels from the earliest beginnings of good news about Jesus until the written documents were fixed in a form that is recognisably like today's copies.

Beginnings

Jesus was known by his followers as 'teacher' or 'rabbi'[1] and the implication there is that they learned from him in a disciplined, ordered way. The teaching that Jesus gave would have been in Aramaic, something that is preserved in various words in the Gospels.[2] While it is possible that the disciples took notes of what was said – people did – we can be certain that they memorised a great deal. That memorised material of what Jesus said and did would have been passed on to others – new converts perhaps – who, in turn, passed it on to others.

To most of us today any idea of anything being passed on by word of mouth would seem to be a guarantee of distortion and confusion.

After all, most of us can't remember more than three or four phone numbers and some of us struggle to remember our car registration. These doubts have been played on by the sceptics who have suggested that what we have in the Gospels is exactly what happens when, in a children's party game, you put individuals in a circle and get them to whisper a short statement to their neighbour. As we all know, by the time the phrase has gone full circle it's been distorted beyond all recognition. In reality, to say that this is what happened with the message about Jesus is naïve and belittles the first believers. No one would have treated news that affected your eternal destiny as a message in a children's game, when to trust the gospel could easily have led to rejection by your family or persecution by your community. Transmitting the faith was a very serious business.

In fact, communities that use oral transmission are well aware of the problems of unintentional distortion. Serious messages are treated seriously and checks put in place to ensure that mistakes are not made. In fact, where we still use oral communication today we do the same. As anybody who has been involved in something like a church prayer chain knows, people tend to adopt what might be call 'error-checking mechanisms'. So after you receive a message to pass on, you may well say to the caller something like: 'Okay, let me check I've got this right before I pass it on: Jane Smith is in City Hospital Ward 10 with a broken leg . . .' Only then, with the message verified, do we repeat it to someone else.

Chris was on the receiving end of an unforgettable instance of the power of oral memory when he started lecturing in geology at the American University of Beirut in 1980. It was a time when there were very few textbooks and accordingly he gave his lectures (in English) at a speed that allowed the students to take full notes. When he gave his class their first test he was surprised to find that when it came to the essay section, dozens of students delivered several paragraphs of response that were identical at a word-for-word level. Deciding that he had somehow failed to spot an inconceivable form of mass cheating, he went with some embarrassment to the head of department who simply laughed and said, 'Chris, the answers are all the same because they've memorised your teaching.' And indeed they had. Actually, when they did get textbooks Chris had students asking him whether they needed to memorise an entire 200-page book. It wasn't just the feat of memorisation that was significant; with it came an extreme reluctance to modify, innovate or rephrase what they had been given. It was an approach that was far from ideal for science but for the transmission of something like the Gospels it would have been very effective. Other people with experience in the same Near Eastern environment have reported a similar phenomenon.[3]

We can probably better appreciate the importance of an oral culture if we try and imagine, in an age before kerosene lanterns and electric light bulbs, what happened in a village when the sun set and darkness fell. Then, as now in many parts of the world, people would have sat around a fire, telling and retelling stories from memory.

In fact, in cultures in which writing was, or is, either difficult or simply not a universal skill, learning by rote becomes essential. For instance it is often suggested by sceptics that the first disciples were illiterate and couldn't have written the Gospels. Actually, the Gospel writers were probably literate in a couple of languages but the overlooked and ironic fact is it is precisely illiterate people who have a well-developed ability to memorise accurately. How else can they keep a record of anything?

We may presume that for at least some time, possibly decades, much of what we have as at least the first three Gospels was passed on by careful memorisation. Indeed it's easy enough to imagine teaching situations, rather similar to those which still operate today in parts of the Middle East and elsewhere, where some authorised Christian leader would have recited – phrase by phrase – an account they had received of what Jesus did and said, to rows of keen students who would have repeated it endlessly until they were letter perfect.

So if there was a period, even a decade or two, where what Jesus said and did was preserved only in oral form, that shouldn't give us too much cause for concern.

Writing down

While a lot of material about Jesus would have been passed on orally for some time, some at least would have been written down. Remember there were Jewish communities – the *diaspora* – scattered around the Mediterranean who kept in touch with each other through writing. Even before the crucifixion, people may well have been sending written accounts of what Jesus was saying to families and friends in Rome, Alexandria or Athens. Another pressure for documents would have occurred when the first followers of Jesus met together, whether in the synagogues or separately. In the synagogue it was customary to read passages from the Old Testament and you can easily imagine that followers of Jesus would have asked to have that supplemented by something of 'what the Messiah had said'. Here a written source would have been vital and, significantly, there are persistent reports amongst writers in the early church of a Gospel (now lost) written in Hebrew, possibly for use in synagogues.[4]

Although surprisingly accurate, oral transmission has its limits. It is time-consuming to memorise Gospel-length material and there's a need for at least a few individuals who can verify its accuracy. By the mid-60s – or even earlier – it would have been obvious that age and persecution was eliminating the number of those who had known Jesus. And anyway, there would have been far too few of those to maintain 'quality control' over the expanding area in which the church now found itself. Persecution would have encouraged the shift to written material. Books can be copied, hidden and easily smuggled; people can't.

Parallel to this shift to writing – and probably starting earlier – would have been the movement from Aramaic to Greek. According to the book of Acts, from the very beginning those who believed in Christ were drawn from around all the Mediterranean and beyond.[5] Aramaic material would have been little use to such believers but Greek, the universal language of the eastern Roman world, would have been ideal. Indeed we may assume that when those first fellowships of believers in Jesus from Gentile backgrounds formed and asked the apostles for more about what Jesus said and did, they would have been given it in Greek.

So at some point, probably far sooner than many people have assumed, someone (and why might it not have been Matthew, Mark, Luke and, later, John?) might well have compiled the various oral and written information they had together into a form that suited them, and this became the basis of our Gospels.

Translation

Translation, as everybody knows who's ever tried it, is a tricky business. For example, try to translate the little English word 'home' into French and you end up with a couple of awkward compromises, none of which adequately carries the richness of the word in English. With this in mind some sceptics say that there must have been a fatal loss of meaning in Jesus' message in going from Aramaic to Greek and then from Greek to our language – presumably here English.

What we can be certain of is that when it came to writing the Greek text of the original Gospels – which presumably involved translating at least some Aramaic – the Gospel writers felt able to use a measure of creative freedom. One illustration of this comes in the context of the unforgettable event where, amid jostling crowds, a paralysed man was lowered down through a roof by his friends for Jesus to heal him. If you compare the two accounts (Mark 2:1–12 and Luke 5:17–26) you find a subtle but significant difference. In Mark's Gospel the friends *dig through* the roof, presumably breaking up the dried clay-covered thatch that was typical of Palestinian roofs. In Luke's Gospel, however, we read that they *removed the tiles*, something that would have been much more comprehensible to readers to the north and west of Palestine. Mark probably recounts exactly what happened, but Luke's adjustment communicates the sense to a different culture. The change has no effect on the message of the story: Jesus has the astonishing authority to both heal and forgive sins.

Of course in most cases today a further translation – from Greek into our own language – has occurred. Here, too, translators face challenges, particularly as we increasingly move into a world in which the agricultural setting of the Gospels is largely lost. So, for instance, pairs of animals such as oxen working together in the field were often linked by a wooden beam – a *yoke*. The yoke became a well-known image for being linked together with someone and occurs six times in the New Testament. Yet when did any of us see a yoke being used? However, with the aid of thoughtful translation and sometimes explanatory footnotes, the meaning of the text in cases like this can be made clear.

One other issue is that language is a moving target. Words, grammar and sentence length change over time. There are many differences in the text between modern English Bibles and the Authorised or 'King James' Version of 1611 but the reality is that most of these reflect nothing more than the fact that the English language has changed dramatically in four hundred years.

These issues of translation may seem major but their importance should not be overstated. For one thing, the message of Jesus occurs in four Gospels and comparing them can often clear up any question over what a passage means. For another, the Christian belief in the power of the Scripture can be extended into the idea that through his Holy Spirit, God can speak to people through translations.

Ultimately, and perhaps far more importantly, Christianity is not about understanding complex philosophical issues that require an understanding of precise shades of meaning. The Christian faith centres first and foremost on us relating to a person: Jesus Christ. The role of the Bible is to point us to the Jesus in whom God has revealed himself fully. To use an image that goes back five hundred years to Martin Luther, 'The Bible is the cradle wherein Christ is laid.' Jesus is the Word of God in person. On this view the Bible is not so much like a painting but more like a window pane of glass through which we see Jesus, God made flesh. Our vision of him is seen best when that pane is clear but men and women can still see through it and come to a faith that saves them even when it is dirty and obscured.

And that is what truly matters.

Transmission

One other challenge is the claim that the original Gospels have, either by accident or design, been altered. After all, the undeniable fact is that the originals of the Gospels no longer exist.

For a start, although the original Gospel manuscripts are no longer with us, we can be certain that they were highly valued and their preservation made a priority. Prior to printing, manuscripts would have been invaluable and probably kept safely for centuries. It is quite possible that, even as late as the second century, people were making copies from the original manuscript that Matthew had written. (St Catherine's Monastery in Sinai holds manuscripts that are 1,600 years old.) The early Christians saw the Gospels as holy documents and would have treated them with the greatest respect.

How accurate the way Jewish scribes copied their religious texts can be demonstrated by the remarkable preservation of some of the Old Testament documents. For example, until 1947 the oldest Hebrew text of the Old Testament was dated to AD 950. However, among the Dead Sea Scrolls was found an entire scroll of the Old Testament book of Isaiah which had probably been written around 100 BC. Careful comparison of the two texts, separated by a thousand years, showed that they were word for word identical in ninety-five per cent of the case. The remaining five per cent are variations in spelling and slips of the pen.[6] The first Christians would have treated the copying of the Gospel manuscripts with similar reverence and care. It's hard to imagine a world without the printing press but it seems much of the copying of the Gospels was done by trained professionals who were painstaking in their labour. The church inherited the long Jewish tradition of giving God's words the utmost reverence. Jewish scribes who made copies of their holy documents went to astonishing lengths to make sure they did not add to or take away from the original. They verified the accuracy of manuscripts by counting words in error-checking methods whose closest parallels today occur in validating computer code. All the evidence suggests that Jesus' followers treated the records of what he said and did with equal respect.

Another key factor in our ability to trust the Gospels as we have them is the sheer volume of manuscript data of whole or fragmentary Gospel portions. Exactly how many texts exist depends on your definition but there are certainly over five thousand manuscripts of the Greek New Testament, varying in size from a few verses to entire books, which can be dated from the second to the sixteenth century. First-century texts are so far absent, second-century texts are largely fragmentary, but by the time we reach the third century we have good texts for almost all the New Testament. This may seem a long gap but when you consider that the two chief works of the Roman historian Tacitus are preserved only in single manuscripts written around a millennium after his death, you realise how good the record of the New Testament is.

From the end of the second century there are also many copies of Latin translations of the New Testament and another twenty thousand or so ancient manuscripts exist that have been translated from Greek originals. One of the fascinating things about these manuscripts is that they come from all around the Mediterranean – Egypt, Rome, Greece – yet they show little discrepancy.

Too much has been made of variations in the manuscripts of the Gospels. Actually the really significant point here is not that the variations exist but that there are so few of them. Almost all modern Bibles will list significant textual variations as footnotes to the text and a glance will show how few and how relatively insignificant these are.[7]

One belief that has gained widespread credence is that originally there were a whole range of Gospels with different variations on the Jesus story but the 'early church' – here the story gets vague as to when and where – erased every version that didn't fit with 'official policy'. Actually there is very little evidence for this. Besides, the church grew so rapidly and spread so widely that the idea of some central church authority rounding up every unacceptable version and destroying them seems highly implausible.[8]

There is, however, one final line of evidence that the Gospels are neither fictionalised accounts created by the early church nor meaningless assemblages of mistranslations and mistakes. We admit it's utterly subjective but it's this: *read them*. Note those extraordinary and often troubling sayings of Jesus, the way that he comforts the weak and challenges the powerful, the self-confidence in which Jesus deals with people and the way in which he alone stays in control through the gory chaos of Good Friday. Yes, it's subjective and not objective and impossible to prove, but the figure that comes out from the Gospels carries with him an extraordinary and authoritative authenticity.

FOR FURTHER READING

The most obvious background reading on Jesus is the New Testament itself. We have used the New Living Translation (NLT) here but the New International Version (NIV) and the English Standard Version (ESV) are also excellent translations.

There are now a number of Study Bibles with introductions to biblical books and help for the reader to understand the text. We recommend the NIV Zondervan Study Bible (renamed recently as the Biblical Theology Study Bible) although there are others such as the ESV Study Bible.

If you have read some of the more popular sceptical material around there are a number of helpful resources that have responded to it. For instance, try the appendix by theologian Ben Witherington in Josh McDowell and Sean McDowell, *Evidence That Demands a Verdict* (Authentic, 2nd edition, 2017). In this area Michael F. Bird, Craig A. Evans, Simon Gathercole, Charles E. Hill and Chris Tilling, *How God Became Jesus: The Real Origins of Belief in Jesus' Divine Nature – A Response to Bart D. Ehrman* (Zondervan, 2014) and the online resource http://ehrmanproject.com/ are very helpful.

GENERAL OVERVIEW

For those who want to study Jesus and his world there are now many good resources. Here are the three we have referred to:

Blomberg, Craig L., *Jesus and the Gospels* (Apollos, 2nd edition, 2009).

Green, Joel B., Jeannine K. Brown and Nicholas Perrin (eds.), *Dictionary of Jesus and the Gospels* (IVP, 2nd edition, 2013).

Keener, Craig S., *The Historical Jesus of the Gospels* (Eerdmans, 2009).

COMMENTARIES

The task of a commentary is to introduce a Bible book and then take you through it verse by verse. There is an enormous range of these, from introductions for those who know little about the text to those designed more for scholars. Here are some suggestions as to series.

Introductory level

Tom Wright, New Testament for Everyone Series (SPCK)

The Bible Speaks Today New Testament Series (IVP)

Higher level

Tyndale Commentary Series (IVP)

The IVP New Testament Commentary Series (IVP)

Pillar New Testament Commentary (Apollos)

Expositor's Bible Commentary (Zondervan)

Understanding the Bible Commentary Series (Baker Books)

NOTES

Introduction

1 Craig S. Keener, *The Historical Jesus of the Gospels* (Kindle edition, Eerdmans, 2009), Kindle locations 9269-9271.

2 N. T. Wright, *The Resurrection of the Son of God* (SPCK, 2003).

3 Susannah Heschel, *The Aryan Jesus: Christian Theologians and the Bible in Nazi Germany* (Princeton University Press, 2008).

4 https://en.wikipedia.org/wiki/The_Sacred_Mushroom_and_the_Cross

5 John 14:6; Matthew 22:16.

1   What we know about Jesus

1 An excellent and readable summary of what we know about Paul can be found in N. T. Wright, *Paul: A Biography* (HarperOne, 2018).

2 Acts 7:58; 8:1–3; 9:1–2; 9:13; 22:4; 1 Corinthians 15:9; Galatians 1:13; Philippians 3:6.

3 Acts 7:58; 8:1–3; 9:1–2; 9:13; 22:4; 1 Corinthians 15:9; Galatians 1:13; Philippians 3:6.

4 See for example Philippians 2:5–11.

5 Craig S. Keener, *The Historical Jesus of the Gospels* (Kindle edition, Eerdmans, 2009), ch. 5.

6 Luke 1:1–4.

7 Compare Luke 24:36–53 with Acts 1:1–11.

8 An accessible compilation of these early Christian writings can also be found in *Early Christian Writings: The Apostolic Fathers*, translated by Maxwell Staniforth, revised by Andrew Louth (revised ed., Penguin Classics, 1987).

9 See Josephus, *Antiquities of the Jews*, 18.63-64, http://www.livius.org/sources/about/josephus-jewish-antiquities/

10 Suetonius, *The Lives of the Twelve Caesars: Claudius*, 25.

11 https://en.wikipedia.org/wiki/Claudius'_expulsion_of_Jews_from_Rome

12 Suetonius, *Life of Nero*, 16.

13 Tacitus, *Annals*, Book 15, ch. 44, https://en.wikisource.org/wiki/The_Annals_(Tacitus)/Book_15#44. There is a full treatment of this, including a defence of its authenticity, in Peter J. Williams, *Can We Trust the Gospels* (Crossway, 2018), p. 22.

14 Pliny, *Epistles* 10.96 https://en.wikipedia.org/wiki/Pliny_the_Younger_on_Christians

15 One website that does this is http://www.bible-researcher.com/parallels2.html

16 There is a thorough treatment of all the issues with the origin of the Gospels in, Craig L. Blomberg, *Jesus and the Gospels* (Apollos, 2nd revised edition, 2007), pp. 83–126.

17 See Craig L. Blomberg, *The Historical Reliability of John's Gospel: Issues and Commentary* (Apollos, 2001).

2   The religious world

1 Genesis 12:1–3; 15:1–21.

2 One result of this is that when the New Testament authors quote from the Old Testament they often use the Greek version. As our Old Testament is translated straight from the Hebrew this can result in mismatches between the New Testament and the original. It's rarely significant.

3 Exodus 34:6–7.

4 For example Numbers 14:17–19; Nehemiah 9:17; Joel 2:13; Jonah 4:2; Psalms 86:15; 103:8; 145:8.

5 For examples see much of Isaiah 24 – 27; 56 – 66; Daniel 7 – 12; and whole chunks of Ezekiel and Zechariah.

6 Matthew 24; Mark 13; Luke 21:5–36.

7 The central business of the Council of Jerusalem around AD 50 recorded in Acts 15 was to rule on how much of the Jewish purity laws were to be obeyed by followers of Jesus.

8 For example Isaiah 27:6; 60:1–14; Psalms 22:27; 45:16–17; 86:9; Habakkuk 2:14.

9 Jeremiah 31:31–34; Ezekiel 37:22–28.

10 Passages about the Messiah can be found in 2 Samuel 7, Psalms 2, 89 and 110, Isaiah 9 and 11, Jeremiah 23:5 and Daniel 9:24–27.

11 Isaiah 42:1–4; 49:1–6; 50:4–11; 52:13 – 53:12.

12 See for example Peter's speeches in Acts 2:14–36 and 3:11–26; Paul to a synagogue audience in Acts 13:16–41.

13 See for example the discussion on the mysterious Melchizedek and Jesus' priesthood in chapters 7 – 8.

14 See 'Land', in Leland Ryken, James C. Wilhoit and Tremper Longman III (eds.), *Dictionary of Biblical Imagery* (IVP, 1998).

15 2 Corinthians 1:20.

3 Place, powers and pressures

1 Good resources on the geographical setting are to be found in various Bible atlases and Craig Blomberg, *Jesus and the Gospels* (Apollos, 2nd edition, 2009), ch. 3.

2 There appears to have been a major drought and famine in the reign of Claudius around AD 45–46, something alluded to in Acts 11:27–30.

3 Matthew 13:55.

4 Matthew 2:1–16.

5 Mark 11:15–17.

6 John 3:1–2; 7:50–52; 19:39–40.

7 Luke 6:15.

8 John 7:49.

9 A good lead into social values can be found in K. C. Hanson and Douglas E. Oakman, *Palestine in the Time of Jesus: Social Structures and Social Conflicts* (Fortress Press, 2nd edition, 2008); various articles in Joel B. Green, Jeannine K. Brown and Nicholas Perrin (eds.), *Dictionary of Jesus and the Gospels* (IVP, 2nd edition, 2013); Craig A. Evans and Stanley E. Porter, *Dictionary of New Testament Background* (IVP, 2000). The works of Ken Bailey, a missionary theologian who knew the modern Near East and its culture very well are also helpful: they include K. E. Bailey, *The Cross and the Prodigal: Luke 15 Through the Eyes of Middle Eastern Peasants* (IVP USA, 2nd edition, 2000); *Jesus Through Middle Eastern Eyes: Cultural Studies in the Gospels* (SPCK, 2008).

10 Luke 7:1–10.

11 Philo, *Laws*, 3.178.

12 Josephus, *The Jewish War*, 6.9.3. Josephus' figures are generally held to be exaggerated; nevertheless it cannot be doubted that the death toll was appalling.

4 Beginnings and birth

1 Luke 1:13–17; 68–79.

2 Luke 1:32–33.

3 Luke 1:35.

4 Isaiah 7:14.

5 Genesis 21:2; 25:21; 30:6, 17; Judges 13:3; 1 Samuel 1:19–20.

6 1 Corinthians 15:45–49; Romans 5:12–21.

7 Gerald O'Collins, S. J., *Christology: A Biblical, Historical and Systematic Study of Jesus* (Oxford University Press, 2nd edition, 2009), p. 294.

8 Craig L. Blomberg, *Jesus and the Gospels* (Apollos, 2nd edition, 2009), pp. 221–229; H. W. Hoehner and J. K. Brown, 'Chronology' in Joel B. Green, Jeannine K. Brown and Nicholas Perrin (eds.), *Dictionary of Jesus and the Gospels* (IVP, 2nd edition, 2013); Andreas J. Köstenberger and Justin Taylor, *The Final Days of Jesus: The Most Important Week of the Most Important Person Who Ever Lived* (Crossway, 2014), Kindle edition, p. 5.

9 Matthew 2:1–12.

10 Suetonius, *The Lives of the Caesars*, 'Vespasian' 4; Tacitus, *The Histories*, 5:13.

11 John 1:1–18.

12 John 1:14.

13 John 1:10–12.

14 A good scholarly resource here is the article 'Angels' by C. Fletcher-Louis, in Joel B. Green, Jeannine K. Brown and Nicholas Perrin (eds.), *Dictionary of Jesus and the Gospels* (IVP, 2nd edition, 2013).

15 Hebrews 1:4–14; Colossians 2:18; Revelation 19:10.

5   The preparation for ministry

1 Luke 3:1–2.

2 Luke 3:23.

3 Luke 2:41–52.

4 Mark 6:3.

5 Matthew 13:55–56; Mark 6:3. There is no biblical evidence for these brothers and sisters being anything other than the biological children of Joseph and Mary.

6 Hebrews 4:15.

7 John 1:19–20.

8 Josephus, *The Antiquities of the Jews*, 18.5.2.

9 Acts 18:24 – 19:6.

10 Matthew 11:7–15.

11 Luke 3:11–14.

12 Matthew 3:11; Luke 3:16.

13 Matthew 11:3.

14 Malachi 4:5.

15 Matthew 11:14 see also Luke 1:17

16 Matthew 14:3–12; Mark 6:17–29.

17 Matthew 3:14; John 1:29, 33, 36.

18 John 1:29–30.

19 John 3:30.

20 Matthew 3:13–17; Mark 1:9–11; Luke 3:21–22.

21 Matthew 3:14–15.

22 Mark 1:9–11.

23 Psalm 2:7.

24 Isaiah 42:1.

25 Exodus 34:28.

26 Numbers 14:33–34; Deuteronomy 8:2; Joshua 5:6.

27 Matthew 4:3.

28 Deuteronomy 8:3.

29 Matthew 4:5–6.

30 Deuteronomy 6:16.

31 Matthew 4:8–9.

32 Matthew 4:10.

33 Luke 4:13.

34 John 12:31; 14:30; 16:11.

35 Matthew 6:13; 13:19

36 John 8:44.

37 John 8:44.

38 Matthew 13:24–30, 36–43.

39 John 12:31.

40 For example 1 Corinthians 10:13; 2 Corinthians 11:14; James 4:7; 1 Peter 5:8; 1 John 4:4.

41 Colossians 2:15; Hebrews 2:14; Revelation 20:10.

6 The ministry of Jesus

1 Craig L. Blomberg, *Jesus and the Gospels* (Apollos, 2nd edition, 2009), p. 225, explains how this is done.

2 See Craig S. Keener, *The Gospel of John* (Baker Academic, 2003); Craig L. Blomberg, *The Historical Reliability of John's Gospel* (Apollos, 2001); Blomberg, *Jesus and the Gospels*;

Colin G. Kruse, *John*, Tyndale NT Commentaries (IVP Academic, revised edition, 2017).

3   For example Jesus' lament over Jerusalem in Matthew 23:37 implies previous visits; see also Luke 5:17; 6:17; 10:38–42.

4   Compare John 2:13–22 with Matthew 21:12–13; Mark 11:15–17; Luke 19:45–46.

5   Luke 8:1–3.

6   Mark 3:7–8.

7   Mark 1:15.

8   Matthew 14:13–21; Mark 6:30–44; Luke 9:11–17; John 6:5–13.

9   John 6:15.

10 For example Mark 1:40–45; 5:43.

11 Matthew 15:1–20; Mark 7:1–3.

12 Mark 8:27.

13 Matthew 16:13–20; also Mark 8:27–30 and Luke 9:18–20.

14 Mark 8:31; see also Matthew 16:21; Luke 9:22.

15 Matthew 16:22.

16 Matthew 16:22–27; Mark 8:34–38; Luke 9:23–26.

17 Matthew 17:1–13; Mark 9:2–13; Luke 9:28–36; see also reference in 2 Peter 1:16–18.

18 Matthew 17:2.

19 Luke 9:30–31.

20 Matthew 17:5.

21 Exodus 19:20.

22 Exodus 24:15–18; 1 Kings 8:10–11; 2 Chronicles 5:13–14; Psalm 97:2.

23 2 Peter 1:16–18; see also John 1:14.

24 Revelation 1:5–8; 5:1–14; 19:1–14.

25 Mark 9:30–32.

26 Matthew 17:22–23; Mark 9:3–32; Luke 9:4–45

27 Matthew 11:18–19.

28 Mark 5:25–34 has the fullest account but see also Luke 8:43–48 and Matthew 9:20–22.

29 Mark 2:22.

30 Luke 4:14–30.

31 Josephus, *The Jewish War* 6.9.3. Here, as elsewhere, Josephus presumably exaggerates.

32 Matthew 12:24.

33 John 10:22–39.
34 Matthew 27:55; Luke 23:49.
35 Matthew 20:17–19; Mark 10:32–34; Luke 18:31–34.
36 Mark 11:11–12; John 11:1.
37 John 11:1–44.
38 John 11:45–53.
39 John 11:50.
40 Matthew 26:1–5; Mark 14:1–2; Luke 22:1–6; Matthew 27:25.
41 John 11:54.
42 John 12:9–11.
43 Matthew, Mark and John all describe what is clearly the same event (Matthew 26:6–13, Mark 14:3–9 and John 12:1–11). Although the impression gained from Matthew and Mark is that the meal occurred in the last week itself, John is the only one who gives it a specific time, placing it just before the entry into Jerusalem.

7   Followers and friends

1   Mark 1:16–20; Matthew 9:9.
2   Mark 3:13–15.
3   Mark 3:13–14.
4   Isaiah 11:10–16; 49:6–12; 56:8; Micah 2:12–13.
5   Mark 10:13; 11:1–3; John 4:8.
6   John 15:13–15.
7   Matthew 26:36–46; Mark 14:32–42; Luke 22:39–46.
8   John 13:18–19; Luke 22:47–48.
9   Matthew 28:10; John 20:17.
10 Matthew 10:1–4; Mark 3:13–19; Luke 6:13–16; Acts 1:13.
11 Mark 1:30; 1 Corinthians 9:5.
12 Mark 3:17.
13 John 20:24–25.
14 John 11:16; 20:28.
15 Matthew 27:56; Mark 15:40; 16:1; Luke 24:10.
16 See Acts 4:13.
17 Acts 12:2.
18 Luke 10:1–20; see also John 6:60–66.
19 Luke 9:57–58.
20 Luke 8:1–3.

21 Luke 18:35 – 19:10; see Mark 10:46–52.

22 K. C. Anson and Douglas E. Oakman, *Palestine in the Time of Jesus: Social Structures and Social Conflicts* (Fortress Press, 2nd Revised Edition 2008), p. 12.

23 John 19:38.

24 Luke 24:1–11, 13–35; 1 Corinthians 15:6.

25 *Against Apion*, 2:25.

26 John 4:27.

27 Luke 8:1–3.

28 John 20:11–18.

29 See for instance Mark 1:29–31; Matthew 9:20–22; Mark 5:25–34; Luke 8:43–48; Luke 13:10–17.

30 Luke 7:11–15.

31 Matthew 5:27–28.

32 Luke 7:36–50.

33 John 8:1–11. As noted in Issue 2, as most Bibles make plain, this passage doesn't belong in here in John. Nevertheless, it is almost certainly authentic.

34 Luke 10:39; see Acts 22:3 where the same phrase in Greek is used.

35 Mishnah Sotah 3.4.

36 John 4:1–26, 39–42.

37 Luke 15:8–10.

38 Josephus, *Life*, 76.

39 Mark 10:11.

8   Miracles

1   See for example Michael R. Licona, *The Resurrection of Jesus: A New Historiographical Approach* (Apollos, 2010), pp. 281–283.

2   Good summaries of Jesus' miracles can be found in Craig L. Blomberg, *Jesus and the Gospels* (Apollos, 2nd edition, 2009), pp. 309–318; G. H. Twelftree, 'Miracles and Miracle Stories', in Joel B. Green, Jeannine K. Brown and Nicholas Perrin (eds.), *Dictionary of Jesus and the Gospels* (IVP, 2nd edition, 2013).

3   Luke 7:22.

4   Acts 2:22.

5   'Miracles', *Dictionary of Jesus and the Gospels*.

6   Matthew 9:27–31; Mark 8:22–26.

7   Luke 5:12–14.

8   John 5:1–15.

9   Mark 1:29–31; John 4:43–53.

10 Luke 22:50–51.

11 Mark 5:24–34.

12 Mark 3:1–5.

13 Mark 5:35–43; Luke 7:11–17; John 11:1–44.

14 Matthew 14:15–21; 15:32–38; Mark 6:32–44; 8:1–9.

15 John 2:1–11.

16 Matthew 8:23–27; Mark 4:37–41.

17 Matthew 14:25; Mark 6:48–51.

18 Luke 5:4–11; John 21:1–11.

19 For example, John 1:47–49; 2:24–25.

20 Mark 1:21–27; Luke 8:26–39.

21 Matthew 9:29; Mark 1:27, 31, 41; 5:41.

22 Matthew 8:4; Mark 5:40, 43; 7:33, 36.

23 Matthew 16:1–4; Luke 11:29–30.

24 Matthew 26:52–54; 27:39–44.

25 Matthew 14:14; 15:32; 20:34; Mark 1:41.

26 John 2:1–11; 4:46–54; 5:1–15; 6:5–14; 6:16–24; 9:1–7; 11:1–45.

27 Matthew 14:13–21; Mark 6:32–44; Luke 9:10–17; John 6:1–15.

28 Acts 2:22; Hebrews 2:4.

29 1 Corinthians 15:12–32.

30 The full list can be found in 'Miracles and Miracle Stories', *Dictionary of Jesus and the Gospels*.

31 As in Josephus, *Antiquities of the Jews* 18.63f; although the passage may have been altered, the reference to Jesus 'doing amazing deeds' is thought to be original. Suggestions that Jesus' miracles were due to black magic can be found in the Babylonian Talmud (Sanhedrin 43a) and are attributed to a Jew, Trypho, in Justin Martyr's *Dialogue with Trypho* and a Greek, Celsus, in Origen's *Contra Celsum*.

32 Craig S. Keener, *Acts: An Exegetical Commentary*, 4 vols (Baker Academic, 2012).

33 Craig S. Keener, *Miracles: The Credibility of the New Testament Accounts*, 2 vols (Baker Academic, 2011).

34 *The City of God*, Book XXI, Chapter 8.

35 See, for example, https://en.wikipedia.org/wiki/Christianity_
and_science; the website of the Faraday Institute https://
scienceandbelief.org/. Useful books include many of the
publications by Alistair McGrath as well as James Hannam,
*God's Philosophers: How the Medieval World Laid the
Foundations of Modern Science* (Icon Books Ltd, 2009);
Rodney Stark, *For the Glory of God: How Monotheism Led to
Reformations, Science, Witch-Hunts, and the End of Slavery*
(Princeton University Press, 2015).

36 John 1:1–14.

37 Luke 23:8.

38 Exodus 16:14–35; Mark 6:30–44.

39 1 Kings 17:17–24; Luke 7:11–16.

40 2 Kings 5; Luke 17:11–19.

41 Luke 24:19.

42 John 3:2; Acts 10:38.

43 Matthew 11:4–5; see also Matthew 8:16–17 (compare Isaiah
35:5; 53:4; 61:1).

44 Mark 5:35–43; Luke 7:11–17; John 11:1–44.

45 Mark 4:41.

46 Psalms 65:7; 107:23–32.

47 Matthew 14:25–33, see Job 9:8.

48 Mark 2:9–11.

49 Matthew 9:32–34; 12:22; Mark 1:21–28; 5:1–20; 7:24–30;
9:14–29.

50 Luke 11:20.

51 Mark 3:26–27.

52 Matthew 8:11; Revelation 21:4.

53 Luke 22:50–51.

54 Exodus 34:6; Psalm 116:5; Matthew 9:36; 14:14.

55 Mark 11:12–14, 20–25; Matthew 21:18–22.

56 John 20:30–31.

57 Matthew 12:24; Mark 3:22.

58 Matthew 11:21.

9   How Jesus taught

1 Matthew 10:24–25; 26:18.

2 John 7:45–46.

3 Matthew 7:28–29.

4   Luke 3:1–2.

5   Luke 13:1–3; 18:15–17.

6   Matthew 7:12.

7   Mark 7:15.

8   Mark 2:27.

9   Luke 12:15.

10 Matthew 6:34.

11 Mark 8:36–37.

12 Matthew 5:6.

13 Matthew 5:3–4.

14 Matthew 10:38–39.

15 Luke 22:26.

16 Luke 20:25.

17 Matthew 5:13, 14.

18 Luke 6:41.

19 John 6:35; 8:12; 10:7; 10:11; 15:1.

20 Matthew 5:29–30.

21 Luke 14:26.

22 Mark 4:34.

23 Klyne R. Snodgrass, *Stories with Intent: A Comprehensive Guide to the Parables of Jesus* (Eerdmans, 2nd edition, 2018), p. 37.

24 Snodgrass, *Stories with Intent*, p. 51.

25 Good summaries about parables can be found in G. P. Anderson, 'Parables', in Joel B. Green, Jeannine K. Brown and Nicholas Perrin (eds.), *Dictionary of Jesus and the Gospels* (IVP, 2nd edition, 2013); Gordon D. Fee, and Douglas Stuart, *How to Read the Bible for All Its Worth* (Zondervan, 4th edition, 2014), ch. 8.

26 Luke 6:39.

27 Luke 10:25–37.

28 Luke 15:11–32. We have written an entire book on this! See J.John and Chris Walley, *The Return: Grace and the Prodigal* (Hodder & Stoughton, 2011).

29 Matthew 13:33 (see Luke 13:21); Luke 15:8–10; 18:1–8.

30 Mark 4:10–12, 21–25, and parallels in the other Gospels.

31 Luke 18:9–14.

32 Luke 15:11–32.

33 Matthew 13:31–32; Mark 4:30–32; Luke 13:18–19. (It also occurs in the Gospel of Thomas, 20.)

34 Ezekiel 17:22–24; 31:3–14; Daniel 4:7–23.

35 Joel Green, *How to Read the Gospels and Acts* (IVP, 1987).

36 See for example John 6:38.

37 John 17:18.

38 Matthew 21:33–46; Mark 12:1–11; Luke 20:9–19.

39 Matthew 9:36.

40 Luke 19:41–44.

41 Mark 10:21; John 11:5; Mark 10:13–16.

42 Luke 12:13–21.

43 Mark 3:1–6.

44 Mark 11:15–17.

45 Mark 10:13–14.

46 Matthew 23:13–36.

47 Matthew 7:24.

10 What Jesus taught

1 Mark 7:1–5, 14–19.

2 Exodus 20:8.

3 Mark 2:23–28.

4 John 2:19–21; John 4:21–23; Matthew 12:6.

5 Daniel 2:44.

6 Mark 1:15.

7 Luke 17:21.

8 Schreiner, Patrick, *The Kingdom of God and the Glory of the Cross* (Short Studies in Biblical Theology) (Crossway, Kindle edition, 2018), p. 87. The book is an excellent and accessible introduction to the idea of the Kingdom of God.

9 John 18:36.

10 Matthew 13:31–32; Mark 4:30–32; Luke 13:18–19.

11 Luke 13:20–21.

12 Mark 4:26–29.

13 Matthew 25:14–30; Luke 19:11–27.

14 Mark 13:24–27; Acts 1:11.

15 Matthew 24:14; Luke 13:29.

16 Matthew 12:28; Luke 11:20.

17 Matthew 13:24–30, 36–43.

18 Luke 11:20; Luke 17:21; Matthew 12:28.
19 Revelation 11:15.
20 Matthew 25:1–13.
21 Matthew 19:28; 25:31–46.
22 Matthew 8:11; 22:1–14; 24:14; 25:1–13; Luke 14:16–24.
23 Luke 13:22–27.
24 See Luke 18:25–30. Here Jesus has been speaking of the difficulties faced by a rich man in entering the Kingdom of God and the disciples reply, 'Then who can be saved?' In the next few verses the Kingdom is linked with 'eternal life'. In Matthew 7:13–14 the 'Kingdom' and 'life' are clearly the same.
25 Matthew 13:45–46; the parable of the hidden treasure (Matthew 13:44) makes the same point.
26 Mark 8:36.
27 Matthew 13:42; 25:30, 46.
28 Matthew 20:1–16; Mark 10:15.
29 Luke 12:32.
30 Luke 8:1.
31 Matthew 7:13–14.
32 Luke 18:16–17.
33 Luke 23:42–43.
34 Mark 1:15.
35 John 8:34; Romans 6:20.
36 Matthew 11:28–30.
37 Matthew 7:21–23; Mark 4:1–20.
38 Matthew 16:24; 19:12; Mark 10:20–27; Luke 9:57–62.
39 John 3:3, 5.
40 Mark 2:21–22.
41 Mark 14:36.
42 Romans 8:15; Galatians 4:5–6.
43 Matthew 6:9–13.
44 Matthew 5 – 7. The title 'the Sermon on the Mount' comes from Matthew 5:1 where we read that Jesus went up on the mountainside to teach.
45 Exodus 20:13.
46 Matthew 5:21–22.
47 Matthew 5:27–28.
48 Matthew 5:48.

49 Matthew 7:17–18.
50 Matthew 15:1–20.
51 Luke 10:25–37.
52 Matthew 22:37–40.
53 John 15:4.
54 Luke 11:13; 24:49; see Acts 1:8.
55 Matthew 5:33–37.
56 Matthew 23:1–35.
57 Matthew 6:9–13; Luke 11:5–13; 18:1–8.
58 Matthew 6:6–8; 7:7–11; Mark 11:22–25.
59 Matthew 6:12, 14–15; 18:21–35.
60 Matthew 5:38–42.
61 Matthew 7:1–5.
62 Luke 22:25–27; Mark 10:45.
63 Matthew 6:19–34; Luke 12:33–34.
64 John 13:34–35.
65 Matthew 6:25–34.
66 Matthew 6:10.
67 Matthew 5:3–10. These are traditionally called the Beatitudes from the Latin word *beatus*, 'blessed'.
68 Matthew 19:4; Mark 10:6; see Genesis 1:27.
69 Matthew 19:5–6; Mark 10:7–8; see Genesis 2:24.
70 Matthew 5:28; Mark 7:22–23.
71 Matthew Parris, *The Times*, August 2003.
72 Matthew 19:11–12.

11 Who was Jesus?

1   Matthew 4:2; 21:18; John 4:6; 19:28.
2   Luke 7:31–34; Matthew 11:16–19.
3   Matthew 18:2–4; Mark 7:24–30; 9:14–27; 10:13–14, 16.
4   Matthew 9:36; Mark 1:41; 6:34; Luke 7:13.
5   Mark 3:5; John 2:13–17.
6   Isaiah 53:3; Luke 19:41; John 11:35.
7   John 12:27; 13:21.
8   Luke 10:21.
9   For example Matthew 7:4; 23:24.
10 Luke 9:51.

11   John 8:46.

12   Mark 1:35; Luke 6:12.

13   Matthew 5:22, 28, 32, 34, 39, 44.

14   John 14:6.

15   The idea that Jesus saves people is a major theme in Luke, e.g. 1:68–79; 2:11; 2:30–32; 5:29–32; 15:3–32; 19:1–10; 23:43.

16   Matthew 1:21.

17   Luke 2:11.

18   Luke 4:18–19; Jesus is quoting Isaiah 61:1–2.

19   Matthew 9:36.

20   Genesis 48:15; 49:24; Psalm 80:1; Ezekiel 34:11–16.

21   Matthew 11:28–30.

22   John 6:35; 8:12; 10:7,9; 10:11; 11:25; 14:6; 15:5.

23   Mark 10:45.

24   Isaiah 42:1–4; 49:1–7; 50:4–9; 52:13 – 53:12. The last passage is the one most commonly referred to in the New Testament. The 'Great Isaiah Scroll' from the Dead Sea Scrolls can be seen in high-resolution with translation on the Internet at the Digital Dead Sea Scrolls: http://dss.collections.imj.org.il/isaiah

25   John 10:11.

26   John 1:29.

27   Matthew 26:26–29; Mark 14:22–25, Luke 22:19–20; see also 1 Corinthians 11:23–26.

28   John 4:25–26.

29   Matthew 16:16, 20; Mark 8:29–30.

30   Matthew 9:27; 15:22; Mark 10:47–48.

31   For example Acts 2:36; 5:42; 8:5; Romans 1:3–4; 2 Timothy 2:8.

32   There is a full treatment of this title in *Dictionary of Jesus and the Gospels*. See also the discussion in Craig L. Blomberg, *Jesus and the Gospels* (Apollos, 2nd edition, 2009), pp. 473–475.

33   Mark 12:6.

34   Mark 12:1-9; Matthew 21:33-41; Luke 20:9–16.

35   John 10:30; 14:9.

36   2 Samuel 7:14; Psalm 2:7–12.

37   Matthew 11:27; see Luke 10:22.

38   Matthew 3:17; 17:5.

39 John 20:17.

40 John 1:14; 3:16; 3:18.

41 See D. L. Bock, 'Son of Man', in *Dictionary of Jesus and the Gospels* and Blomberg, *Jesus and the Gospels*, pp. 470–472.

42 See for example Mark 2:10; 2:28; Luke 9:58.

43 Daniel 7:13–14.

44 Mark 14:62–64.

45 Matthew 24:30; Mark 13:26; Luke 21:27.

46 Blomberg, *Jesus and the Gospels*, pp. 474–475.

47 Mark 11:3.

48 Acts 2:36.

49 Philippians 2:9–11.

50 Romans 10:9; Philippians 2:11.

51 John 20:28.

52 John 6:35; 8:12; 10:7, 11; 11:25; 14:6; 15:1.

53 John 8:58.

54 Exodus 3:14.

55 John 8:59.

56 Matthew 26:26–30; Mark 14:22–26; Luke 22:14–20.

57 Matthew 12:6.

58 John 2:18–21.

59 Matthew 7:24.

60 Mark 2:5–7.

61 Matthew 5:31–32, 38–39.

62 Mark 7:1–23.

63 Matthew 12:38–42; John 4:12; 8:53, 56.

64 Hebrews 3:3.

65 Matthew 26:53. The Letter to the Hebrews develops the idea of the superiority of Christ over angels.

66 See for example Matthew 8:16; 15:21–28; Mark 1:21–27; 5:1–20.

67 Matthew 4:1–11; Luke 4:1–13.

68 Matthew 12:8.

69 Mark 13:31.

70 Matthew 11:27; 28:18–20.

71 Matthew 10:32–33; 25:31–46; Mark 8:34–38.

72 Matthew 7:22–23; 25:31–46.

73 Luke 14:26.
74 John 14:13–14; 16:23–24.
75 John 12:44; 14:1; Matthew 11:28.
76 Matthew 10:40; Mark 9:37.
77 John 3:13; 17:5, 24.
78 John 6:62; 16:28.
79 Matthew 28:20; see also Matthew 18:20.
80 John 1:1–14.
81 James 2:19.
82 John 4:6.
83 Matthew 4:2.
84 John 19:28.
85 Matthew 26:53.
86 Matthew 12:25; John 1:48; 2:24; 16:30.
87 Matthew 24:36.
88 Luke 2:52.
89 1 Corinthians 15:45–49.

12 The last week

1 The phrase goes back to the German theologian Martin Kähler (1835–1912).
2 One book-length attempt to do this is Andreas J. Köstenberger and Justin Taylor, *The Final Days of Jesus: The Most Important Week of the Most Important Person Who Ever Lived* (Crossway, 2014). While there might be disagreements over some of the details of this reconstruction it demonstrates that it can be done.
3 John 19:30.
4 Matthew 21:1–11; Mark 11:1–11; Luke 19:28–40; John 12:12–19.
5 Craig L. Blomberg, *Jesus and the Gospels* (Apollos, 2nd edition, 2009), p. 61; Eckhard J. Schnabel, *Mark*, Tyndale NT Commentaries (IVP Academic, revised edition, 2017), p. 343.
6 Zechariah 9:9.
7 Mark 11:9–10.
8 John 12:13.
9 1 Maccabees 13:51; see also 2 Maccabees 10:7.
10 Matthew 21:18–19; Mark 11:12–14, 20–21.
11 Hosea 9:10; Jeremiah 24:5; Luke 13:6–9.

12 Matthew 21:12–13; Mark 11:15–17; Luke 19:45–46.

13 Malachi 3:1.

14 Isaiah 56:7–8; Jeremiah 7:1–15.

15 Mark 11:27.

16 Matthew 21:28–32, 33–46; 22:1–14; Mark 12:1–12; Luke 20:9–19.

17 Matthew 24:1–51; Mark 13:1–37; Luke 21:5–36.

18 Matthew 24:2.

19 Matthew 24:3.

20 Matthew 24:36.

21 Matthew 26:3–5; Mark 14:1; Luke 22:1–2.

22 John 18:31.

23 Acts 7:57–60.

24 Deuteronomy 21:22–23.

25 Matthew 26:14–16; Mark 14:10–11; Luke 22:3–6.

26 Luke 22:24.

27 John 13:2–17.

28 Jeremiah 31:31–34.

29 Luke 22:19.

30 Matthew 26:28.

31 Exodus 24:8.

32 Exodus 24:9–11.

33 Luke 22:19.

34 John 13:18–30.

35 John 14 – 16.

36 John 17.

37 Matthew 26:36–46; Mark 14:32–42; Luke 22:39–46; John 18:1–9.

38 Matthew 26:37–38; Mark 14:33–34; Luke 22:44.

39 Mark 14:35–36.

40 Galatians 3:13.

41 Luke 22:42.

42 1 Corinthians 15:45–47.

13 The trial and the cross

1 Matthew 26:47–56; Mark 14:43–52; Luke 22:47–53; John 18:1–11.

2 Matthew 26:57 – 27:31; Mark 14:53 – 15:20; Luke 22:54

– 23:25; John 19:12 – 19:16.

3   On Joseph: Matthew 27:57; Mark 15:43; Luke 23:50–51; John 19:38. On Nicodemus: John 3:1–21; 7:50–51; 19:39–42.

4   John 19:5, King James (Authorised) Version.

5   Matthew 27:6; John 18:28.

6   Luke 11:42.

7   Josephus, *Antiquities* 20.198; John 18:19–24.

8   Matthew 26:57–68; Mark 14:53–65; Luke 22:66–71.

9   Isaiah 53:7.

10   Matthew 26:63.

11   Matthew 26:64.

12   Daniel 7:13; there is also an incorporation here of Psalm 110:1–2, widely recognised then and now as referring to the Messiah.

13   Matthew 26:65.

14   Matthew 26:58, 60–75; Mark 14:54, 66–71; Luke 22:54–62; John 18:15–18, 25–27.

15   Matthew 27:3–10.

16   See H. K. Bond, 'Pontius Pilate', in Joel B. Green, Jeannine K. Brown and Nicholas Perrin (eds.), *Dictionary of Jesus and the Gospels* (IVP, 2nd edition, 2013).

17   Matthew 8:5–13; Luke 7:1–10.

18   Luke 23:6–12.

19   Matthew 27:15–21; Mark 15:6–11; Luke 23:18–19; John 18:38–40.

20   John 19:6.

21   John 19:7.

22   John 19:12.

23   John 19:15.

24   Josephus, *Jewish War*, 2:21, 5.

25   Matthew 27:27–31; Mark 15:16–20; John 19:1–3.

26   Matthew 27:32–56; Mark 15:21–41; Luke 23:26–49; John 19:17–37.

27   Quintilian, *Declamations*, 274.13.

28   Matthew 27:32; Mark 15:21; Luke 23:26.

29   Matthew 27:34, 38; Mark 15:24; Luke 23:32–33; John 19:18, 23–24.

30   Matthew 27:39–41; Mark 15:29–32; Luke 23:35–37.

31   Matthew 27:37; Luke 23:38; John 19:19–22.

254 · JESUS CHRIST – THE TRUTH

32 Acts 7:60.

33 John 19:27.

34 Joel 2:2; Amos 8:9.

35 2 Corinthians 5:21.

36 John 1:29.

37 See John 17:4.

38 John 19:34.

39 Matthew 27:51; Mark 15:38; Luke 23:45.

40 On Joseph, see note 3 above. Matthew 27:57–61; Mark 15:42–47; Luke 23:50–56; John 19:38–42.

41 Matthew 27:62–66.

42 Hebrews 2:11.

43 Galatians 4:5; Romans 8:14,23; 9:4; Ephesians 1:5.

44 Matthew 27:42.

45 Matthew 27:45; Mark 15:33; Luke 23:44.

46 John 1:4.

14 The resurrection

1 1 Corinthians 15:14, 17.

2 John 21:9.

3 Acts 17:31.

4 1 Corinthians 15:3–8.

5 Galatians 1:18.

6 Acts 7:58; 8:1–3; 9:1–2; 9:13; 22:4; 1 Corinthians 15:9; Galatians 1:13; Philippians 3:6.

7 Matthew 28:1–10; Mark 16:1–8; Luke 24:1–12; John 20:1–10.

8 John 20:5–7.

9 Compare Mark 3:21 and John 7:5 with Acts 12:17, Galatians 1:19; 2:9.

10 Josephus, *Antiquities of the Jews*, 20:9, 1.

11 John 20:5.

12 On the significance of names in the Gospels see Richard Bauckham, *Jesus and the Eyewitnesses: The Gospels as Eyewitness Testimony* (Eerdmans, 2nd edition, 2017).

13 John 20:17.

14 It's widely available on the Internet in a variety of translations. We've accessed: http://www.earlychristianwritings.com/text/gospelpeter-brown.html

15 See the discussion in T. P. Henderson, 'Gospels: Apocryphal', in Joel B. Green, Jeannine K. Brown and Nicholas Perrin (eds.), *Dictionary of Jesus and the Gospels* (IVP, 2nd edition, 2013).

16 Acts 1:21–22; 2:22, 32; 3:13–15.

17 Babylonian Talmud, Baba Kamma 88a.

18 Josephus, *Antiquities*, 4:219.

19 1 Corinthians 11:20–30.

20 Romans 6:4.

21 See for example Michael R. Licona, *The Resurrection of Jesus* (Apollos, 2010) and at a more popular level Josh McDowell and Sean McDowell, *Evidence That Demands a Verdict* (Authentic, 2nd edition, 2017).

22 Matthew 3:17; see also Matthew 17:5.

23 Revelation 1:7.

24 2 Peter 1:19; Revelation 2:28; 22:16.

25 1 Peter 1:20; 2 Peter 3:3.

26 1 Corinthians 15:20–23.

27 Luke 24:32.

15 Not the last word

1 Acts 10:37–43.

2 Acts 1:1–2.

3 Matthew 16:15.

4 Matthew 6:9–13.

Issue 1: Can we trust the Gospels?

1 The indefatigable Craig S. Keener discusses ancient novels at length in his commentary on Acts. *Acts: An Exegetical Commentary, 4 vols* (Baker Academic, 2012), vol. 1, pp. 62–83. See also R. F. Hock, 'Romances/Novels, Ancient' in Craig A. Evans and Stanley E. Porter, *Dictionary of New Testament Background* (IVP, 2000).

2 On this question of the accuracy of the Gospel accounts in respect of culture and geography, the treatment of Peter Williams in *Can We Trust the Gospels?* (Crossway, 2018) is very helpful.

3 Mark 13:32. See also Matthew 10:5–6; Mark 9:1.

4 For example, Matthew 24:15–22; Mark 13:14–20; Luke 21:20–24.

5 Richard Bauckham, *Jesus and the Eyewitnesses: The Gospels*

as *Eyewitness Testimony* (Eerdmans, 2nd edition, 2017). Aspects of this work are summarised in Peter Williams *Can We Trust the Gospels?* (Crossway, 2018).

Issue 2: How did the Gospels come to us?

1 Matthew 10:24–25; 23:8; John 13:13–15.

2 For example Mark 5:41; 15:34.

3 A very helpful writer on this is Ken Bailey who was able to write from years of missionary activity within the Middle East. See K. E. Bailey, 'Informal Controlled Oral Tradition and the Synoptic Gospels', at https://biblicalstudies.org.uk/article_tradition_bailey.html

4 James R. Edwards, in *The Hebrew Gospel and the Development of the Synoptic Tradition* (Eerdmans, 2009).

5 Acts 2:9–12, 41.

6 You can verify the accuracy for yourself by comparing a modern Bible translation with a high-resolution photographic reproduction of the entire Dead Sea Scroll of Isaiah at http://dss.collections.imj.org.il/isaiah. Mercifully for those of us not fluent in Hebrew, it includes a translation.

7 If we compare modern versions such as the NLT (New Living Translation) and the NIV (New International Version) with the much revered Authorised Version of 1611 we find that only two substantial blocks of text in the Gospels have been rejected in over 400 years. The first includes various verses added to Mark's Gospel to smooth out its abrupt ending. These have been considered questionable summaries for centuries and their omission causes no problem. The second is the passage in John's Gospel (John 7:53 – 8:11) about the woman caught in adultery. It certainly doesn't fit in John but nevertheless there is a widespread acknowledgement that this is an authentic account of an incident in the life of Jesus. It's not hard to imagine why someone found it convenient to omit a story in which a sexually immoral woman is shown leniency and the religious leadership is humiliated! Actually some manuscripts include it after Luke 21:38 and both its language and sympathy with women fit very much with Luke's interests.

8 A detailed refutation of the idea that the New Testament is corrupted can be found in Daniel B. Wallace, *Revisiting the Corruption of the New Testament – Manuscripts, Patristic and Apocryphal Evidence* (Kregel, 2011).